Luigi Barzini

THE
EUROPEANS

SIMON AND SCHUSTER · NEW YORK

LIBRARY OF CONGRESS CATALOGING IN PUBLICATION DATA
BARZINI, LUIGI GIORGIO, 1908–
    THE EUROPEANS.
        1. NATIONAL CHARACTERISTICS, EUROPEAN.   2. EUROPE—
CIVILIZATION—1945–   I. TITLE.
D1055.B27   1983   940.55   82–19655
ISBN 0–671–24578–3

To V.C.

CONTENTS

Prologue

T HERE ARE SO MANY simple and obvious reasons why the venerable and illustrious countries occupying the jagged western rump of Asia, occasionally pecking at each other like irritable hens or quarreling with the United States, should form what the Americans (who, by their very nature, have never been satisfied with mere perfection) would call "a more perfect union," and why they should do it immediately, today, tomorrow morning at the latest, without wasting one more hour or waiting for one more windy and inconclusive meeting of experts, that only a few fanatics are left who bother to exalt or mock the idea.

There is, to begin with, one irrational emotional reason, which should not be entirely disregarded. Irrational emotions move bigger multitudes and shape events more easily than cold economic, scientific, or sociological motivations. It could be called "the European Dream." It is many centuries old. Dante described, in *De Monarchia*, the vague hope of seeing the Continent pacified under one sovereign. It was proposed as a cure-all by great princes, emperors, statesmen, thinkers, poets, and starry-eyed idealists down the centuries. Nothing ever came of it, yet it never died. It was advocated (I quote only a handful of names) by Kant, Novalis, Voltaire, Rousseau, Lamartine, Michelet, Victor Hugo, Cobden, Saint-Simon, Bentham, Mazzini, Cattaneo, Gioberti, and Garibaldi. The European cause was embraced equally by obdurate conservatives such as Klemens Metternich and revolutionary apostles such as Pierre Proudhon. Aristide Briand, the French foreign minister, solemnly proposed the creation of the United States of Europe to the League of Nations on September 5, 1929, in a memorable speech written for him by his *chef de cabinet*, Marie

René Auguste Alexis Saint-Léger Léger, who is better known as St.-John Perse, the poet who won the Nobel Prize for literature in 1960. The project was duly entrusted to a committee and was heard of no more.

And yet it is still at the bottom of the heart of every European, this ancient desire to see Europe pacified and merged into one political unit; to admit openly once and for all what we knew all along and what foreign visitors perceive immediately; that in spite of the infinite diversities, the many separate histories, religions, and cuisines, the innumerable languages and patois, we are all basically the same kind of people, comfortable in each other's countries and in each other's homes. It is admittedly a heartwarming idea. It makes people's eyes shine. If national frontiers were to be abolished, every war fought by Europeans in the past would be transformed ipso facto into a bloody but insignificant internal family squabble, in which there would be no longer losers and only one winner, Europe. There would also be a pool of all our great men. We could all be equally proud of our common European countrymen (to name only a handful), Dante, Shakespeare, Cervantes, Goethe, Victor Hugo, Tolstoy, Byron, Leopardi, Molière, Goldoni, Beethoven, Mozart, Verdi, Wagner, Michelangelo, Rembrandt, Reynolds, Constable, the Impressionists, Modigliani, de Chirico, and thousands of others.

This Europe of the Dream is by no means limited to great men and solemn historic occasions. We can recognize it now in the landscapes that ignore all frontiers: Normandy, Artois, and Picardy slowly merging into Flanders; Savoy imperceptibly becoming Val d'Aosta; the Po Valley resembling here and there the flat lands of Belgium and Holland; the snow-hooded impassive Alps, indifferent to flags, stamps, police uniforms, and customs barriers, that look majestically the same whether French, Italian, Austrian, Swiss, or German. We recognize our common fatherland everywhere, in busy village streets, the smiling faces of children and old men, the tidy bourgeois households with polished floors and shining windowpanes, the swinging walk of girls, the majestic flow of all our big rivers between wooded banks. Europe is the penumbra in candlelit little churches; white and gold opera theaters lit by sparkling crystal chandeliers in all our cities, large or small; the little lake boat, as white and pompous as a swan, tooting as it calmly approaches the landing stage; the small inns. Above all, I think, we recognize it in the wines. Wine is perhaps the essence of our continent. It is a rebellious product. The best cannot be homogenized and mass produced. It varies from place to place and from year to year. To make it, man must submit to ancient unvarying disciplines, trust his instinct, follow nature, preserve the ancient arts of the vintner unchanged in spite of the scientific and convenient instruments invented to ease his work. Even the European countries that do not produce wine, or produce a little in good years, the Germans, the Dutch, the Belgians, the Scandinavians, the Irish, feel compelled to show an almost religious respect for it, as if they too recognized it as one of our sacred symbols, as sacred as the flag of Europe that nobody has yet bothered to invent.

Besides this inebriating, instinctive, and poetic feeling, which has unfortunately never generated any concrete results and could be ignored, there are today other serious, sober, and objective reasons for the immediate creation of a European union. The West is in danger, as everybody knows. Europe is where Western ideas and hopes were born. It is their home. We want to defend them simply because we know that life without them is not livable. The greatest nation in the West, the United States, should also be included among the European nations (it is even proudly producing and drinking more and more excellent wines). It is a *dépendance* or annex, philosophically speaking, of Europe. This is also proved by the fact that when the chips were down and western Europe was on the verge of collapse, the peaceloving Americans, who are at best reluctant if valorous soldiers, whose "business," as Calvin Coolidge said, "is business," or their own affairs, rushed to the rescue with bugles blowing and flags fluttering like the U.S. cavalry in Western films. They saved Europe at great expense of lives and gold twice in twenty-three years. They too knew life without the common Western values was not livable.

Nevertheless, one must admit the United States is a peculiarly

European nation, shaped as it has been by its own unique history. It can be alarmingly optimistic, compassionate, incredibly generous. It can be, at times, apathetic or impulsive or irascible. Its political decisions and way of handling foreign relations are often surprisingly heterodox. It likes to see problems in black and white. (This may be inevitable. The United States must always simplify complex issues so that the common ill-informed man may understand them. Ill-informed men include those who are extremely well informed in their particular fields but innocent of anything just outside their perimeters, and unfortunately also at times certain inexperienced political office holders, including a few presidents, who have rarely dabbled in the conduct of international affairs before their elections.) The United States may appear uncomfortably tactless and arrogant at times. (It is the arrogance of the man who knows that he is right, that the problem at hand has only one possible solution for a righteous man, and that anybody who disagrees is wrong.)

Europe has the contrary defects. It is pessimistic, prudent, practical, and parsimonious, like an old-fashioned banker. It has learned not to rush into anything, even if it is the obviously necessary or advantageous thing to do. It always prefers to wait and see. It enjoys delving into the complexity of things; the more complexities it can find the better. Europe looks for nuances, the bad side of anything good, the good side of anything bad. It believes the devil is never as ugly as he is painted, the future is never (or seldom) as appalling as one fears, but never, never as wonderful as one hopes. It sometimes believes that old inequities are preferable to new inequities. It is sagacious, and its frequent miscalculations are often the product of its excessive sagacity.

Its wisdom, or what Europeans think is their wisdom, has been gained down the centuries at the price of untold millions of corpses, people killed in wars, some of them dynastic or theological, in persecutions, riots, pogroms, revolutions, famines, sacks, plagues, epidemics, massacres, or being burned at the stake. It has been enriched by numberless ruinous mistakes, delusions, insane experiments and failures, myths, fanatical attempts to force society into schemes invented by philosophers. Its wisdom has also immensely benefited in the end from the lessons its past history has taught it, by moral, political, economic, scientific, and religious improvements, by ingenious technological inventions, by prodigious advances in thought, by achievements in all the arts, including the humble art of enjoying life. And it is comforted, with Benedetto Croce, by the knowledge that history has but one meaning, the slow, bloody, meandering progress of human liberty. Europeans believe that their combined wisdom, their long and painful experiences, and their folk memories possibly could prevent others, in this case the United States and the Soviet Union, from repeating some of the same mistakes, and save themselves and the world from catastrophic delusions and suicidal collective follies.

It is evident that if one day a united Europe could collaborate with the United States as equals, respecting each other's character, compensating for each other's defects, and combining each other's virtues, the consolidation of peace and the defense of the West would become a much easier matter. The appalling economic, political, and military burden the United States is carrying would become lighter. The added responsibilities, it is hoped, would give back a certain amount of pride to Europe, a new sense of its unique heritage and of the need to preserve it. Europe would discover that to entrust the task of its defense mainly to its Atlantic cousins and their nuclear armaments, for the shoddy, unconfessed reason that it saves money and trouble, is unworthy of its name and history. Europe is (as Denis de Rougemont said in 1946) *"la patrie de la mémoire."* It is the ultimate fruit of man's millenarian endeavors, in fact civilization itself. No sacrifice should be too great to preserve it.

Each man and woman is unique, different from all other men and women on earth as each leaf is different from all others on the same tree, but all human beings are recognizably human beings. In their infinite varieties, under the many different colored skins, they have common instincts, traits, virtues, and foibles. They are attracted by more or less similar temptations, capable of the same noble sacrifices, sublime heroism, abject cowardice, abominable acts, and ruthless cruelties. This is why great art (Greek lyric poetry, memorable American movies, the best painting and music, old Russian novels, and so on), as well as minor accomplishments (French, Chinese, and Italian cuisine and some American TV serials), are instinctively recognized as their own by all men everywhere. This is also why the slightest departure from the common norm is called "inhuman."

Nevertheless, most men grouped in nations, speaking more or less the same language, are born or are unconsciously compelled to model themselves on a national pattern, so that they may appear on the surface different from all foreigners. Those unfortunates who are born different and cannot adjust are profoundly unhappy, lead lives of quiet desperation, and often write poetry. Some commit suicide.

Nations (even those that do not have a state of their own) could be compared to living organisms, and their inhabitants to programmed cells. Like all living organisms, nations and their people change, but usually very slowly and gradually, down the centuries. They flourish, wither, and die so slowly and gradually that they seem immutable within a limited period of time. Like all living organisms their existence is rigidly restricted by Nature within a narrow range of possibilities. Experts know that the acrobatic tricks that seem against nature that are done by Lipizzaner horses in the Vienna Spanish School are what horses often do spontaneously when they are free and frisky. Gardeners know there is a narrow range of ways within which a plant can be made to grow. It may not be impossible to study and predict the behavior of nations as if they were creatures with *almost* fixed characters, inclinations, and preferences.

Cola di Rienzo (1313–54) made himself a dictator in Rome and tried to revive the glory of the Roman Empire. He counted years from his coming to power. He believed that florid eloquence, arrogant and threatening letters to foreign sovereigns, parades, ceremonies, flags, and uniforms could take the place of a well-stocked treasury and powerful armies. After he was driven out of Rome by a revolt, he was brought back by a foreign enemy army. The enraged populace killed him and hanged him by his feet in a public square. Six centuries later another Italian, Benito Mussolini, tried the same path to greatness and met with the same fate.

The French Revolution did not correct the fundamental defects of French life. It magnified and perfected them: from the rigid centralization of Louis XIV to the bureaucratic straitjacket that Colbert created to the concentration of economic power in the hands of a few. The Russian Revolution exaggerated the worst traits of czarist autocracy: secret police, mass exiles to Siberia, forced labor camps, the concentration of all the economy in the hands of the state. The Soviets dedicated the largest percentage of the national income to armaments and starved the peasantry, as had been done in Russia for centuries. In the end the Communist regime turned out to be a caricature of what had existed before. To understand the Soviet Union today, it is surely more useful to read Astolphe de Custine (1790–1857), Lermontov (1814–41), Turgenev (1818–83), Dostoevsky (1821–81), and Tolstoy (1828–1910) rather than the collected works of Marx and Lenin.

Perhaps, in order to understand a little better the elusive and dangerous European situation today and to try to peer through the impenetrable dark future, it might be helpful to study the national character of each European nation and the laws that govern their behavior, particularly of the five principal members of the European Common Market, Britain, Germany, France, Italy, and Benelux. They are the protagonists. They formulate decisions, are responsible for relations with the rest of the world, and inevitably drag the others, Greece, Ireland, and Denmark behind them. Americans are clearly baffled by the Europeans' behavior, are constantly tempted to withdraw their armed forces from the Continent and to forget the whole thing. I have included here too a study of the somewhat distorted conception of the United States that Europeans have always preserved. This is important, for it is the reason why exchanges across the Atlantic often turn into sterile *dialogues de sourds.*

Maybe we can begin to understand why the process of European integration ground drearily to a standstill, after having got off to a brilliant and luminous start, and why there persist continuous misunderstandings between the Americans and their Allies.

ONE

The
Elusive Europeans

T HE KNOWLEDGE THAT Europe must rely on itself and share an equal burden with the United States would, one hopes, retard its decadence, its gentle decline into sweet but vaguely inglorious Sybaritic impotence, and its concentration on squalid quibbling about money. It would give the people, one also hopes, a new sense of responsibility, consolidate governments, and placate social unrest. Could Walloons and Flamands still hate each other with such passion when they knew they must man the common ramparts? Could the British coal miners, French steelworkers, or Italian railway men go as easily and as often on unjustified strikes if they were aware they were enfeebling their countries and endangering their own security? Would governments go on casually distributing billions to mollify malcontents?

If a united Europe were authoritative and strong enough it would no longer be taken for granted as a docile, occasionally recalcitrant, vassal by the friendly superpower, nor could it, one day, be intimidated by the other's guns and missiles pointed against it into the craven acquiescence of a resigned surly serf. A unified Europe could also prepare itself in time for the dangerous, turbulent, and violent decades ahead, possibly the most treacherous times since the fall of the Roman Empire. Besides the confrontation between East and West, it must keep watch on the contortions of the Third World. Europe is uniquely prepared for this role. Most of the developing nations are former European colonies. There are Europeans who know their languages and patois, their histories, their people, their religions, taboos, and customs. Obviously this is a field in which the United States needs a helping hand, for it never has had much success with underdeveloped nations, not even with its neighbors in Latin America. In spite of its well-meaning intentions and its generosity it does not really understand them and, for some reason, it seldom follows the advice of Americans who do. It tries to mold Third and Fourth World people into its own kind of political organization as if everybody were a potential American at heart. The result is often the words that can be read on walls: "Yankee go home."

The situation is explosive. Hungry masses must be fed. Primitive people must be trained for the almost impossible task of governing themselves without periodic recourse to military coups d'état. Some of them must be taught the arts of agriculture, husbandry, fishing, management, and the simpler industrial activities, as well as the polite manners and hypocrisies of international behavior. Then there is the frightening problem of the free flow of armaments, which sooner or later will inevitably tempt some of these countries to start wars. Such wars may spread like wildfire on dry grassland. It is a well-known fact that recently industrialized nations (as well as some desperately retarded ones) often resort to war as a diversion for their anguishing domestic problems. As soon as they acquire enough armaments (some may even succeed in constructing their own nuclear bombs with the help of foreign scientists), credit, a patchy ideology, and a Great Invincible Leader, they invade one of their neighbors. There is not even the need to find a valid excuse. Anything will do. Journalists and historians will later invent suitable philosophic, historical, or economic motivations. That's their job. The examples of this are numerous and well known. Here are a few: As soon as it was strong enough, troubled Japan attacked China in 1895 and Russia in 1904; weak and unstable Italy attacked the Turks in Libya in 1911, Ethiopia in 1885, 1896, and 1935; Iraq made war on Iran in 1980; Libya invaded Chad the same year. Wars are notoriously the best possible way to make suffering people forget unsolved and unsolvable problems and their own wretchedness. If successful, they placate unrest like oil on stormy waters, justify repression, prevent revolutions or counterrevolutions and the possible dissolution of shaky recently formed states. Evidently, if the shah of Iran had been allowed to conquer some weaker neighbor with his massive American armaments, he would have saved his throne and his empire. It is easy to foresee that Europe (as well as the Soviet Union and the United States) must and probably can prepare itself for imminent unprecedented and unpredictable nightmares.

To do all this, Europe should clearly evolve one common will, speak with one calm majestic voice, have a clear idea of its identity and goals, cultivate and defend its economic prosperity, and pursue a single foreign policy in its own interest (and the world's). It should therefore forget its trivial disputes and rivalries, put its own house in order, set up authoritative common democratic institutions, arrange its financial affairs according to more or less uniform criteria, adopt one common currency, and set up one redoubtable defense establishment.

All this is almost too easy on paper. It could be decided in a couple of months. Statesmen, diplomats, staff officers, politologists, bankers, jurists, journalists, and economic experts have pointed out for almost half a century now in innumerable speeches, interviews, articles, essays, reports, and books; in gatherings, conferences, and congresses; how simple the unifying process could be. Hundreds of hypothetical blueprints and possible timetables are available. Treaties have been drafted, signed, and ratified, some institutions have been established, bureaus organized and manned. A European parliament has been elected. In reality nothing much has happened. All serious efforts have been somehow defeated. In spite of the verbiage, the rhetoric, and the elegant euphemisms, Europe is no nearer integration today than it was, say, after 1815, when it was somehow held together first by the Holy Alliance; later by the blood ties among sovereigns, most of whom were cousins; and by what was then known as the "European concert." On the eve of Sarajevo, no passport was needed to go from one European nation to another (it was indispensable only for travel to the United States, Turkey, and Russia). The 1911 *Baedeker* for London says: "Passports are not necessary in

England, though occasionally useful in procuring delivery of registered or *poste restante* letters." When German police officers broke into my father's hotel room in Munich in 1910 and asked him to prove he was not the dangerous anarchist they were looking for, he could not produce a document. To prove who he was, he showed them the letters in his coat pocket, addressed to the same name his tailor had written in indelible ink on the label in the inside pocket of his coat and inside the waist of his trousers. The policemen apologized and left. In 1911 Belgium alone had adopted *l'heure anglaise* or Greenwich time, which was nine minutes behind Paris time, four minutes behind French railway time, and twenty minutes behind Dutch time; but one year later all clocks were synchronized on Greenwich or set exactly one, two, three, four or more hours ahead or behind it. Few institutions today can be compared to such durable European creations of yesterday as the *Union des Gaz Universelle*, the *Compagnie Internationale des Wagons Lits et des Grands Express Européens*, the *Union Postale Universelle*, the international acceptance of uniform decimal weights and measures (based on a platinum meter deposited in the cellar of the French National Archives), and the currency agreements, known originally as the *Union Monétaire Latine*, founded in 1865. Give and take a few pennies, most currencies—the French, Belgian, and Swiss francs, the British shilling, Austrian crown, German mark, Spanish peseta, Italian lira, and two U.S. dimes—were then roughly equivalent and did not fluctuate unexpectedly.

Ominous parallels come to mind. The ancient Greek cities, the brightest flower of civilization at the time, could not form an alliance robust enough to resist the brutal advance of the Macedonian phalanxes, in spite of Demosthenes' eloquent pebbly warnings, and the Roman conquest later. In the fifteenth and sixteenth centuries the Italian *fritto misto* of city-states and principalities did not (like other great European countries) form a unified nation under one sovereign and one law, a state capable of defending itself; they could not preserve the civilization of the Renaissance, far more advanced than any other in Europe, as well as their own great wealth, from the ironclad armies of brutal Nordic soldiers who rode down the Alps in the springtime to murder men, rape women, destroy works of art, burn libraries, and loot elegant cities.

Could it be, one asks, that more advanced, polished, cultured, gentle, and intelligent peoples are always doomed? The better the cuisine, the more defenseless and unfortunate the cooks? Must the best cheeses and wines or the well-roasted ducks always be protected by weak Maginot lines or Great Walls of China? Could it be that the more delicate the poetry, lucid the prose, liberal the laws, dazzling the paintings, polished the manners, and harmonious the music, the more fragile the ramparts? Are the more civilized inevitably condemned to become (like Imperial China or Imperial Byzantium) the degraded serfs (and patient teachers) of loutish and ruthless outsiders? Can Athens be saved from the Romans, Rome from the Ostrogoths, and Imperial Vienna from defeat and gentle disintegration? Is Europe like the thousand-year-old Republic of Venice, which was abolished in 1797 by the on-the-spot decision of a twenty-seven-year-old cuckolded Corsican adventurer? Don't the nice people ever win? Must they always finish last?

In principle, as you listen to after-dinner speeches, to official statements by solemn spokesmen at formal press conferences, or read the multicolored propaganda booklets issued in eight or nine languages on glossy paper, you almost believe the points of agreement between Europeans are infinitely more numerous than the points of disagreement and that the integration of the Continent (or its western tail) is but a matter of time, perhaps only a few months or years away. There are, after all, a Common Market, a European Executive Council, a freely elected Parliament, and a bureaucracy of hand-selected, experienced men. But when you look closer, you see the Common Market is bogged down in innumerable petty, inglorious disputes, some as small as grains of sand, a few more important. There is, for instance, no agreement on the shape and size of European lawn mowers, the wording on a future European passport (only the color has been agreed on: Bordeaux red, possibly in homage to the memory of Jean Monnet, who was from Bordeaux, and started life as a salesman for his family's cognac firm), the thickness of fishing nets, the seas in which to use them, the free exchange of eggs, chicks, potatoes, wines, lambs, and piglets, and many other things. One fierce argument that has separated the French and the Germans is worthy of mention. The French have been disputing for years the Germans' right to call a dubious synthetic dressing in jars, which contains not a trace of egg yolk, olive oil, and lemon juice, "mayonnaise."

There are also, to be sure, more vital disagreements—the vast sums the British refuse to pay to the common coffers; the impossibility of persuading armaments factories to standardize weapons and their ammunitions; the choice of one capital city instead of three makeshift ones, Brussels, Strasbourg, and Luxembourg (documents, files, archives, functionaries, experts, and secretaries travel from one to the other, as the need arises, in long caravans of trucks and cars like a circus company); the reluctance of northern countries to stop producing at everybody else's expense Himalayas of unwanted butter that have to be sold at bargain prices to oil-producing Arabs or the Soviet Union. All these problems, large and small, which must be taken seriously because they have slowed all progress practically to a standstill, obviously could be solved with some common sense and some amiable give-and-take in a few hours. But they are in reality mere pretexts. There is something else that stops the integration of Europe, something few people ever mention, that really makes these trivial disputes insurmountable obstacles. What is it?

The parallels with Greece, *Graecia capta*, and Renaissance Italy are enticing, but like all historical parallels not entirely reliable. There may still be hope. Civilized and amiable people do not always lose. To begin with, not all Europeans have reached the *faisandé* or gamy stage. A large number of them are still practically untouched by the more epicurean forms of their own civilization. Peasants in distant provinces, industrial workers newly recruited from the farms, and the recently emerged affluent bourgeois are often as uncouth as the citizens of the emerging or of the totalitarian nations. There may still be a vast reserve of local barbarians in Europe to challenge the primacy of outside barbarians and possibly defeat them. (This is the secret Hitler discovered.) Then, if it is indubitably true that a confederated or federated or united or integrated or whatever Europe does not yet really exist, and what there is is in no better shape than the Greek cities or the Renaissance Italian principalities to resist, without massive outside help, the onslaught of invading armies, it is nevertheless heartening to observe that there is a united Europe of sorts, a small inarticulate Europe, to be sure, but lively and spontaneous, *l'Europe réelle*, so to speak, not yet to be found in almanacs and yearbooks. How solid it is nobody knows. A number of ill-informed local inhabitants, who do not read newspapers with adequate attention, believe, to be sure, they are citizens of their native country, but also proud citizens of Europe, real Europeans. Some of them who would hesitate to die for their small fatherland, as their fathers did, would probably be willing to fight and die for this nonexistent Europe. They live in (and love) this premature, almost imaginary confederated polyglot nation as unquestioningly and unconsciously as fish live in water.

In their youth they learn (or absorb) each other's languages (and some argots) almost effortlessly, as a matter of course. Language schools spontaneously spring up everywhere like pimples on an adolescent's face or mushrooms after the warm autumn rains. For the first time in history the British (some of them anyway) speak French, Italian, or German without a condescending heavy accent. More and more people are able to listen to each other's television broadcasts across borders or seas (one sees France's Antenne 2 rebroadcast in Rome from Corsica); more and more people study, work, enjoy life, travel, sightsee, swim, ski, eat, drink, and make love in each other's countries. A large number marry other Europeans and raise bilingual children. It is almost impossible to tell what part of Europe the young you meet are from; they appear identical, belonging to the same tribe. (All you can be sure of is that the very blond are probably not Italian or Greek.) It is no longer possible, either, to distinguish one European from another by the cut of his or her clothes. Frenchmen and Germans are almost as elegant, for the first time in more than a century, as only Italians and Englishmen used to be. Germans are thinner than they have ever been. English girls are chic, more so than their mothers and grandmothers, who favored sensible dowdy clothes. Only specialists can tell one country's military uniforms from those of other European countries. Industries merge across frontiers and exchange technical tricks as schoolboys exchange stamps. Merchants flock to each other's fairs as they went long ago to Nizhni Novgorod and to Samarkand.

Financiers, film and TV producers, singers, con men, musicians, terrorists, journalists, smugglers, actors, professors who teach with equal skill in their own or other universities, gamblers, and courtesans ignore boundaries and operate easily all over the Continent. At one time a French citizen was elected leader of an Italian political party, the Partito Radicale. Customs inspectors and border policemen often yawn, play cards, and do not bother to check the passage of fellow European travelers, their passports, and their baggage. High foreign service officials rarely write stuffy ambiguous notes to each other as they used to, notes that could be read from left to right or from right to left; they now consult chattily by telephone as if they were all in one big city to agree on possible common lines of action, and they call each other by their first names. Staff officers meet informally all the time to exchange ideas and bring plans up to date. The secret services and the police forces have belonged to an imaginary united Europe for years. More and more people are even deserting the last refuge of patriotism, gastronomy, and fearlessly eat each other's national specialities. The Germans are spending vast sums to persuade reluctant Italians to eat their sausages and cheeses. Pizza and the little Italian restaurants have conquered Europe; pizza now dominates the Avenue des Champs Elysées, of all places. Supermarkets are filled with more or less identical products everywhere; only the signs and the prices in local languages and currencies are different.

All this, I admit, is also true almost everywhere else in the world today, part of a universal homogenization. Pizza and little Italian restaurants have conquered the globe, not Europe alone. All this is not entirely new either. It was also partly true in the past. Musicians, merchants, opera singers, conductors, millionaires, aristocrats, spies, journalists, gamblers, scientists, swindlers, adventurers, diplomats, financiers, anarchists, and magicians rarely operated in one country alone. Even British sovereigns could often be found somewhere on the Continent—on the Riviera, in Florence, or at famous watering resorts. Long before World War II even the suspicious and obdurate French secretly ate foreign food. They merely called Italian specialities *à la niçoise* (e.g., *ravioli à la niçoise*), German food *à la alsacienne* (e.g., *choucroute à la alsacienne*), and stubbornly mispronounced and misspelled the names of English dishes (*le bifteck, le rosbif, le boudin de Yorkshire*). True enough. Nevertheless, it is evident that these phenomena are now more prevalent than in the past and in Europe more than anywhere else. Exchanges are infinitely easier. Countries being shoulder to shoulder with each other, languages change after but a few hours train or plane ride, and every European must have a working knowledge of his neighbors'. Outside pressures, economic, political, or military, force the people and their governments to stick closer together whether they want to or not. What is also true (and unprecedented) in Europe today is that these trends are accelerating rapidly and no longer involving an exiguous minority of restless, cosmopolitan, adventurous characters such as the Orient Express clients, the drinkers of miraculous mineral waters in international spas, idle aristocrats, or the gamblers at the Baden-Baden or Monte Carlo casinos, but each year larger and larger numbers of people of all classes, millions and millions of them, young and old, obscure, poor, rich, and very rich alike.

This tranquil (and unfounded) certainty of many Europeans that their continent is already One, or on its way shortly to becoming One, a solid, cohesive, awe-inspiring entity, may also be seen in the fact that people unquestioningly call "Europe" what is officially and cautiously known only as the European Economic Community, little more at the present time than a fragile customs union, a mosaic of myopic, national, sacred egotisms badly harmonized, that any robust historical breeze or a serious economic crisis could easily overwhelm (as the German *Zollverein* vanished overnight at the outbreak of the Austrian-Prussian war in 1866), and a network of flimsy and mutable agreements on agricultural prices. These people speak of Europe as confidently and prematurely as the Americans called their country "America" from the beginning, when it consisted only of a ludicrously small fringe on the northeast coast of an immense continent. This free and easy and optimistic appropriation of the name might also be due to the fact that Europeans dream of embracing one day, as soon as historically possible, other contiguous countries, all of them definitely European: Switzerland and Austria, to begin with, which are in the very heart of Europe, Switzerland being the polyglot democratic model and Austria formerly the ancient feudal polyglot prototype of it all; Spain, Portugal, partly European Turkey, and possibly later swallow also some countries to the East, one after another, as far as the Soviet border one fine day, and perhaps later, as de Gaulle wished, even as far as the Urals, where most geographers authoritatively, if arbitrarily, affirm Europe ends and Asia begins.

These Europeans also delude themselves that their Continent already inspires deep respect, wields some authority, and can make its weight felt at crucial moments. They are hurt when the president of the United States, whoever he may be at the time, forgets to consult them or disregards their advice, or when the

Kremlin disdainfully and insultingly overlooks their existence. Better-informed and more skeptical Europeans (as well as non-Europeans) know that the influence of divided Europe is today merely moral, admonitory, and quite negligible. Europe is at best a finger-wagging and foot-dragging entity. As things stand now, it cannot save itself, let alone save the world. The diplomats know, of course, that the original hope to see the Continent united rapidly from above by far-seeing statesmen acting like gods from Olympus has been proved a failure. Many of them now timidly put their trust in the coral-like instinctive construction (notoriously an extremely slow process) of millions of hard-working, tenacious Europeans. Perhaps they may one day produce an impregnable atoll, surrounded by dangerous defensive shoals. If this were to happen, possibly one or two generations from today, surely statesmen will later adorn the result with legal documents ceremoniously signed in historic halls, vaunt their own providential achievements, and be monumentally rewarded in their own countries with suitable statues in bronze. The obscure and occult forces blocking the unification of Europe will then have to disarm in front of a fait accompli, a massive, collective, spontaneous phenomenon, as irresistible and as slow as an Alpine glacier. Unless a great crisis comes too soon, a worldwide economic collapse or a premature confrontation with the Soviet bloc, these self-made Europeans might save themselves. Will they be on time?

TWO

The Imperturbable British

BLACK BECAME the predominant color of men's clothes on the Continent of Europe after the third decade of the nineteenth century. The funereal fashion (which survives in our contemporary evening, morning, and dinner clothes, and in the uniforms of hotel concierges and waiters) came from Britain. Only the continental aristocracy and elite abandoned at first the glossy silks or the vivaciously colored worsteds of previous generations for opaque fuliginous wools, generally imported from across the Channel. Slowly but inevitably the gloomy hue, the symbol of respectability, percolated all the way down to the middle and lower-middle class. In the end, everybody—statesmen, bankers, kings and emperors in mufti, scientists, rentiers, revolutionary thinkers, musicians, professors, lawyers, novelists, poets, clerks, accountants, and shopkeepers—all dressed like clergymen, undertakers, seconds at a duel, or as if in mourning for departed close members of their families.

Something similar had happened in Italy in 1530. The Spaniards had become the dominant power in Europe. That year, Charles V came to Bologna to be crowned both king of Italy and Roman emperor by the Pope and to pose for a portrait by Titian. He and his retinue paraded on horseback through the city streets. The gay Italians, dressed in silks of all colors, brocades, velvets, and damasks, cheered their guests and tossed flowers from balconies hung with multicolored cloths and tapestries. All the unsmiling Spanish dignitaries, as pale as El Greco saints, wore black with white ruffled collars. A few months later the Italians, most of them, wore black too, as if to show their sorrow for the end of the Renaissance and the loss of their liberties and joy of life. "Nero

colòr traditoresco" Tomaso Campanella (1586–1639), Domini-
can monk, poet, philosopher) contemptuously called it in one of
his sonnets, or "black traitorous hue."

Three centuries later there was admittedly no traitorous oppres-
sive significance to the shift in fashion. The wearing of the black
was neither a foreign imposition nor a sign of mourning. It was a
spontaneous homage, a flattering imitation. The imitation was not
quite accurate, to be sure. The model was largely imaginary, the
"Milord" of continental folklore, popular novels and plays, who,
Mussolini contemptuously said several times, "ate five times a
day." He survived till the second half of the twentieth century in a
song of Edith Piaf, "Je vous salue, Milord." Most of these nineteenth-century Englishmen (all Britons were called that on the
Continent) were well educated, well behaved, and incredibly
richer than almost all Continentals. Only Russian grand dukes and
American railroad builders and bankers beat them. Many of their
qualities were not necessarily national traits but the result of
wealth and good upbringing. "It's their confidence," Aldous Huxley said of them in *Antic Hay*, "their ease, it's the way they
take their place in the world for granted, it's their prestige, which
the other people would like to deny but can't" that made them
admired models. The model was enriched by the observation of
the English colonies in Paris, Florence, or the Riviera, idlers, literati, and art lovers; by the embellished souvenirs of homesick
nannies bringing up continental children; or of spinsters and retired Indian army officers enjoying the favorable exchange rate;
and of debauched wastrels, kept by their families as far away as
possible, longing for home.

The imitation could not be accurate because it was dictated
mainly by admiration and envy. The virtues Continentals admired
and envied at that time were those they feared they and their
countrymen lacked; those they thought they needed in order to
cope with the new iron and coal age and to defend themselves
from British overbearing domination; those they believed had determined the inexplicable success of the empire. At the same time,
the wearing of the black was once again, as it had been in Italy

during the sixteenth century, the symbol of the acceptance of an alien code, the rigorous religious code of the Protestant and devout British middle class, but also of a code imposed by the secular necessities (closely related to the religious code) connected with running mines and industries, building railways, administering the world's treasures, winning wars, conquering entire continents and governing them with but a sprinkling of soldiers and civil servants, allegedly in order to improve the natives' lot, patrol the seven seas, explore and open up dangerous unknown lands. The code also included unbending rules of etiquette and manners, the use of forks and knives, but above all, a strict sense of duty. The British model imposed (or forced many incredulous and unwilling Continentals to feign) such unwonted virtues as earnestness, parsimony, prudence, diligence, discipline, perseverance, honesty as the best policy, correct accounting, punctuality, selfless patriotism, courage, the acceptance of death in battle, tenacity, self-control, fair play but, at the same time, the survival of the fittest, loyalty, the pursuit of profit, the practice of vigorous and competitive physical exercises. Incidentally, Continentals also felt obliged to adopt constitutions, parliamentary democracy, and freedom of the press. Maybe, they thought, they were indispensable ingredients of the British secret. The imitation was inevitably precise because it was not really an imitation. The black suit was merely a symbol, a tacit admission of British supremacy in almost all fields, with the exception of abstract philosophy, music, cuisine, and love-making, the admiration and envy for their wealth, power, sagacity, and brutal ruthlessness, whenever necessary. Hadn't the Duke of Wellington, the very personification of all his nation's virtues, chosen to wear a black civilian hunting coat on that fateful day at Waterloo?

To be sure, more important signs of British moral and material influence were to be found in other fields, many of which signs are still with us. Some continental railways keep to the left today because the first lines were built by the English and all others had to follow forever. Sailors still wear variations of the British Victorian uniform which, in some cases, incongruously includes the black neckerchief worn to mourn the death of Horatio Nelson. Royal guards in several countries, including the Vatican until a few years ago, were and still are the imitation, bearskin and all, of the British model. Continental plumbers still use pipes and valves whose diameter is calculated in inches and fractions of inches because the first were imported from Britain, all successive ones had to fit the old in a perennial chain, and there was no way ever to change the system into centimeters. Corduroy is still called "Manchester" in Germany today. There is a hunt club in Rome, founded by a Lord Chesterfield in 1830. The members, dressed impeccably, top hats, pink coats, and all, behaving according to strict nineteenth-century hunting etiquette, crying "Tallyho" when opportune with a Roman accent, still pursue a pack of English hounds and local foxes twice a week in the Campagna. Tailor shops in continental cities are still named "Old England" or "High Life Tailor." Hotels are still called "Bristol," "Oxford et Cambridge," "d'Angleterre," "Prince de Galles," "St. James et Albany," and "de Grande Bretagne." In old-fashioned provincial hotels, signs in faded letters still announce "Five o'clock tea" for long-dead English travelers. Seamen of all countries still navigate the less frequented parts of the oceans using the charts drawn by Sir Francis Beaufort (1774–1857) and estimate the strength of the wind by means of his renowned scale. Distances at sea still have to be measured in British nautical miles, depths almost always in fathoms.

The adoption of English ways (or what the Continentals wanted to believe were English ways) was in the end so widespread as to go practically unnoticed and unquestioned. People automatically chose the best and the best was British. Only a few were so insanely ardent in their pursuit as to be noticed. They were known as "Anglomaniacs" or "dandys" (pronounced à la Française, with the accent on the "y"). "Le Dandysme est fait de flegme, de cant, d'impertinence polie," says a contemporary authority. Napoleon III, who had been a wealthy and smart bachelor in London in his youth, was one of them. Tailors naturally considered London their holy city. My grandfather, the best tailor in

Orvieto, ironed his trousers, like everybody else, with reverse creases at the sides, but added some horizontal creases too because he had noticed English travelers always wore them that way. He did not realize the horizontal creases appeared because travelers had to fold the trousers to pack them in trunks and suitcases. An Italian count, who prided himself on the meticulous perfection of his English elegance, once went to London accompanied by his manservant. He sent him out the first morning to see how the natives were dressed in the street. The man came back perplexed. "Signor conte," he said, "there's nobody in London dressed like an Englishman except you and me!" Count Camillo Cavour, like many wealthy managers of their own farms, went to Britain not only to buy clothes but also the newest agricultural machinery, newly improved breeds of sheep and cattle, and to learn scientific techniques, which included the growing of newly developed grasses, root crops, and proper methods of cultivating grains. He also carefully studied parliamentary procedures at Westminster, just in case. Entrepreneurs bought machines for entire factories in England. Some of these are still intact and functioning today in the Soviet Union. The Russians produced their own spare parts all along, thus keeping historical equipment hard at work after almost a century.

Sports and their terminology were naturally imported from where almost all had been invented. Distinguished Swedes or Greeks or Hungarians or Andalusians in white flannels cried, "Ready?" and waited for the opponent to answer, "Play," before serving a tennis ball across the net. Gentlemen in tweeds went shooting with a recently invented English gun known everywhere by the English term "hammerless." Improved breeds of dogs were also bought in Britain. (There was even one which the French called "le dogue.") The elite rode English saddles the English way wearing English clothes ("la redingote," as everybody knows, is a French corruption of "riding coat"). Distinguished sportsmen, members of one of the Jockey Clubs scattered all over the Continent, raced thoroughbred horses, direct descendants of the original English mares and Arab stallions. English jockeys and trainers came from Britain in large numbers. Their distant descendants, English surnames intact, can still be found today living near racetracks all over the Continent. In Italy, a few inhabit Barbaricina, a village on the coast near Pisa, where in the last century race horses spent the winter months galloping on the sandy beach. Scottish surnames, belonging to the descendants of the engineers who brought the first steamships to the Continent, are still to be found in many ports. Smart carriages and coaches were also imported from across the Channel or built in imitation of chic English models. Most of them preserved their English names, tilbury, victoria, brougham, coach, break, cart, and one, in France, was even known as "la charrette anglaise." *Anglaiser*, or to Englishize, meant cutting the muscles that lowered a horse's tail, thus forcing it always into a smart raised position. The high stepping of a carriage horse was known in Italy as "steppare" or "stepper" in France, and the horse itself "steppatore" or "steppeur." It was as if the Continentals had never bred, ridden, driven, or raced horses, and had never built elegant carriages in the past, which was patently absurd. Didn't the queen of the United Kingdom and empress of India sometimes go to state ceremonies in a carved and gilded coach which had been made by Italians in Italy in the eighteenth century?

English wives were as popular among continental aristocrats as English horses and dogs. (The number of English wives in the entourage of Kaiser Wilhelm II, himself the son of an English princess, was so high as to make anti-British political decisions occasionally hard to take.) Well-born children were brought up by English nannies and often dressed with clothes ordered from London. Vladimir Nabokov once went to the shop in Old Bond Street from which his childhood clothes had been mailed to Saint Petersburg and looked at his name and measurements in the old clients' book with tears in his eyes. The upper class spoke French and English as a matter of course. The more difficult to please sent their shirts to be laundered and ironed in London. I never found out why, English laundries not being noticeably better than others, during my lifetime, anyway. Some gentlemen went on sending their shirts to London until just before the Second World War, even from Nazi Germany. Among such aficionados of English laundering was the chief of staff of Mussolini's ragtag Fascist army during the march on Rome. On that fateful day in October 1922 he wore a starched collar that looked as if it had been cut out of shining black oilcloth. The attraction of other British perfections in the past century is proved today by the existence in many old country houses from Spain to Germany (and possibly still, here and there, in eastern Europe) of bound collections of *The Illustrated London News* of the time, and of Victorian porcelain toilet bowls, evidently imported from where they had been invented by Mr. Crapper. They are usually decorated with tasteful pre-Raphaelite or William Morris patterns of flowers, writhing carnations or irises, and modestly enclosed in elegant mahogany or teakwood boxes with polished brass hinges. The English water-closet bowl of my childhood proudly bore the name "Favoria" and the arms of the United Kingdom, "Dieu et Mon Droit," lion and unicorn and all, exactly where one had to direct one's stream. Continental butlers no longer dressed as in the past in colored liveries, no longer considered themselves part of the family, and no longer took part, while serving at table, in the general conversation. ("Take some more of this, it's very good," or, "I would put on a heavier suit if I were you. It's a chilly day.") They wore black *à l'Anglaise* (they still do where they survive) and became deaf and dumb, with the expressionless smooth faces of marble statues.

This frivolous upper-class urge to impersonate fictive Englishmen and ape imaginary British ways and fashions was only the visible sign of a much deeper state of mind, the certainty that Britain knew best; that its overwhelming power and wealth would take care of most of the world's public problems, military, political, and economic; that private problems could be controlled by the British moral code and rules of good manners; that Britain could prolong the *status quo* indefinitely, and that there was nothing to worry about. Most Continentals accepted the situation with relief and gratitude, some with resignation, a few with a feeling of revolt against what they thought was a demeaning tutelage. Everybody envied, first of all, the impressive and inexplicable stability of the United Kingdom. Foreigners, of course, knew little of the struggles between the parties, and groups within the parties, of the appalling problems, domestic and imperial, and the terrifying social turmoil that troubled British life. As the stormiest sea when observed at a distance from a mountaintop looks like a placid unruffled lake, Britain seemed from across the Channel a perfect, unblemished, and harmonious commonwealth. To be sure Continentals who had never visited the islands could best preserve this illusion, but even those who visited them saw mostly the chic quarters of London, the best hotels, and the houses of upper-class friends. The British themselves often shared this idea of their own country. "I was brought up in a faith untroubled by doubts . . ." says Mr. Cardan, a character modeled on Norman Douglas in Aldous Huxley's *Those Barren Leaves*. "We were all wonderfully optimistic then; believed in progress . . . in Mr. Gladstone and in our moral and intellectual superiority. . . . And no wonder. For we were growing richer and richer every day. The lower classes, whom it was still permissible to call by that delightful name, were still respectful, and the prospect of revolution was still exceedingly remote." Many Britons attributed all social disturbances to sinister outside influences. The political clashes, the high society scandals and the gruesome murders that occasionally filled the popular press were generally dismissed as "inexplicable," mostly owing to foreign importations, to French novels or German political theories. Labor unrest was deemed in puzzling contrast to "the general amiability, on the whole, of the social structure to which later generations of Victorians had grown accustomed. . . . Our strikes, like our crimes, were becoming disturbingly un-English," lamented a puzzled contemporary observer (R. H. Gretton, A *Modern History of the English People*, page 45).

Inevitably, people whose countries were periodically shaken and terrified by revolutions, whose sovereigns were from time to time forced to flee or abdicate, and whose constitutions were continually modified, envied the apparently uncanny harmony and immutability of English life, the condition sine qua non of the national power. They looked with awe at the unquestioned prestige of the Crown, the authority of governments, the universal respect for the unarmed policemen, the Olympian majesty of Parliament, and the durability of the unwritten constitution. They wondered at the affectionate deference with which the upper class was treated by the lower classes, those same lower classes, which, in other countries, were always on the verge of mutiny, hated their betters, dreamed of hanging kings, noblemen, landowners, bankers, and priests to the nearest convenient lampposts, or chopping off all their heads with an ingenious machine. Professor Lawrence Lowell of Harvard put this in a few words in his introduction to his *Government of England* (1908): "Measured by the standards of duration, absence of violent commotions, maintenance of law and order, general prosperity and contentment of the people, and by the extent of its influence on the institutions and political thought of other lands, the English government has been one of the most remarkable in the world. . . . The typical Englishman believes that his government is incomparably the best in the world. It is the thing above all others that he is proud of. He does not, of course, always agree with the course of policy pursued . . . but he is certain that the general form of government is well-nigh perfect."

Continentals also admired and envied the ubiquitous invincible fleet, the famous regiments, the mysterious knack the British had of dominating inexpensively a motley empire inhabited by hundreds of millions of people. The diabolical British Intelligence Service, which infiltrated its agents unnoticed everywhere and ferreted out the world's most jealously kept secrets, was particularly admired and feared. As late as the last war, General Walter Schellenberg of the SS, who built up an independent foreign intelligence service for Himmler, was awed by his British opponents. "Like so many Germans," writes H. R. Trevor-Roper (*The Last Days of Hitler*, chapter 1)—and he could have added, "and all other Continentals"—"he [Schellenberg] was an admirer, a despairing admirer, of the British Intelligence Service—an organization of which indeed he knew very little, but of which he had read evidently much in those amazing novelettes which filled the reference library of the Gestapo. From these he had learnt much about the all-pervasive, incessant engine which, founded by Edward III and perfected by Oliver Cromwell, had secured the otherwise unaccountable success of British diplomacy and politics, and which, operating through the YMCA, the Boy Scout Movement, and other dependent organizations, had overthrown dynasties, altered governments, and assassinated inconvenient ministers throughout the world."

Envied, above all, was the sagacity of British statesmen, who, fully informed by their secret agents of what went on behind the scenes in foreign countries, managed to preserve the peace of Europe and the world (or, some said, occasionally provoked a small useful war) by relentlessly pursuing (or sometimes disrupting) the balance of power, with the unruffled steadfastness of the gambler who alone possesses a fool-proof scientific martingale. They appeared to be upright, far-sighted gentlemen, impeccably dressed, on whose word one could always rely, famous for their honesty and truthfulness, their encouragement of liberty and the redressment of injustice everywhere in the world but in their own kingdom and empire. They took their prestige and authority for granted. This, of course, infuriated foreign statesmen. Prince Felix Schwartzenberg, the Austrian chancellor, wrote, in 1848, after Lord Palmerston had sent him a note defending the rights of the inhabitants of Lombardy to freedom and independence, "It would never occur to us to impose on Lord Palmerston our advice on the Irish problem. He should spare us his on the problem of Lombardy." Incidentally, Queen Victoria was of the same opinion, possibly because of her foreign blood. On October 10, 1848, she wrote her uncle-by-law, King Leopold of Belgium: "It is indeed immoral to force Austria to abandon her legitimate possessions in Italy when we hold Ireland in our power."

At the same time, the impeccable British statesmen could,

whenever necessary, resort with equal ease and elegance to what seemed to foreigners Levantine duplicity, Greek ambiguities, Florentine intrigues, and, but more rarely, outright treachery. This unexpected flexibility offended the French in particular, perhaps because they alone felt entitled to resort to such dubious techniques. They condemned the British, not out of moral prejudices, but because of the incoherence between gentlemanly pretenses and actual performance. They called Britain *"la perfide Albion."* Stendhal wrote, "Les Anglais sont, je crois, le peuple du monde le plus obtus, le plus barbare. Cela au point que je leur pardonne les infamies de Sainte Hélène. Ils ne les sentaient pas" (The English are, I believe, the most obtuse, most barbaric people in the world. This to the point that I forgive them the infamies of Saint Helena. They were not aware of them [*Souvenir d'égoisme*, chapter 1]). Even Jules Verne had it in for the English. He had one of his characters say: "Si le monde savait toutes les injustices que ces Anglais, si fiers de leur guinées et de leur puissance navale, ont semées sur le globe, il ne resterait pas assez d'outrages dans la langue humaine pour leur jeter dans la face" (If the world knew all the injustices those Englishmen, so proud of their guineas and their naval power, have scattered over the earth, there wouldn't be enough insults in the human language to throw in their faces [*L'Etoile du Sud*, chapter 5]). Few Continentals realized that a gentleman was, according to a well-known English definition, "a man who does things no gentleman should do as only a gentleman can."

This evoking of faded clichés, this thumbing through old photographic albums is not an idle exercise in nostalgia. It is essential in order to understand recent and contemporary events and to peer into the future. Everybody knows Britain is no longer what it was. Nobody wears black unless he has to. The empire has gone the ways of Nineveh and Tyre, its domination of the world is over, the awesome fleet and the tentacular intelligence service are but memories, and the sagacity of its statesmen almost (but not entirely) vanished. Everybody knows the British working class is in en-

demic revolt against the strictures of the industrial society, and the
upper class pleasurably relieved to be finally rid of its uncomfortable sense of duty, the white man's burden, and the straitjacket
code of yesterday. Everybody (including many Britons) now
knows the English are more or less like many other people. They
make the same mistakes, commit the same crimes, and show some
of the same weaknesses. Like everybody else, they have been
trying in vain to find a way to work less and less and to consume
more and more. They are broke and confused.

Nevertheless, their old prestige, like embers under the ashes the
morning after, is not yet dead. Foreigners still expect them to
show something of their ancient firmness, resourcefulness, diplomatic dexterity, and to perform miracles. This has irremediably
influenced the Continentals' views in the last decades. De Gaulle
refused to admit the British, who, he thought, were perfidious and
treacherous, to the European Common Market for years, because
he naturally feared they would infiltrate it with unscrupulous
agents and astute officials, keep a "special relationship" with the
United States behind Europe's back, lead Europe with their authority, and eventually turn it surreptitiously into a British domain. Others, the Italians, for instance, and the smaller nations,
badly wanted Britain in from the beginning for the same obsolete
reasons. They hoped it would counterbalance the political weight
of France, especially since France was allied to the economic
weight of West Germany, and guide all western European nations
as soon as possible toward some sort of federation or confederation, thus one day turning Europe into the third superpower. Italians and others remembered the ancient fame the British elite had
deserved as foreign secretaries and diplomats, with their skeptical
knowledge of man, classical culture, balanced judgments, prudence, easy manners, and capacity to inspire trust, as well as their
ability to utilize devious stratagems when necessary, which the
Italians admired. They also thought the British "special relations"
with the United States (or what was left of them after the Second
World War) not at all a disadvantage, as de Gaulle did, but a
convenience for everybody. The European point of view could be

explained in Washington with greater clarity and, it was hoped, treated with greater respect when expounded with a slight, hesitant, upper-class British accent.

How had the British done it? How, in the first place, did a peripheral island rise from primitive squalor to world domination? And how did they, between the wars, still manage to keep their rickety empire together with little visible effort? What was their secret? The search for it has vital contemporary relevance. The apparent disappearance of the British knack for greatness is one of the keys to understanding not only their decadence and their weakness, but also the disarray and impotence of Europe. The question of how they had achieved world supremacy haunted most other nations for a long time. The hope of isolating the formula, to duplicate it and reach the same results, obsessed foreign kings, emperors, dictators, presidents, and prime ministers for generations. This political Anglomania was the cause of much restlessness and tension in international relations in the nineteenth and twentieth centuries and not the least of the causes of the two world wars. Every self-respecting European country (including the United States at the turn of the century) felt compelled to acquire a powerful navy and colonial possessions as the British had done. Mussolini himself got around to conquering Ethiopia— thus endangering the stability of Europe—much too late, when the imperial fashion had faded, Kipling had long been dead, and other nations were beginning to shed with relief some of their more expensive, ungrateful, and ungovernable domains. Wilhelm II also acquired African colonies and built a mighty fleet just to emulate and defeat the nation he most admired, loved, and feared, and by which he longed to be admired, loved, and feared. In the end, he was compelled to go to war in 1914 by the sheer weight of his country's armaments, the size of its costly fleet, and the logic of his anti-British rhetoric. The Japanese fleet at Tzushima in 1905 was a meticulous reproduction of British models and had British naval officers-advisers on board some of the ships. Hitler himself never concealed his hope of wresting the domination of Europe from the British while preserving their empire, which he considered one of the great political achievements of white Aryan man. "Like so many foreigners . . ." wrote James Morris (*Farewell the Trumpets*, page 432), "Hitler thought of the Empire as it had been. . . . He conceived of it as aristocratic, ubiquitous, imperturbable, immensely experienced. . . . 'I do not wish the Crown of the British Empire to lose any of its pearls, for that would be a catastrophe for mankind. . . . an Empire which it was never my intention to harm,' he wrote."

What was the British secret? Were they supermen?

Military and naval supremacy, moral authority, technical proficiency, wealth, and the possession of colonies were not the answer. They were more the result of greatness than its cause. I tried to study the problem many years ago when I was a young, naive, and eager journalist in London. I listened to debates in the House of Commons, read books, sometimes in the British Museum Library like Karl Marx, bought and borrowed more, and saw as many eminent persons as would receive me. There was no mystery about the past. Everybody agreed the empire had somehow come about through a felicitous convergence of rare heterogenous factors at a favorable period in history. The people, first of all, who were brave, stubborn, ruthless, industrious, pragmatic, and inventive; their proverbially excellent seamanship; their desire for wealth generated by the relative poverty of their land; its appallingly bad weather; their desire for adventures and excitement because of the boredom of their lives; their uncanny ability as merchants, bankers, and underwriters; their capacity, in older days anyway, to accept discipline and follow their leaders to hell if necessary; their jealous defense of their liberty; their belief that they were, if not always the best, surely unique; and, in the end, their coal mines.

None of these explanations was really satisfactory, I concluded. There were other hardy, adventurous, and industrious people all over Europe, whose countries were poor and dull, who were condemned to live in appalling weather, brave, disciplined people who were jealously proud of their liberty, vaguely contemptuous of foreigners, but who never managed to extend their empires (and their languages) to the ends of the earth, hold them more or less intact for centuries, and strike the fear of God in all foreigners' hearts. Most of these hardy people, in fact, were resigned to staying put and being unhappy in their own countries. The British Empire had grown so gradually that it had been possible to cultivate an imperial elite of sailors, soldiers, adventurers, administrators, diplomats, bankers, jurists, engineers, linguists, teachers, scientists, and cartographers to cope with the problems as they arose, and poets to sing the glory of their people. An Italian could not help comparing the British to another miraculous maritime merchant empire, the Most Serene Republic of Venice, which had also declined mysteriously and ineluctably. It too had started on islands, depended for its growth on skilled seamanship and a flair for commerce, established and defended trading routes, created commercial beachheads in distant countries, accumulated vast fortunes, fought its enemies victoriously on land and sea for centuries, occasionally lost some of its colonies but conquered others. It too developed a capable and virile elite conscious of its mission and responsibilities, but also eager to amass wealth for themselves and the Republic, an elite whom the people were proud to obey and under whom they fought bravely.

But what I was interested in in those years was the present. I tried to discover whether the British really were inordinately intelligent or whether there was an inordinate number of intelligent men among them. Like all Italians, most Frenchmen, and Mediterranean people in general, I then believed a nimble mind, quick reflexes, eloquence, and brilliant improvisations were the essential requisite for success. The Italians firmly believe this even after their cleverness has repeatedly led them to catastrophes. I studied the eminent, gray-haired, distinguished gentlemen in their offices, where great historic decisions had been taken in the past and would surely be taken again in the future. I studied them in their ancient clubs. They received me with stiff courtesy and some bewilderment. Some let their monocles drop in astonishment (nature too often imitates clichés), and let them oscillate at the end of black silk cords, at my more indiscreet questions. They cleared their throats, said, "Er, er," thought awhile, then solemnly expressed some banal truism with the tone of a man quoting the wisdom of the ages. They said, for instance, "His Majesty's government is in favor of every initiative that might further the cause of peace in the world," or "The key to peaceful international relations is good faith, mutual respect, and loyal adherence to treaties." Once, on the day the papers had announced that Mussolini had nominated one of his henchmen to a cabinet post, an expert in foreign affairs I was interviewing asked me, "Is this new minister a man of principle?" The Englishman I was talking to was not naïve. He surely must have known that a dictator, no matter how powerful, only wanted weak, malleable, docile men in his entourage and banished men of principle as if they were the devil's spawn. Was this Englishman dull-witted or was he pulling my leg?

In the end I concluded there was no sure way to ascertain if an Englishman was intelligent or stupid. My colleagues in Fleet Street pubs and some of my friends were evidently quick-witted. They were almost the exact equivalent of the Roman wits who gathered at Aragno and the French at Les Deux Magots or La Coupole. They conversed freely with me. None of them, however, had imperial responsibilities. The important gentlemen I interviewed naturally had to be laconic and prudent. They were evidently conscious that they faced an inquisitive foreign journalist. They wrapped themselves up in the traditional mantle of British reserve, which became almost impenetrable in my particular case. I was not only a dark-haired Roman Catholic, an Italian, by definition capable of all the iniquities so aptly described by Elizabethan dramatists, but at that moment also the treacherous representative of a hostile totalitarian regime. I never tried to explain that I was no Fascist and that I disagreed vigorously with my government. (I ended up in jail not many years later.) They would scarcely have believed me. In the improbable case that they did, they would have considered me in an even worse light, as a traitor, a traitor to a despicable cause, to be sure, but still a traitor.

Furthermore, I learned, the British code of behavior made it almost impossible for any well-mannered person to seem intelligent or well informed even at an informal dinner or in a casual conversation. As they were forbidden to talk about themselves, their families, personalities, children, servants, the things they did, the things they knew best, religion, and politics, they were therefore limited to noncommittal generic statements and vague banalities. To fill the silence, they were trained to ask bland questions and make other people talk. I found myself once explaining Dante to an attentive man I discovered too late was a renowned Dante expert. Another time I talked at length at dinner about China to two women. They did not, because they could not, tell me that one of them had lived there many years and had written a famous novel, *Peking Picnic*, and that the other was the inventor of an arcane theory, which bore her name, to explain the shape of the Chinese jade scepter. Well-mannered people were also strictly forbidden to say anything witty or clever. If anything of the kind was said, usually by a foreigner or a famous Irishman, at a dinner table, silence followed. Nobody laughed. As Lord Chesterfield had written, "There is nothing so illiberal and so ill bred as audible laughter." All faces turned in mild embarrassment in the direction of the uncautious witty man. Then conversation resumed haltingly.

My first conclusion was that the English, like most Nordic people, were not very sharp as a whole, and that the secret of their success surely was not exorbitant intelligence. Later I discovered that some of them were definitely intelligent and that a few were exceptionally so, more than the average Continental, but that it was practically impossible to separate the dull from the acute, the Sherlock Holmeses from the Doctor Watsons, as they all behaved and spoke alike. On the other hand, all of them, the dull and the acute, somehow knew how to act bravely, splendidly, and usually successfully in critical or difficult circumstances, as if they had all been intelligent and that this capacity of theirs was the secret that made their country great, the secret they now apparently wanted to forget.

A friend of mine, Bernardo, a Roman born of an English mother, who had lived and worked in London for years, tried to explain the mystery to me. He was thoroughly Italian, but his family was thought to be English enough for George V and Queen Mary to stay for one night in their palazzo during a state visit to Rome. At that time, a visit to King Victor Emmanuel and a visit to the Pope had to be kept neatly apart, as there had been no relations between the Quirinale and the Vatican since 1870. A foreign sovereign had to make believe he was leaving Italy, bid a formal good-bye to the King, usually spend the night in his own embassy, which was foreign soil, and leave the morning after for the Vatican as if he had just arrived from abroad. In the case of George V, Bernardo's house was probably considered more comfortable than the embassy.

Bernardo warned me first of all that I, an Italian, couldn't reach any valid conclusion, because the English behaved in a particular way when there were foreigners present. He told me that as a boy after the First World War he spent many summers with various aunts, uncles, and cousins in Britain. One of these houses was by the sea and the children went bathing every day. On the way to the beach they followed shortcuts across a war cemetery, changing itinerary every time, and made up a pool based on the sum of the dead soldiers' ages marked on the crosses they passed. They did this as a lark, laughing and joking. One morning, however, they were silent and solemn. No pool. Bernardo asked how come. He was told that that day one more cousin had arrived, the son of a Hungarian father, and that it was not *bon ton* to have fun based on the ages of British war-dead in front of a former enemy.

My friend Bernardo, after mulling over the problem for many years, had developed a theory that explained everything. He believed that it wasn't important for Englishmen to be intelligent (intelligence could be a hindrance) because, as I had discovered, they all could behave intelligently when the need arose. This is how it worked. They all had a few ideas firmly embedded in their heads. He said "seven ideas," but his figure was probably too low. Whatever the number, the ideas were exactly identical and universal. That was why in older days, in distant lands with no possibility of communicating with their superiors, weeks or months by sailing ship away from London, admirals, generals, governors, ambassadors, or young administrators alone in their immense districts, captains of merchant ships, subalterns in command of a handful of native troops in an isolated outpost, or even common ordinary Englishmen, facing a dangerous crisis, had always known exactly what to do, with the certainty that the prime minister, the foreign secretary, the cabinet, the queen, the archbishop of Canterbury, the ale drinkers in any pub, or the editor of the *Times* would have approved heartily, because they too had the same seven, or whatever, ideas in their heads and would have behaved in the same way in the same circumstances. He mentioned Fashoda as an illustration. Kitchener did not have to ask anybody what to do when Major Jean-Baptiste Marchand arrived. He raised the flag (the Egyptian flag in this case), risking a war with France, possibly a European war. The fact that the British knew they all had the same "seven" ideas in their heads made it possible for the authorities in London to trust the men on the spot blindly, those who surely knew more about the local situation than anybody else.

How were those "seven" ideas implanted in the British heads? Bernardo explained that what he could talk about was the people he knew best, the elite, the quintessence of Britishness (the Nobil 'Uomini of Venice, the people inscribed in the Golden Book), whom the crowds used to follow, as they did in Venice until the end, sometimes enthusiastically, and the elite, open to new talent in each generation, was mainly formed of people who were related or related to relations, had known each other from childhood, had gone to the same schools and universities, called each other by their first names, spoke with the same accent, as if the upper class were a distinct province. The "seven" ideas had been driven into their heads in their mothers' laps, in the nursery, in the classrooms, in the playing fields of whatever public schools they had gone to. But, he said, all other Britons of all classes shared the same ideas, absorbed in childhood from their parents at home, from ministers in church, and from the teachers in whatever school they went to. As long as problems could be solved and crises faced with those ideas, the empire and the peace of the world had been secure. Now (we were talking in the thirties) the world was changing, other nations were successfully competing with the British, problems had become sticky and incomprehensible, brutality had taken the place of dexterity, colonial possessions wanted to give up the placid prosperity of alien rule in exchange for independence, poverty, and interminable internal wars: the magic of the "seven ideas" no longer worked. This was confirmed to me, just before the Second World War, by an old *Times* correspondent, in Rome, McClure. He was a lanky and tall elderly man, baffled and embittered by the current crisis. He said, "You know, this Mussolini, this Hitler, these threats of war . . . they are signs of bad manners, *cattiva educazione, au fond.*"

In 1954 the European idea looked irremediably dead. The French Parliament had rejected, not without some British relief, the creation of a European Defense Community, which ironically had been invented especially to please France. (The French wanted, it was said, a German army strong enough to defeat the Soviet Union but weak enough to be kept in its place by Luxembourg.) The EDC had looked like a way to rearm Germany, safely locked in a straitjacket within a unified European defense system. At the same time, it had been of course a surreptitious attempt to arrive at a unified foreign policy (without which a unified defense force made no sense) and eventually also one day at a unified European supergovernment (without which a unified foreign policy made no sense either). A few months later the European idea was resuscitated by Gaetano Martino, the Italian foreign minister. He was one of the most intelligent Italian statesmen of the time, which is not saying much, as there were (and still are) not many of them. He was a man of great integrity, a doctor in private life, a university professor of physiology and a brilliant scientist, whose vast culture extended to history, sociology, economics, and political science. He spoke several languages fluently.

Martino chose Messina for a meeting of his European colleagues for electoral reasons. Messina was his birthplace and his constituency. The Sicilian town was of excellent auspice: it was the port where Crusaders had gathered a few times before sailing to the Holy Land and where the Christian fleets had waited for each other before sailing to Lepanto, where they destroyed the Turkish fleet and freed Europe for a while from the Eastern menace of that day. (In reality the delegations met at nearby Taormina, a much more scenic and pleasant place, where excellent hotels had always catered to fussy foreign guests.) The British didn't accept the invitation and declined to send anybody. Martino's apparent purpose was the creation of some sort of customs union or common market, something to which the French surely, and the British possibly, could not seriously object. Everybody agreed with him in principle, the French with some reservations and the Germans, the Dutch, and the Belgians enthusiastically, in the hope of dumping the costly products of their patriarchal farms on captive customers, which they managed to do in the end. They all decided to meet again in Brussels later, once more asking the British to take part in the debates, to formulate the best possible practical project. This (the Spaak Report) eventually became the foundation for the Treaty of Rome, signed in 1957, which gave official birth to most of the existing EEC institutions.

The British, however, rejected the Spaak Report and did not sign the treaty. This withdrawal of theirs was crucial. They did not care to assume their historic role as arbiters of continental politics (probably because they thought they had never lost it) and did not use their authority and experience to lead Europe toward the future. They cut themselves off from inevitable developments, disastrously both for themselves and for the other Europeans. When they tried later, in 1963, to enter the Common Market, they were rebuffed and humiliated by the French as impoverished supplicants and were finally accepted much too late, under conditions gravely unfavorable to them, which they had not helped to formulate.

Most delegations in Brussels in 1955 were headed by foreign ministers or eminent persons of comparable rank. The British sent a senior civil servant from the Board of Trade, Russell Bretherton, as if to proclaim the fact that they believed the meeting was solely what it purported to be, a dreary, sterile gathering of economists and treasury officials and not a political reunion of vast significance one way or another. He was surprised and flattered to join such an elevated company. "I have never before or since been called Your Excellency," he recalled. His superiors in London thought nothing would come of the meetings anyway, except more verbiage and communiqués ambiguously worded to please friends and foes. They trusted the French would block dangerous progress, if any, toward real integration. Therefore Bretherton had instructions "to cooperate but avoid all commitments." He behaved accordingly. He spoke very little, smoked his pipe incessantly, was polite and attentive but cold, evasive, ironic, and openly skeptical. One of the participants, Robert Rothschild of Belgium, *directeur de cabinet* of his foreign minister, Paul-Henri Spaak, described Bretherton, years later in an interview with Michael Charlton, a veteran foreign correspondent and BBC commentator (*Encounter*, August, 1981). He said, "Bretherton usually had a cynical and amused smile on his face. He looked at us like naughty children, but not really mischievous, enjoying themselves, playing the sort of game which had no relevance and no future." Bretherton objected to concrete proposals, usually for excellent technical reasons, and pointed out that any good idea that was approved by everybody else would not please the British government and would be surely voted down by the House. One day he vanished altogether and was seen no more. "I think it was the last and the most important bus that we missed," said Anthony Nutting, who had been responsible for European affairs in the Foreign Office at the time. "I think we could still have had the leadership of Europe if we had joined in Messina."

The British stand particularly disappointed the Italians, the Belgians, and the Dutch. Many were the attempts made during the following years by everybody to convince the British they had acted against their own interests. One desperate effort was made personally by Spaak, who traveled to London to win over "Rab" Butler, chancellor of the exchequer, an old-fashioned John Bull Englishman and one of the most resolute opponents of European integration. Robert Rothschild, who was present, recalled later, "It was obvious Spaak was not convincing Butler. I can still see him, very immobile, looking at Spaak without saying a word, and the colder he became the warmer Spaak became, and the warmer Spaak became the colder and colder Butler obviously became. After a while we realized it was no use going on. We said goodbye and went off. . . . As we walked back, Spaak turned around to us and said, '. . . I don't think I could have shocked him more, when I tried to appeal to his imagination, than if I had taken my trousers off.' "

The Brussels deliberations were a turning point, the opportunity that would never return. Evidently the British could have collaborated to formulate the recommendations in their own interest, incorporate their ideas in the Treaty of Rome, and be among the founding fathers of the kind of Common Market they preferred. Even Bretherton later admitted, "If we had taken a firm line, that we wanted to come in and be a part of this, we could have made that body more or less into whatever we liked." They were still considered the moral leaders of Europe, if only because their rivals were too enfeebled to count. Germany had no political influence, Italy and Benelux were too weak, and France was in disarray.

It is surely too simple to think that had the British got in on the ground floor among the promoters and founders of Europe, and among the drafters and signers of the Treaty of Rome, the unification of the Continent would be by now a fait accompli. This is a mere exercise in idle nose-of-Cleopatra speculation, the futile exploration of one more "if" of history. Surely the British could not easily have cut through the tangle of complex problems, preconceptions, and contrasting interests. They could not have performed miracles. As Hegel might have said, and possibly did, "Whatever is had to be." Nevertheless, there is no doubt that in the fifties, Italy, West Germany, and Benelux needed an authoritative ally to balance the stubborn and overbearing power of the French, who wanted to cut down the dream to a mere customs union of separate *patries* to serve above all some of their separate national interests, and more precisely, sell their agricultural products at a high price to keep the *paysans* happy. There is no doubt either that an early British contribution would at least have simplified the topheavy, intricate, and awkward institutions, and distributed advantages and disadvantages to all participants a little more equally. Some of the Britons' native virtues (or what Continentals believe to be their native virtues) would have been extremely useful, such as their capacity not to be swept away by emotional storms, their tenacity and stubbornness. Surely the efficiency of their high civil servants, their ability to handle foreign affairs deftly, the weight of their ancient prestige, their knowledge of trade and finance, and their flexibility would have made a great, possibly a definitive, difference in the outcome.

Curiously enough, it was the Britons' most traditional virtues and prejudices (or what was left of them), those very virtues that would have been most useful, that had paralyzed them and prevented them from believing in the project and cooperating. First, of course, was patriotism. Most of the men who at the beginning rejected the European idea had had responsible roles in World War II. They kept on considering their country what it had been indisputably only a few years before, one of the three great powers. England had paid fully for its place alongside them in ruins, human lives, courage, gold (all foreign holdings amassed over centuries had been sold without hesitation within weeks), and by the unique political and strategic sagacity of its leaders. Such men naturally found it unthinkable to join a condominium of defeated, weak, frightened, and impecunious second-rank nations. The leaders' patriotism (and that of most other Britons) included faith in the innate absolute superiority of their people, not necessarily always of single men, but surely always of the nation as a whole. History had confirmed this often enough in the past, remote, recent, and very recent, to be doubted only by isolated cranks. Were they not still better than any Continental in every—well, practically every—field that really counted? Didn't the ordinary inferior humans still begin at Calais? To be sure, some individual Continentals could be brilliant and sometimes admirable, but most of them were bizarre, slippery, and often incomprehensible. They ate incdible things such as octopuses, frogs, and snails. "Only foreigners waltz backward," Englishmen said contemptuously in the past, when the waltz was still fashionable. (All these prejudices used to be expressed openly. Now they are politely kept hidden or lightly alluded to. Some Britons go so far in their attempt to understand foreigners as to speak Continental languages fluently, cat octopuses, frogs, and snails from time to time, all seasoned with lots of garlic.) Englishmen thought it was best to have as little to do with Continentals as possible in the present as they had done in the past, and to be extremely cautious when they dealt with Continentals. In a way, Britain still sees itself as the sceptered isle, cut from the Continent by divine will. If God had wanted to tie it to the rest of Europe, He would evidently not have dug the Channel. Wasn't it therefore sinful and somewhat sacrilegious to attach Britain to the terra firma by treaties, tunnels, or bridges? Added to this then was the feeling the British were somehow still responsible, morally at least, to their own former empire, more tied to it than to the rest of Europe. In their old domains, the language, institutions, culture, and traditions of Britain were still alive, cricket was still played, and some judges still wore wigs. Could such intangible ties be easily cut?

All this made them particularly wary of being imprisoned in any durable organization that might one day acquire supernational powers. As Palmerston said, "England has neither eternal friends nor eternal enemies. She has only eternal interests." Britain had always been a jealous guardian of its freedom of action, proud of its solitude. The British preferred at all times to be the victims of their own mistakes rather than to trust the judgment of other people. This is one of the reasons why their expeditionary forces in France in two wars were strictly autonomous, collaborating with, but not subordinated to, the French high command. Added to all this was the fact that their interventions in continental affairs in peace and war down the centuries awakened extremely hideous memories. To be sure they always had to watch what was going on across the Channel and to intervene when necessary. They accepted a few continental kings and, more often, continental queens, for political reasons, conducted elaborate negotiations, participated in international conferences and congresses, and occasionally landed armies across the Channel to fight Philip II, Louis XIV, Napoleon, the Kaiser, and Hitler, among others. These wars cost them millions of pounds and a heavy toll in human lives, but always in the end prevented one power or another from dominating Europe uncontested. Clearly, Britain could not pursue its own ancient and well-tested technique of preserving the peace by adding its weight to this or that plate of the scales if it were organically and indissolubly tied to one side. Added to this was the British innate aversion to vast, noble, and vague political designs, especially when formulated by foreigners. It was at all times one of their more useful and enviable virtues. Their socialists were the only ones in Europe who ignored Karl Marx, whose doctrine was based on a study of their own society and the thinking of their own economists. Their great-grandfathers had recoiled from joining the Holy Alliance in 1815 and the great-grandsons felt the same way about a united Europe. The British thought, rightly, that the Holy Alliance would never work and, wrongly, that the European project would die stillborn. They believed it was therefore a waste of time to worry overmuch about it.

When they finally joined the European Common Market, disastrously, too late, too expensively, at the wrong moment, they did so reluctantly and somewhat squeamishly, though politely concealing their feelings, like decayed aristocrats obliged by adverse circumstances to eat in a soup kitchen for the needy. They made it very clear they did it because of force majeure but that they were ready to leave at the first opportune time. It was disagreeable for them to admit that, yes, participation was costing them a lot of money and was raising the price of their food, but that their departure would cost them even more. According to the *Economist*, since Britain joined, its exports to the community had risen by 560 percent while those to the rest of the world by only 290 percent. Two-fifths of its exports went to their market partners and some two and a half jobs out of ten depended on access to it. Curiously enough it was not the old elite who thought of Britain in proud ancient terms and wanted to keep it isolated behind its moat, not tied "with inky blots and rotten parchment bonds" to deceitful foreigners, but a large part of the working class, especially the left of the Labour party.

The fact is that the traditional and admirable virtues of the British people, Bernardo's "seven ideas," have become obsolete or are at best premature. They cling, or rather all of them used to cling and many of them still cling, to the virtues that made them great and powerful, the virtues they distilled from their native land, the surrounding seas, the weather, and the vicissitudes of their history. They are the virtues of sailors on sailing ships who face raging seas and hurricanes or wait weeks for the windless calm to end; farmers on inhospitable land, resigned to the unpredictable weather; fishermen on the stormy and fog-bound seas of the North; lonely shepherds on deserted moors; hunters in the wilderness; adventurers in all parts of the world; soldiers in squares unflinching under the enemy's cavalry charges; corsairs; horsemen. (Perhaps such virtues are more evident in the case of the horsemen. This is obviously why the animal has always played such an important symbolic role in the intimate and public life of the country. To calm a difficult, spirited animal over jumps, in the hunting field or in the littered chaos and tumult of the battlefield, a rider must avoid the quick reflexes of the Latin and show imperturbable steadiness. His hands must be still, his body at ease, his weight straight on his buttocks.) Surely it was their hard life that taught the British to be brave, resourceful, patient, far-seeing, self-controlled, or to act as if they were. In one word, they are stoics.

Most of them were stoics to begin with long ago with but few hedonistic exceptions. Later most of them still behaved like stoics, whether they were or not, because that was the way to be and it was inconceivable to be anything else. Later still, as their belief in their historic mission gradually waned, the number of genuine stoics diminished, until in the end they seemed obsolete figures of fun to the ironic and irreverent young. Nevertheless, when facing a life or death national crisis, they always found their real nature again, as in Flanders in the First World War, in Dunkirk, in the skies of Britain, in the Cyrenaican desert, daring German submarines' attacks to convoys, during the Second World War, or in the Falklands in 1982. It is probable that should they be put once again to the test, they would show themselves to be what they have always been, what their ancestors were.

The fact that most of their churches contain variations of stoicism does not necessarily mean they were taught the ancient code of behavior and philosophy in church. Religions often are the codification and sanctification of a people's native character. (It was the Italian people who created the Counter Reformation Church in their image, and not, as some think, the other way around.) Stoics believed (I quote the *Britannica* for the sake of brevity and to avoid controversies) that "the universe was rational, despite appearances; that man could regulate his life by emulating the calm and order of the universe, learning to accept events with a stern and tranquil mind and to achieve a lofty moral worth." They believed "man, as a world citizen, was obliged to play an active part in public affairs. . . . Thus, moral worth, duty, and justice were singularly stoic emphases, together with a certain sternness of mind. For the moral man is neither merciful nor shows pity, because each suggests a deviation from duty and from the fated necessity that rules the world." Demonstrations of the fundamental stoicism of the British can be culled abundantly from archives, political documents, history books, anecdotes, literature, and poetry. In my youth their stoicism was proved by individuals sitting on the roofless tops of London buses in the rain, by students' quarters at Oxford, by the appalling cuisines of provincial inns, by the heating arrangement and the plumbing of houses without *chauffage central* and with outside drains that froze in winter. Nowadays, their stoicism is proved by the patience with which they put up with absurd government regulations, inefficiency, and above all, the recurrent miners' or railway men's strikes, which paralyze the country for weeks. (Italians also have to put up with strikes, probably more strikes than any other country in the world, but theirs is not stoicism. It is pessimism. They are always resigned to the worst and are gratified and relieved to discover that things, as bad as they are, are not as bad as they could be.) Kipling's "If," a sacred text a few generations ago, and still embedded in many British hearts, could have been written by Marcus Aurelius. The embarking at Dunkirk of the British expeditionary force and the Battle of Britain, as well as the reconquest of the Falklands, must have been applauded in a stoic heaven by Zeno, Marcus Porcius Cato the younger (who killed himself at Utica not to fall into the hands of the tyrant), Cicero, Seneca, Marcus Aurelius, Kant (whose concepts of duty and imperturbability are notoriously drawn from stoicism), and Kipling himself. Definitely stoic were the sober newspaper comments on the brilliant, skillful, and daring Falklands war, in which most ancient British virtues surprisingly shone once again. It was a highly pragmatic operation undertaken in defense of international law and morality and surely not for gain. I will quote only one comment, Alexander Chancellor's in the *Spectator* after the victory. It began, "A little rejoicing is now in order, but only a little. We may rejoice that the Falklands war did not end in a bloodbath at Port Stanley. . . . We may rejoice at the performance of our armed forces who have conducted themselves with great skill and with as much humanity as is possible in war." It is clearly inconceivable for anybody not a Briton to write so soberly after such a brilliant and risky military performance.

Clearly such virtues, admirable as they still are, are outdated, unfit (except for rare occasions) for the complex and corrupt times we live in, or at best, as I pointed out, should one day the world change for the better, which is unlikely, premature. They surely have not aided in the construction of an integrated Europe. Take but one of the stoic virtues, imperturbability. In the past it made the British dangerous adversaries in negotiations, on battlefields, or when governing turbulent mutinous colonies. It was this virtue that enraged Napoleon at Waterloo, who cried, "This man Wellington is so stupid he does not know when he is beaten and goes on fighting."

Roberto Ducci, a brilliant man, Italian ambassador to London for years, one of the team who wrote the Treaty of Rome, and a *desenchanté* believer in Europe, thought imperturbability was today one of the main impediments to efficient collaboration with the British. He discovered it was always difficult, if not impossible, to make the Foreign Office aware of the gravity of an approaching crisis and of the necessity of taking some immediate decisions. The British foreign secretary or high official, who evidently considered him an excitable and emotional Latin to be humored and calmed like a jittery horse, told him there was no crisis, not really, no need to rush into rash decisions, and that the best thing to do was to keep cool, do nothing for the time being, and wait for the murky situation to clear up. This approach, the very best in the days of sailing ships and armies marching on foot, is clearly inadequate in a world in which events follow each other at dazzling speed and opportunities vanish forever within hours. Lord D'Abernon (quoted by Geoffrey Madan in his *Notebooks: A Selection*) put it this way: "An Englishman's mind works best when it is almost too late."

This is but one of the reasons why the British missed the European bus, which was not only to their detriment, but everybody else's too. They thought there was always time to catch it. They were imperturbable by nature and tradition but also because they did not really believe Europe was their business. Still today, when one asks a Briton, any Briton, pointblank, "Are you European?"

the answer is always, "European? Did you say European? Er, er"—a long thoughtful pause in which all other continents are mentally evoked and regretfully discarded—"Yes, of course, I'm European." This admission is pronounced without pride and with resignation.

THREE

The
Mutable Germans

THE FUTURE OF Europe appears largely to depend today once again, for good or evil, whether we like it or not, as it did for many centuries, on the future of Germany. It is still, as Madame de Staël wrote, *"le coeur de l'Europe"* (the heart of Europe). Destroyed, defeated, humiliated, arbitrarily reshaped according to angry and frightened foreigners' punitive ideas, mutilated of some of its most fertile provinces in the East and of their 17 million inhabitants, it has laboriously climbed back to the top. It has become once again the richest, strongest, most efficient, orderly, productive, scientifically and technologically advanced, as well as the most populous nation of western Europe. In prosperous years, it is the first up; in lean years, the last down (and not all that much down). Italy is too tired, skeptical, unruly, and confused to count. Victorious Great Britain has seen its arrogant pride fade away along with its wealth, power, and prestige. France, of course, firmly and loudly proclaims itself Number One, but too firmly and too loudly at times.

It is therefore once again essential for everybody, the French, the British, the Italians, the other Europeans, as well as the Americans and the Soviets, to keep an eye across the Rhine and the Alps and the Elbe in order to figure out, as our fathers, grandfathers, great-grandfathers, the ancient Romans, and remote ancestors had to do, who the Germans are, who they think they are, what they are doing, and where they will go next, wittingly or unwittingly. This, of course, was always impossible to fathom. How can one tell? Germany is a trompe l'oeil Protean country. As everybody knows, only when one tied down Proteus, the prophetic old man of the sea, could one make him reveal the shape of things to come. But he couldn't be pinned down easily; he continued to change. He could be a roaring lion, a harmless sheep, a slippery serpent, a charging bull, or in turn, a rock, a tree, a brook, a bonfire.

I read about Germany, sporadically and in a desultory manner, all my professional life, and I had to visit the country frequently during the last half century. (There is nothing like seeing people or nations at intervals to be made aware of even the smallest changes.) Surprisingly, all the successive chapters of the history books I read seemed to describe a different country from the one a few pages back or the ones that followed. Not even the geography stayed put. Borders advanced and retreated like tides. Flags changed. Titles changed. The very language varied somewhat from time to time and from place to place. So did the name of the country itself. It was known as "Germania" to Tacitus, "Germany" in English, an empire that included until the last century most of the German-speaking people, Austrians too (but not the German-speaking Swiss), as well as millions of non–German-speaking people. Germany was then short for the "Holy Roman Empire of the German Nation." (This is why, until the beginning of this century, Italians kept on familiarly but erroneously calling the Austrians "Germans.") It was "Deutschland," "Allemagne," "Germania" (inhabited by "Tedeschi"), and sometimes "Das Reich." It was "Niemcy" to the Poles, "Niemets" in Russian (the Slavic words mean "people who do not speak," intelligibly, that is), "Saxland" to the Scandinavians, "Saszka" to the Finns, and so on. For centuries the German empire had a movable capital, or "Pfalz." It was where the emperor and the court pitched their tents, sometimes in the open country or in hamlets which have been forgotten, like Goslar and Wittenberg. For a long time, the only thing that did not vary was the national anthem, its boastful proclamation, "Deutschland über alles," echoing unchanged down the corridors of time. And every time I was there on a journalistic mission I saw a startlingly new country, only vaguely resembling what I had seen before or what I had read about.

To be sure, under the mutable appearances, the provincial differences, the fascinating disguises, the enthusiastic acceptance of the newest ideology (liberalism, romanticism, Hegelian state worship, imperialism, democracy, and fascism), under the Protean transformations, I was aware there must have been a constant basic Germany, whose virtues and vices practically went unchanged from one metamorphosis to the next, from one regime to its successor, from one political, philosophic, or aesthetic fashion to another. But it was difficult, particularly for a hurried foreign traveler, an outsider, to isolate this perennial Germany. It is still difficult for foreigners, and for the Germans themselves. What is the shape of Proteus when caught unaware at rest? "It is characteristic of the Germans that one is seldom wholly wrong about them," wrote Friedrich Nietzsche despairingly (*Beyond Good and Evil*, paragraph 244). "The German soul has corridors and interconnecting corridors in it, there are caves, hiding-places, dungeons in it; its disorder possesses much of the fascinating and mysterious; the German is acquainted with the hidden paths to chaos. . . ."

Germany seemed once, in the nineteenth century, to have been a peaceful Arcadia, cut up like a patchwork quilt into a large number of sovereign fiefs. Even after Bismarck united it in 1871, it still consisted of four kingdoms, five grand duchies, many principalities, and three free cities. Enraptured travelers described the intact picturesque medieval towns, the villages all sparkling windows, the blond children, the top-hatted statesmen in frock coats, the brass bands, the fairy-tale primeval woods, the happy housewives, the hard-working peasants. The people were tenderly sentimental, moral, God-fearing, in love with children, folk tales, and music. Germans were earnest. Stendhal wrote, "Il me semble que l'on fait plus de plaisanteries à Paris pendant une seule soirée que dans toute l'Allemagne en un mois" (I believe more witticisms are bandied about in Paris in one single evening than in all Germany in a month [*Racine et Shakespeare*, chapter 2]). The country gave birth to great poets, great composers, savants, writers of tragedies, and sedulous collectors of legends. It was the schoolteacher to the world, "la patrie de la pensée," Madame de Staël called it. It produced the greatest thinkers, beaverlike constructors of all-embracing philosophic systems, first-class theologians, philologists, archeologists, linguists, physicists, and chemists galore. None of them could be safely ignored by their colleagues in the rest of Europe and the Americas. Italians had to study their own Latin authors and their own more obscure dialects from German texts. All good foreign scholars (Luigi Pirandello, who studied in Bonn, among them) had to spend a few years in Heidelberg, Jena, Berlin, Bonn, or Göttingen. In fact, no serious academic or scientific work could be published anywhere during the last century without an ample German bibliography and German footnotes.

Only from the military point of view did Germans count for little. "Nothing is odder than the German soldiers," wrote Madame de Staël in her book published, strangely enough, after Waterloo, where Blücher and his Prussians carried the day (*De l'Allemagne*, I, chapter 2). "They fear fatigue or bad weather, as if they were all shopkeepers or literati. . . . Wood burning stoves, beer, and tobacco smoke create a heavy and warm atmosphere around them which it is difficult for them to leave. . . . Resolutions are slow, despondency is easy. . . . Imagination, which is the predominant quality of the Germans, inspires a fear of danger. . . . Among them a general who loses a battle is more assured of obtaining forgiveness than one who wins of being applauded." Machiavelli agreed with her. He says in *Ritratto delle Cose della Magna*: "E così si godono questa loro rozza vita e libertà; e per questa causa non vogliono ire alla guerra." (They thus enjoy their rough life and liberty and do not want to go to war.) To be sure, one of the great military leaders and strategists since Alexander, Frederick the Great, had been king of Prussia, and the greatest military theoretician of all times, Karl von Clausewitz, was born at Burg, near Magdeburg; nevertheless, German soldiers frightened nobody. Even George Washington overcame the Hessians on occasion with little difficulty. Not only did Napoleon defeat Germans easily many times almost until the end, but so now and again did some of his more inept marshals.

Then as you turned a few pages in the history book, the Germans suddenly appeared completely transformed. They emerged from the stove-heated rooms filled with pipe smoke in 1870. They crossed the border of France as a gray tide of faceless, disciplined soldiers with spiked helmets, a relentless unstoppable war machine. Where had they come from? Only a few Germans and no foreigner had suspected what the imminent metamorphosis would be like. Heinrich Heine was one of them, and he wrote: "Denk ich an Deutschland in der Nacht, bin ich um meinem Schlaf gebracht!" (When I think of Germany in the night, I am robbed of my sleep!) The well-drilled, well-armed, and well-commanded hordes outmaneuvered, surrounded, and defeated the most glorious army in Europe in a few weeks, captured the old and sick French emperor, Napoleon III, and went on to Paris and triumph in Versailles. Nothing and nobody could stop them. The German soldiers left behind ineffaceable memories of brutal, unfeeling cruelty. Weeping French writers went on for decades telling innumerable heartbreaking stories of how ruthless, rapacious, and contemptuous the invaders had been. How could these Germans be so dissimilar from those harmless and peaceful people Madame de Staël had described, those whom Europe had known and loved only a few years before? How did they, as Friedrich Nietzsche wrote (*Beyond Good and Evil*, 241), "sacrifice their old and sure virtues for the sake of a new and doubtful mediocrity?" And, I would add, for power? "Ma," we say in Italy, "who knows?"

In the beginning the new empire carried itself with some prudence. It seemed to fear its own power. The leader, Otto von Bismarck, dreaded a Germany that would, if left to its own new tactless arrogance, dominate Europe with catastrophic results. He tied the new empire in a web of contradictory secret alliances that made all wars, if not impossible, at least improbable. He managed to divert his countrymen's nationalism into less ruinous channels, such as the struggle against the Poles in eastern Germany, against the Catholic Church, or against the Social Democrats at home. Above all he dreaded a war on two or three fronts simultaneously: against France and Russia on land; and on sea, against Britain. He was careful not to provoke too many enemies at the same time. A few years later, however, when the old statesman had been forced to retire to his country estate, nothing could restrain the Germans. Success had gone to their heads. Steelworks vomited a steady stream of improved weapons; shipyards launched one terrifying warship after another; the army was awe-inspiring, the most modern and best trained of all; the general staff elaborated vast ingenious plans of invasion in all directions. The emperor wore a shining cuirass and a golden imperial eagle on his silver helmet. He believed himself (and his people) chosen by God to punish his Uncle Bertie, King Edward VII, and his cousin Nicky, the czar; to dominate, improve and educate all Europe and, eventually, the whole world. He believed what a German poet, Emanuel Geibel (1815–84) had prophesied: "Am deutschen Wesen soll die Welt genesen" (the German spirit will heal the world). In the end the kaiser committed all the errors Bismarck had warned his countrymen against, and it all ended very badly in November 1918.

Confusion followed: disarray, civil strife, moral decay, violence, inflation, misery, unemployment, and hunger. This is where I came in. As a young journalist I visited Berlin a few times and saw the end of this period, just before Hitler came to power and rang the curtain down. I too was in the Kurfürstendamm with George Grosz, the painter, so to speak. (Actually, I met him only in 1954, on the day he had returned from America, an American citizen, dressed in shop-new clothes like a dapper Midwest Rotarian. That evening, Melvin Lasky and I took him back to the Kurfürstendamm for the first time after twenty years of exile. We were vaguely moved. It was like taking Kipling back to India, Stendhal to Parma, Proust to Illiers, or Dante to the Inferno. We sat in several cafés in succession, we visited two or three famous cabarets. Melvin and I spied the people's faces, which, in a sense, Grosz had invented [or at least artistically immortalized]. Nobody recognized him. Nobody knew who he was.] In 1931, Berlin surely was the artistic capital of Europe, full of brilliant theaters, cabarets, avant-garde art shows, trail-blazing films, experiments of all kinds. The Kurfürstendamm, the famous tree-lined boulevard, a pretentious imitation of the Avenue des Champs Elysées, was filled with characters dreamed up by de Sade, Havelock Ellis, Sacher-Masoch, Krafft-Ebing, and Sigmund Freud. There were men dressed as women, women dressed as men or little schoolgirls, women in boots with whips (boots and whips in different colors, shapes, and sizes, promising different passive or active divertissements). I saw legless veterans on crutches, *culs-de-jatte*, armless or blind veterans wearing iron crosses, and the hungry unshaven unemployed, all of them begging. I saw pimps offering anything to anybody, little boys, little girls, robust young men, libidinous women, or (I suppose) animals. (The story went around that a male goose of which one cut the neck at the ecstatic moment would give you the most delicious, economical, and time-saving frisson of all, as it allowed you to enjoy sodomy, bestiality, homosexuality, necrophilia, and sadism at one stroke. Gastronomy, too, as one could eat the goose afterward.)

I couldn't help wondering where all these monsters had come from, which Germany had generated them. Had they been there all the time, and if so, where had they been hiding? To be sure, under the parade-ground perfection of Wilhelmine Germany (as under the impeccable comme il faut appearance of Edwardian Britain) there always was some concealed corruption of one kind or another. Scandals had occasionally broken out in public—a famous homosexual one in the kaiser's entourage—or had been murmured about with raised eyebrows in upper-class drawing rooms. Distinguished Germans (and Englishmen) had resigned from exalted positions, fled to Dieppe, Capri, or Taormina, to live in a delectable, perpetual, and obscure exile. But both countries had been healthy and wholesome as a whole. Nothing had prepared observers for that massive outbreak of freaks in Germany. I must confess the show bewildered and frightened me. What did it mean? Who were (I asked myself) the listless apathetic customers without natural appetites who had to be titillated and tempted with such an outlandish array of horrifying variations?

The young Italian journalist was by no means theoretically opposed to sexual freedom. In fact he welcomed it with relief and enthusiasm. But he limited his concupiscence strictly to young, well-washed, and pretty girls. To sleep with elderly bearded men, hunchbacks, mutilated veterans, blond soldiers, schoolboys, to whip or to be whipped, and to savor excrement seemed to him forms of diabolical and unendurable torture, suitable for the souls of sinners in hell, and by no means paradisiacal delights. He therefore abandoned himself gratefully to his middle-class provincial preferences. The young, well-washed, and pretty females were abundantly available. They could be had for the asking, sometimes without asking at all, often for the mere price of a dinner or a bunch of flowers: shopgirls, secretaries, White Russian refugees, nice girls from decayed good families. Some of them pathetically wept on the rumpled bed after making love when they accepted money. Old Germans remember those days with nostalgia as the *goldenen Zwanziger*. Naturally, I told myself, Kurfürstendamm was not Germany (as Americans tirelessly point out that New York, and Times Square in the heart of it, is not America). But what *was* Germany?

In the sooty industrial suburbs sporadic street fighting went on, which foreign correspondents described diligently without really understanding. Armed men in all kinds of strange uniforms or in overalls and caps, singing anthems, flying old imperial flags, Nazi flags, red flags with hammer and sickle, or red, black, and yellow Weimar flags (which had been invented by liberal revolutionaries in 1848), sometimes paraded the streets. I saw one of their skirmishes by chance one day. The men on my side, in some sort of uniform and steel helmets, with campaign ribbons on their chests, crouched behind street corners, inside doorways, behind masonry

pillars, tree trunks, and the pedestal of the monument to an unknown statesman in a bronze frock coat, and cooly aimed their
rifles before pulling the trigger. The chattering of a machine gun
could be heard in the distance, as well as shouts, the screams of
wounded men, and the occasional explosion of a hand grenade.
The opponents, evidently working men, started to advance carefully, one man or two at a time, from one shelter to the next as
they had been taught in the army, while the men on my side
retreated just as carefully. They carried their bloodstained
wounded men with them. I helped one of the fighters limp down a
side street to a doctor's office, whose metal sign was visible on his
door, a white enamel plate with red Gothic lettering. The man had
sprained an ankle as he jumped from a truck. His name was
Heinz.

What the screaming and fighting was all about and how it all
would end nobody really knew. The speeches at street meetings,
the slogans, the posters, the newspaper articles, the plays, the
witticisms in the cabarets, the conversation with colleagues in
cafés made no sense. My impression was that all this merely expressed the anger of a defeated people, the rage of men who
thought they had been betrayed, men who had lost the old comforting faith in their great Vaterland, the omnipotent kaiser, the
invincibility of the military, all the things for which they had been
willing to die, and now sought relief in one desperate and insane
hope or another. This bewildered and frightened me. What had
happened to the rational, efficient, disciplined, sober Germans of
yesterday, the Germans all Europe admired and feared?

A few years later (it must have been in 1934) I visited Kurfürstendamm again. Hitler was in power then. The long tree-lined
boulevard shone with new municipal pride. It was carefully mani-
cured by gardeners and kept dust-free by hard-working street-
sweepers. Paternal and severe policemen, their black leather
shakos bent forward, watched over it. A new set of people prome-
naded up and down with gravity, stiff men in spotless uniforms,
honorable families, businessmen carrying briefcases full of vital

documents, rich gentlemen with shaved heads and the fat backs of the Grosz-like necks bulging like pillows over the starched collars, a feature typical of their breed that nobody else in Europe managed to acquire, shopping housewives and supercilious chic women, aristocrats, actresses, or haughty courtesans who looked almost unapproachable. It was definitely and bewilderingly another country.

I met the newly appointed chancellor at that time (I never saw him in person again). Adolf Hitler received a small group of foreign journalists, four or five of us, in the foyer of the Kroll Opera House, during a parliamentary meeting, among incongruous gilded furniture and red velvet draperies. The Reichstag had been destroyed by a famous fire and the deputies were sitting for the time being in the stalls and boxes of the theater. None of us, of course, could foresee that day how Hitler would end, where he would drag the world, our countries, and each of us, and how many million deaths he would cause. To me, then, he merely looked like an improbable funny burlesque character, a sinister clown, with his bang plastered diagonally across his forehead (he probably thought it gave him a Napoleonic air), a more preposterous and ridiculous man even than Mussolini and surely less human. Definitely, I thought, the new *Reichskanzler* did not have to be taken seriously. He did not look like the portraits of one of the great characters of history, not like Bismarck, Cavour, Gladstone, Clemenceau, or Wilson, men who had led their countries sometimes in the wrong direction but always with gravity and prudence and authority. He was, I concluded, too improbable to last; there was nothing to worry about. He would vanish shortly, as quickly as he had appeared from nowhere, dragged back behind the wings by the hook of history. His ideas were so outlandish, his programs so absurd, primitive, and barbaric, so unsuited for the twentieth century, that I believed he would not have the slightest chance to implement them, no more of a chance than Mussolini's operatic attempt to reconstruct the Roman Empire.

Hitler was wearing the mustard-colored uniform of the S.A. with armband. I noticed his ill-fitting breeches entered his too-large boots with concertinalike folds. His mustache surprised me. It had a third dimension that was not apparent in photographs. It was thick and bristled horizontally forward, somewhat like the quills of a porcupine, almost as far as the tip of his nose. The nose was triangular, vaguely shaped like the hood of a fireplace. I was fascinated, above all, by his tearful eyes. I imagined the author of *Mein Kampf*, the leader of an army of thugs, the persecutor of the Jews (who were law-abiding, indispensable, and patriotic German citizens, many of them heroic soldiers in the previous war) should have had cold, dry eyes, set in the mask of a cruel Roman emperor, not watery eyes in the face of a postman. And why the tears? (Later that evening at dinner, I told an old friend, a good German journalist, I was bewildered by Hitler's tear-filled eyes. I said he had the eyes of a bird-dog or a hound. My friend corrected me. "No. He has the eyes of an orphan." Of course.)

When my turn came, Hitler shook my hand, held it for a while between his two, looked steadily at me, and delivered a short statement for my benefit. Very probably, I imagine, he was expressing admiration for Il Duce (and gratitude, too, for Il Duce had amply financed the Nazi party in the 1920s), admiration for his model, protector, and older brother. Sometimes I like to think he delivered to me personally a pregnant political proposal which, if relayed to the right persons, followed through, and made the basis for negotiations, could have prevented World War II. Whatever his short speech meant, it was wasted on me. I did not understand a word. I knew only enough German to read headlines, order meals, and persuade young ladies to sleep with me. Needing little coaxing (much less than Italian girls, who at the time were still under their mothers' close watch and afraid of the fires of hell), they could be persuaded by two or three simple words at the most, or by a meaningful gesture.

Later I had to go to Germany every few years. I saw the strangely malleable country gradually given a new shape by the Nazis. The phenomenon was disturbing. Even intelligent old friends, men who spoke foreign languages and had lived abroad, diplomats and journalists, seemed now and again to go out of their minds. You drank beer and chatted pleasantly about this and that, the job, cuisine, girls, books, money, until the talk turned to Germany, the Führer, or the Western democracies. Then their faces suddenly froze and they took on a determined expression. They clenched their teeth. Their eyes looked toward a radiant future. Being myself the inhabitant of a presumably totalitarian country, corroded (as the wits said) by the almost complete disregard of all laws, I knew from personal experience that some of my German friends were unfortunately sincere. They honestly hoped Hitler would somehow avenge the honor of their fatherland, restore its pride and dignity and its place in the concert of nations, solve the economic problems, and eventually, one day, unite all Germans under one flag. Many also wanted to believe that the latest outrageous decision, heinous speech, monstrous challenge to the world, or appalling decree would be the last, that Hitler and his accomplices would not go any further because they were satisfied and placated, and that then the country would shortly return to normality. Others (like many Italians at that time) were only ambiguously sincere. They wanted badly to deceive themselves, to believe in the opinions they were expressing, the only safe ones, in order to preserve their self-respect. Some were evidently faking their Nazi faith, or keeping silent. Later, just to keep silent became an act of courage. One cabaret comedian used to keep silent for a minute or two, looking at his public. Then he said, "Now that we have discussed the political situation, we can talk of something else." He soon ended in a concentration camp.

At this point I went to Germany more and more rarely. The feeling of constraint and deceit was becoming heavier and unbearable. The persecution of minorities and dissidents, of which the regime openly boasted, was growing more barbaric and demented. To be sure, the economy flourished and order reigned supreme, but at what price? Preparations for the next war were arrogantly flaunted in violation of treaties. The ostentatious display of brand-new tanks and guns, the parades of infantry and cavalry in impeccable formations through city streets, the planes flying overhead in formation were ominous and frightening. Frightening above all were the young, healthy, well-washed faces of the soldiers, their eyes shining with fanatic faith as they marched by, singing martial songs. The proud, unconcealed show of military might was, of course, the message. Other countries (Italy included, at the time) had to be intimidated, forced by fear to let the Nazis achieve their goals without firing a shot. But war was not excluded. In fact, the German people (or what journalists then called "the German people") seemed as a whole to look forward to it without fear if not with relish. Whether they really did or did not was difficult to tell. Even your best friends lied to you, and it was of course impossible to meet opponents of the regime. They were already rotting and dying in concentration camps. What I could discern was the perfection of everything, the drilling of the soldiers, the design of the weapons and machinery, the thorough enforcement of all laws and regulations. Was the perfect functioning of everything really a sign of acquiescence? It seemed as if each German refused to raise his head to look where he was being led and diligently concentrated his attention on the small job entrusted to him. Was it *die prinzipielle Ordentlichkeit der Deutschen* at work, "that basic thoroughness of the orderly German," as Johannes Gross wrote of his countrymen in 1981; was it, as he said, "the pride in doing something so efficiently that one can be pleased with oneself?"

That many Germans were still human beings, civilized Europeans and Christians in spite of everything, was evident in Italy only toward the end of the war. In the few months before the liberation of Rome, I lived with my wife and two baby daughters in an isolated white house on the sea outside Porto Santo Stefano. I was supposed to be under constant police control as an anti-Fascist condemned to *confino*. But the situation was too confused for me to be really watched. There were more pressing things. The little port was being used to unload German supplies for Cassino.

It was bombed day and night, during the day by the Americans and during the night by the British; the town was reduced to gaping holes and masses of dusty ruins. Inevitably, I had to become acquainted with many Germans. One day, a naval officer with an arrogant supercilious manner visited us. He had received the order to blow up our house as it was presumably used at night by Allied bombers as a guidepost on their flight to their objectives. He ordered us to get out immediately while his men prepared the mines. Then he noticed a Scotch terrier bitch of ours which had given birth to three pups. He smiled, petted the black mother, lifted one of the tiny dogs in his arms, and finally proposed he would forget the whole thing, our evacuation and the blowing up of the house, in exchange for a male puppy. (I remember the dog's name. It was Rollo. I have forgotten the officer's.)

In an antiaircraft battery not far from us was a strange elderly soldier who paid us a visit one night after sundown. He introduced himself, Doktor Nassau, a medical doctor from somewhere near Hamburg. He spoke good English. He had started the war as a captain, he told us, but, because of some unguarded remarks he had made had been tried, demoted, and sent as a medical orderly to a very dangerous place where the authorities hoped he would die any day. He offered us his services. He visited us always at night. He explained, "I come to you after dark not to compromise you. You will not be accused later of having had contacts with a German soldier." And he chuckled. He watched over our two baby girls (they fortunately enjoyed good health). He brought us medicines we needed. We gave him an omelette, a glass or two of wine, and some fruit every time he came. We talked about the war. Dr. Nassau (God bless him wherever he is) had no illusions. He knew what his country had done. He said, "Doctor Goebbels explains to us why we cannot lose this war. He forgets to tell us how we can win it, ha ha . . ." His political ideas were those of an elderly gentleman. He was certain that once Germany was rid of Hitler and the party, the Hohenzollern would come back and there would be once again a kaiser in Berlin. "Wilhelm might have been a bad and tactless emperor and made many horrible mistakes," Dr. Nassau used to say, "but he was infinitely better than our present Führer. To begin with, Wilhelm was a gentleman, after all, a grandson of Queen Victoria." We knew that many Germans in uniform secretly shared Dr. Nassau's doubts, if not his hopes, perhaps more than half of them, surely the sailors and the naval officers. But none of them could help obeying orders like automatons. They were born obedient. An Italian friend of mine, who was fighting in the underground and visited us once in a while during the night to get supplies and news, used to say, "I would hate to be shot by a firing squad composed of men who had my same ideas."

I returned to Germany after the war where I diligently interviewed the Allied high commissioners and Dr. Konrad Adenauer on the future of the country. What I wanted to know was what everybody wanted to know, what was the real nature of these people? Were they ineluctably condemned to make wars? Could they be trusted? Could they become free men, conduct themselves responsibly as members of the western community?

André François-Poncet, the French high commissioner, was pensive and preoccupied. He had a little mustache, wore a wing collar and a polka-dotted bowtie like Adolphe Menjou. He saw one great danger. "Suppose," he told me, "the Germans come to an agreement with the Russians. They did it after the First World War at Rapallo. They did it in 1939. We all know that every time they come to an agreement with the Russians they arrive in Paris."

Konrad Adenauer, whom I saw the following day, asked me what François-Poncet had said. I repeated his words. Adenauer snorted. "Paris? They go much beyond!" he said with some pride. This was, of course, not quite true. They went beyond only once, in 1940. However, he excluded the possibility of his country's coming to an agreement with the Russians within the near future. "Impossible," he said.

John McCloy, the American high commissioner, was full of

hope and doubts. "Can they become democratic?" I asked. (The German regime was then called *Kanzlerdemokratie* by clever journalists, a democracy completely dominated by the chancellor.) "There are many heartwarming signs," McCloy answered. "To be sure a great number of Germans, like Konrad Adenauer and millions of others, had been secretly democratic all the time. Many have now discovered the value of democratic ideas at their own heavy cost. Defeat is a great teacher. Many more are willing to learn. The American overwhelming success in peace and war is an impressive example." But he pointed out it was not a simple question of indoctrination and the enforcement of treaties. It was a deeper and more complex problem. Sometimes old German prejudices cropped up, McCloy said; and he told me this story. A few weeks before, a German count had invited American officers to go shooting on his lands; they came dressed as Americans do in shabby old clothes and not in the chic new hunting outfits the Europeans prefer. One of the American officers, taken by mistake for some animal or other as he was crawling behind a bush, was killed, and the count was arrested and tried. His lawyer offered two defenses: (a) the count did not know the victim was an American; (b) the count did not know the victim was an officer. But this, McCloy said, was not typical. It was only a residue of past feudal ways of thinking, going back to the times when it was considered an unfortunate but forgivable error to kill a peasant or a private, and a serious crime to kill a gentleman and an officer, especially if he belonged to a conquering army.

To compare, as all of us journalists did in those years, Berlin under the Weimar Republic, Berlin under the Nazis, with Bonn, in an attempt to measure the change in the German soul and way of life after the defeat, was deceptive and dishonest. One had always been an ugly, bustling, cosmopolitan capital, fermenting with new ideas, the other a sleepy garden city on the river, built for scholars and retired apoplectic old people. (The depressive climate notoriously lowered their blood pressure.) Nevertheless, the very choice of Bonn (a fortuitous choice, to be sure, as many fatal choices are in history, the consequence of the fortuitous decision of some obscure American officer to nominate once again Adenauer as mayor of Cologne, and later the fortuitous decision of some obscure British officer to dismiss him as too old and politically incompetent, which gave him time to organize a brand-new party; Adenauer lived across the river from Bonn and chose Bonn as a convenient temporary capital, convenient for him) could be interpreted as the symbol of the new start. It was as if the little town on the Rhine had really been selected by a divine film director (or designed and built by his divine art director) as the perfect background for a tale full of nostalgia, yearning for the old-fashioned virtues, for tranquillity, amiability, security, gemütlichkeit, law and order, a life among books and flowers and children and dogs and good wines; the very antithesis of the Nazi ideals. The two cities, of course, had been there all the time, two opposite and irreconcilable aspects of Protean Germany, as mutable as the sea. One, the seat of the mighty, mystical, loquacious, imprudent, unpredictable kaiser and of the demented, diabolical Hitler, murderer of millions; and the other the civilized retreat for the sagacious, patient, firm, and prudent old *Oberbürgermeister* of Cologne and people like him.

Like many other hurried observers I did not penetrate below the surface and investigated only the most evident aspects of postwar Adenauer Germany. Maybe a deeper knowledge would have blurred my impressions. I merely tried to meet as many people as I could from all walks of life, visit their houses, eat their food, listen to reminiscences and hopes. What interested me above all was to explore the ease with which they had adapted themselves to be proper characters in the Adenauer show. Maybe, as McCloy said, some of them had been all the time, under the uniforms, what they now appeared to be, and did not have to adapt themselves so much as reveal themselves. Who knows? My impressions were surely also influenced by the architecture. Most of the town (it was fairly intact then, without skyscrapers and modern ministerial buildings) appeared to have been designed by the artists who made nineteenth-century German Christmas cards, *Ad-*

ventskalender, or valentines, adorned with rococo decorations festooned with flowers, birds, and paper lace. Other parts of town, the old ones, were designed by the artists who made steel engravings of squares with fountains and old buildings and carriages for tourists to take home as souvenirs. When you visited one of the old-fashioned little villas you were struck by the 1900 decor, the oil portraits of grandfather and grandmother, he in his uniform with imperial decorations and she in her ball dress, by the fringed draperies and curtains, the potted plants, the fretwork furniture in the living room or the heavy dining room furniture of elaborately carved walnut. In the entrance hall you usually found felt pads on which you were asked to place your feet and not to walk but slide (as a long-distance skier does), so that you did not mark the well-waxed floors but increased their sheen. Everything that could be was washed, shined, varnished, polished, rubbed, gleaming. Evidently Adenauer, the Restorer, had somehow led his people back to his youth, more than a half-century before.

There has always been a mysterious capacity of rulers in many centuries and countries to shape their people physically and morally. Frenchmen wore whiskers à la Napoleon III and their women Eugenie's crinolines until 1870; Italians cut their hair short and flat on top alla Umberto I until 1900 and wore mustaches like Victor Emmanuel III later. Most high officials in Vienna looked like Franz Joseph, with a shaven chin and sidewhiskers joining their mustache in a graceful curve. Great Britain adopted Queen Victoria's and Albert's style of life and moral virtues. English dandies left the last button of their waistcoats unbuttoned like Edward VII. Piedmontese families today still unthinkingly give their children their grandparents' names, those of long dead princes and kings of the House of Savoy: Charles Albert, Humbert, Emmanuel Philibert, or Amadeus. And of course, vice versa, foreign princes who have not one drop of their subjects' blood in their veins somehow acquire national traits to the point of becoming national caricatures, more typical of their country than any native. The Hapsburg-Lorraine grand dukes of Tuscany were so Tuscan they could be used as sociological specimens in textbooks. The Bourbon kings of Naples, of French and Austrian blood, spoke their people's dialect and had the natives' quick and irreverent wit. The present king of Spain, whose Spanish ancestry is tenuous, looks and behaves like a hidalgo from way back.

It is therefore not surprising that Dr. Adenauer managed to transform the malleable Germans into his image, after his likeness. He himself did not look like a German. His old and wrinkled face reminded you of an ancient turtle or a Japanese mask. Morally, however, he was the archetype of a West German, the inhabitants of the Rhineland-Palatinate, born within the borders of the old Roman Empire, beyond which the grapes, Roman civilization, and Roman law did not take root. In fact the northernmost vineyards in Europe are to be found in Rhöndorf, Adenauer's own village. The physical difference between the two Germanys is sometimes perceptible especially to a Southerner's eye. The great forests, the wild moors, the barbaric romantic landscapes are in contrast to the tidy man-made civilized landscapes of Roman Germany. Many Germans from his region and farther south traditionally thought their countrymen beyond the Elbe still belonged to wild unpredictable tribes and had to be kept at a distance. (This is one of the two reasons why the chancellor bore the separation from East Germany with great fortitude. The second was that there was little he could do about it.) He was definitely a European, a *German* European, a Catholic, a drinker of fine wines (and dry martinis), a cultivator of prize roses, and a man of his times. There was nothing Nibelungian about him.

Adenauer was elected chancellor by a slim majority: one vote. When asked if he had voted for himself, he said proudly, "Yes, of course I did. And it turned out to be a happy inspiration." His influence as a founding father was fundamental. He was old enough to remember and had had the time and leisure to analyze all the mistakes made by the framers of the Weimar constitution in 1919. He avoided them all. He created the new Federal Republic as a solid, durable, and practical machine. He inspired its fundamental laws, its guiding philosophy, and, as I said, the manners and beliefs of its citizens. He chose its friends and allies.

He did all this with an ease and thoroughness that were baffling to an Italian. I could not help thinking (for instance) of the ease and thoroughness with which in the eighteenth century German princelings had adopted French tastes. They spoke French, wrote French, ate French, danced French, built imitation rococo French châteaus all over the country, all curlicues and contorted statuary, some actually designed by French architects. Or the ease and thoroughness with which the Hamburgers imitated the English. Or the ease and thoroughness with which Germans had all apparently become Prussians almost overnight after 1871. Or the ease and thoroughness with which Munich was filled with scholarly copies of Florentine, Venetian, and other Italian Renaissance buildings in the last century. All this, of course, was due to one puzzling quality, the people's adaptability, their blotting-paper capacity at all times to absorb and improve alien conceptions. Was not nazism (among other things) a thoroughly perfected and efficient copy of disorganized and ramshackle fascism, down to the Roman salute? (Nobody really knows if the Romans saluted each other and the emperor by raising their right arms. The salute was probably invented at the beginning of the century by the forgotten director of a silent movie version of *Quo Vadis* or *Fabiola*.) Nevertheless, in spite of rococo châteaus, Renaissance palazzi, American skyscrapers, or the rigidly extended right arms, there always was and is something perennially and unchangingly German. The Germans call it *Deutschtum*. What was it? What *is* it?

The later model for all things evidently was (after Dr. Adenauer's resurrection of Wilhelmine Germany) the United States, the conquering superpower that had destroyed nazism in 1945 (and most of Germany at the same time) with the might of its industries, the efficiency of its machines, the courage of its people, the intelligence of its leaders, and the infallibility of its political ideas. This was not surprising. Nations at all times have adopted

the customs, fashions, and ideas of the predominant power. European armies, which had gone to war in three-cornered hats and
powdered wigs against the revolutionary French in the 1790s,
ended up a few years later in their own short and unpowdered hair
and Napoleonic uniforms against Napoleon. American skyscrapers,
of course, are the symbol of a desire to belong to the modern
world, not in Germany alone, but everywhere. President Pompidou
incongruously filled corners of noble Paris with them. They rise
like asparagus in Latin America, proof, strangely enough, not of
servile imitation of, but proud independence from, the Yankees'
"rapacious hegemony." Skyscrapers rise in all or almost all oil-
producing countries; in capitalistic countries and in the Soviet
Union; and, one or two, for reasons of prestige, even in miserable
underdeveloped countries that cannot afford them, where starving
people die like flies in the streets. Similarly, American airport-
style hotels and supermarkets have been generously scattered all
over the world. But nowhere was the imitation and emulation of
American buildings, ways, fashions, styles, habits, techniques, so
meticulous as it was in West Germany. Entire city quarters were
diligently rebuilt from the rubble according to the chosen model.
(Of course, Germans told you, the architecture was not purely
American, but partly a derivation of the German Bauhaus, whose
creators emigrated from Germany to the U.S.A. in the early thirties. Perhaps.)

Scientific research centers (there are many of them) were lovingly planned exactly like western American university campuses.
The specialized buildings, laboratories, lecture halls, and libraries,
spread around landscaped estates amid vast lawns, artificial lakes,
and woods, are connected not only by roads but by shorter foot-
paths on which scientists, aides, students, and workmen walk or
ride bicycles, as they do in similar establishments in the United
States. All these people are dressed alike. One cannot tell where
they stand in the hierarchical scale by their clothes. In summer-
time they wear open lumberjack shirts or T-shirts, jeans, and
slacks, and in wintertime, peajackets or parkas. They call each

other by their first names. They slap each other's shoulders. They all eat side by side, Nobel Prize winners, professors, engineers, janitors, workers, and distinguished visitors, in a rigorously democratic one-class cafeteria, oddly called kasino, at least in the research center I recently visited. (The name means brothel in Italian, gambling house in French and English, and regimental officers' club in German.) There are no executive dining rooms. (In the Soviet Union, a country pledged to egalitarianism, there are six or more categories of eateries in all establishments, as well as six or more categories of WCs, to separate the big bosses from the middling and inferior chiefs, the employees of various ranks from skilled workers and unskilled workers.) The food in the kasino was eatable, probably nourishing, evidently harmless, but not particularly interesting, as in similar American establishments. Certainly nobody dawdles over it. No alcoholic beverages and beer were available.

In hotels, office buildings, and many other places, one is perpetually awash in soft music, as in America. Plaintive arias leak from the walls in elevators, waiting rooms, bars, and lavatories; the music comes from nowhere, like a ventriloquist's voice. In new hotels there is no concierge (an effete European institution) and shoes are polished by electric machines placed in the corridors. Doors from the street are opened by ghostly hands. After the war, Hamburg proudly adopted an American specialty it had never even heard of before, the hamburger. *Und so weiter.*

As always, the meticulous German imitations of the U.S.A., like most German imitations of foreign models in the past, went much beyond the originals. They were definite improvements—the United States as it would have liked to be and managed to be only sporadically, with difficulty, only here and there. Surely it was never as tidy, clean, law-abiding, disciplined, well-administered, docile, punctual, rigorous, and prosperous a country as its German copy. This is because of, for one thing, the perennial German compulsion to surpass their teachers. German firms bought supermarkets in the United States and ran them better and more efficiently than the Americans themselves, who had invented them. German publishers launched mass circulation magazines for women in the American market, American imitations of German imitations of American prototypes. One cannot help remembering how Prussian military thinkers analyzed Napoleon's victorious but somewhat unchanging and unimaginative maneuvers on the battlefield, discovered his secrets, and bettered them in the end; how much more efficient and deadly was the German imperial fleet in 1914 than the British fleet it was built to rival and destroy but did not.

It was also symptomatic and possibly pregnant with future developments that the American model the Germans had idealized, imitated, and perfected and clung to was a little behind the times, yesterday's America, *l'Amérique de papa*. The model was the neat, sedate, industrious, and confident America of a few years before, Truman's and Eisenhower's America, a solid and somewhat predictable country. The choice of the older model was inevitable. To save their pride and honor, the Germans could only admire and imitate the two superpowers that had reduced their country to rubble, destroyed the best fighting machine the world had known, led by the best generals tradition and training and rigorous selection could produce, manned by the best soldiers in history. In the East the Germans obediently adopted and definitely improved on the Soviet model. East Germany is the only eastern "People's Democracy" that has managed to solve a few of the impossible problems of a bureaucratic economy that works nowhere else. In the West the model had necessarily to be the United States as it appeared to the defeated, humiliated, and hungry Germans at the time of the occupation and the reconstruction.

The United States surely was at that time, immediately after the war, the most advanced country in practically all fields that mattered. The dollar was the world's lodestar; U.S. industries still dominated all competition. The Republic was solidly founded on firm certainties, moral, political, and economic. It knew it was right; its institutions and principles being the best could not be improved much and were perfectly adaptable to changing times and to foreign countries anywhere. It knew its armed forces were invincible because its weapons were the most advanced and also because it had always fought on the side of justice. Furthermore America was generous and magnanimous and humanitarian, securely guided by its ideals and virtues. It was capable, time and again when necessary, at critical moments, to produce from the sleeve of history elites of *homines novi*—noble, committed, and competent leaders, occasionally even one great man, a great or nearly great president. These men were capable of leading their nation to prosperity in times of depression. The generals could lead it to victory in great wars and, after the last world war, were capable of firmly facing the Soviet threat. Its statesmen could protect, defend, reassure, and lead the free world with ease.

This America, of course, was not entirely imaginary. But it was never as good as the Germans and many foreigners imagined or wanted to imagine it. Its foreign policy was never as far-seeing, enlightened, and coherent, its elites as competent and imaginative, its economy as free from flaws. Later, in fact, some cracks began to show even from a distance. Particularly the severe strains and delusions of the last decades impaired the image of the United States. Somehow the elites did not seem as capable, the ideas as valid for all seasons, the armed forces as invincible, the presidents always as admirable as some of their famous predecessors; foreign policy seemed at times more undecided, ineffectual, and contradictory, particularly under Jimmy Carter. There were widespread doubts in western Europe (and in Germany above all) whether a more mature and wiser but weaker and more uncertain America, the post-Vietnam and post-Watergate America, or the more abrupt, belligerent, defiant, and impatient America of Reagan's administration, might be willing or capable of protecting Europe —and first of all the *Bundesrepublik* which is manning the ramparts—from Soviet aggression.

The time had perhaps come for Germany gradually to abandon the comforting security of the past decades, the idea that to imitate the United States, take care of the economy, leave most decisions to the Americans' wisdom and the protection of the West to their nuclear weapons was enough to secure tranquillity. To be sure Europeans (including Germans) have to stick with their great ally. They certainly cannot get along by themselves. The Allies could not in 1917 and the United Nations in 1941. But this time everybody in Europe had to reexamine all contemporary problems from scratch. The heaviest burden naturally fell on Germany's shoulders, once again the strongest nation in Europe. This alarmed all history-conscious Europeans a little. It alarmed the Germans most of all. They were scared (as Bismarck was) to see their country acquire once more an indisputable hegemony over the Continent and the responsibility for its future.

Rightly proud of their miraculous resurrection, proud too of their unprecedented economic renaissance, the people were at the same time uneasy, anxious, and often frightened by their own wealth, power, and responsibilities. Nietzsche's 1874 warning to them acquired an ominous contemporary significance. He wrote (*Notes*, VII, paragraph 145): "One must seek to make amends for one's superiority. To be ashamed of one's power. To use it in the most salutary way. . . . Awe-inspiring power. The only way to use the present kind of German power correctly is to comprehend the tremendous obligation which lies in it." They had learned that their best political plans often went awry because it was easy, almost inevitable for them to provoke envy, resentment, suspicions, fear, hostility, and sometimes hatred among their neighbors. This they had always dismissed as not very important in the past. In fact they liked it. It confirmed their exalted conception of themselves. As Frederick the Great, king of Prussia, used to say, repeating an old saying, "Many enemies, much honor."

It was, however, a pointlessly heavy and expensive added burden to bear. One of the two main reasons (to mention the most evident example) why the Russians cling hysterically to the German eastern provinces and the German Democratic Republic; govern them nervously through subservient political henchmen;

keep a vast armored army in them ready for instant war; control them through occult and visible police; and fill the border zone with a wall, mine fields, fortifications, beamlights, electronic traps, armaments, trained dogs, and soldiers is the terror (and admiration) Germany has inspired in Russian hearts for centuries. Russians have always been dazzled by the Germans' superior scientific knowledge, perseverance, orderliness, and their unique diabolical military proficiency. (The other reason is the delusion shared by all military experts that it is possible to reinforce one's defenses by means of a glacis. One glacis notoriously needs another glacis in front of it for its own protection, and so on, ad infinitum, one glacis after another, until theoretically the only real safety is a chain of glacis circling the earth, the possession and control of the whole world. This seems fatally to be the Soviets' ultimate unreachable goal.)

Now the Germans have at last discovered that this capacity of theirs to provoke at times the hostility and hatred not only of their enemies but also of their friends and allies has decisively contributed to their defeats. This capacity has its roots not only in their less amiable traits—arrogance, tactlessness, and obtuseness—but also in their great virtues, their excellence in almost all fields. When they are at war they do the job, as they do it in peacetime, as thoroughly, efficiently, and expediently as possible, without looking left or right, like the good obedient workmen they are. They never bother about what the rest of the world will think. Scruples and doubts might slow them down. Thus they sent armies across neutral Belgium twice, as a matter of course, shocking the world; were the first to use poison gas in World War I; practically allied themselves to the Soviets in 1939 and then attacked them without warning in 1941; righteously shot thousands of innocent hostages in all wars; the SS murdered millions of people who their superiors thought might have retarded national progress; and in Africa, retreating in a hurry from the Egyptian border, the Germans borrowed all Italian transport at the point of guns and left their Axis allies to make their way back on foot in the desert, without food or water, as best they could. What else was there to do?

Their professed aim during the last war was to unify and pacify all Europe forever, but they did not bother to charm the Europeans with lies. They candidly made it clear instead that they considered all foreigners inferior, contemptible, and irresponsible, to be governed with an iron hand. Naturally their prospective subjects did not like the idea at all. They could not convince themselves how much gayer and lighter the life of helots could be under German tutelage. Many Europeans, in fact, preferred death to a well-regulated future and a Nazi peace lasting one thousand years. As a result, they did what they could to see Germany defeated. Even its allies fought half-heartedly or did not fight at all. They were infinitely more frightened of winning than of losing.

After World War II, the Germans, evidently appalled by the hatred directed toward them, worked hard to make friends and influence people. It was a new experience. They really needed to be liked this time. Therefore they tried to be as inconspicuous as possible and to demonstrate the fact that they were just a western European nation like all the others. It was one of their Protean transformations—but it was not entirely a dishonest ruse by any means. It was the Reich that foreigners had disliked and feared, Germans en masse and in uniform and their leaders, but not the individuals who, with some appalling exceptions, have always been rather affable human beings. The head of state and the chancellors no longer wore tight frock coats or uniforms, top hats, spiked helmets, steel helmets, or helmets surmounted by a golden bird. On state visits Helmut Schmidt wore an accountant's Sunday best of the previous year (when he had been leaner) and the incongruous but obviously pacific cap of a Hamburg fisherman (though Helmut Kohl accepted his election to the chancellorship by the Bundestag wearing formal morning clothes). Presidents of the Federal Republic are carefully chosen from among reassuring, white-haired grandfatherly professor or family-doctor types. Everybody smiles, like Rotary club members, and is cordial and cheerful. Nobody clicks heels or bows deeply anymore, as they used to, the body bent mechanically in two rigid halves, head low. When a picture appears in the papers of a German dignitary forgetting himself and bowing the old-fashoned way, he is fustigated by commentators and angry letter-writing readers the next day. No officer wears a monocle. There is no such thing as a *Generalstab* anymore, the famous military planning group once headed by the old Moltke, Schlieffen, the young Moltke, and Ludendorff. The chiefs of staff are now inconspicuously called "inspectors," the title of obscure police officials in other countries. Speeches, editorials, diplomatic toasts, and policy pronouncements are always in favor of indisputably good things, such as peace, democracy, the brotherhood of man, détente, economic development, the war on inflation and unemployment, international control of slavery, the extermination of terrorists, the suppression of drug traffic and contagious diseases, aid to the hungry Third World, and so on. All this, as I said, is not entirely a public relations show. The sane, pacific, democratic, and civilized Germany, a Swisslike Germany, did not have to be invented. It was, as I said, always there, hibernating at times, concealed by the bellicose and truculent Second and Third Empires. The operation, after the Second World War, was simple, a shifting of projector beams to the democratic aspects of the country, and quite easy, as the other Germany was buried in Berlin under the rubble of the chancery bunker.

Elderly Europeans with good memories still suspiciously watched out for, in those years, small signs that might reveal the immutable nature of the people or the reawakening of their worst instincts. They did not realize that Germany could change into something entirely different within a short time. A retired British ambassador, who had spent his youth in Berlin, kept on repeating, "All this is too good to be true. I'm afraid if you scratch a German you will find a German underneath." At a party given a few years ago by the French consul-general in Stuttgart for a group of French businessmen, one of them noticed with alarm a ramrod-stiff gentleman with an Erich von Stroheim haircut, a supercilious expression, and a monocle. The businessman tugged at the sleeve of Professor Alfred Grosser (the celebrated bilingual academic authority on Germany in France, on France in Germany, and on French-German relations in the rest of the world) and said in a stage whisper, "There they go again, they are back at their old trade, they cannot change." Grosser was glad to reassure his nervous countryman. The bemonocled, ramrod-stiff, supercilious gentleman with the Erich von Stroheim haircut was the French consul-general himself, the host.

The Germans had to be on the qui vive since they discovered for the first time that it was their more admirable characteristics that somehow provoked the foreigners' diffidence and hostility. They therefore moved on leaden feet, in those years after the war, looking East and West, with extreme circumspection and prudence, with what is proverbially known as the *deutsche Blick*. This made the conduct of foreign affairs particularly difficult and delicate for them. Their statesmen and diplomats perennially walked an oscillating slack rope in the dark. Their problems are, indeed, unique and terrifying. Their country is divided into two separate states, with relatives of many families on both sides. Bonn must always keep in mind that it has 17 million hostages in Soviet hands. Germans in both Germanies naturally dream of some sort of unification. They know they will not be at peace until it is achieved somehow. They know it cannot be brought about by force. A war of reunification might inevitably turn into a nuclear world war, the obliteration of both Germanies, Europe, the United States, and the rest of the world. Statesmen therefore talk vaguely of "reunification by peaceful means," whatever that might mean. Germans could console themselves by repeating in private to each other what the French said after 1870 (and the loss of Alsace-Lorraine) until 1918: "N'en parler jamais, y penser toujours," and "On les aura!" (Let's not talk about it, but let's think of it always, and, We'll get them!)

Germans worry, of course, about their own defense, which is after all the defense of western Europe whose outposts they man.

After the end of the Americans' nuclear superiority and their growing natural reluctance to be the first to launch a nuclear weapon, NATO has now to be also prepared eventually to fight a believable conventional war, and not, as before, just a holding action until the nuclear weapons are fired. A wholly conventional war, while improbable, cannot be entirely excluded at this point by military planners. The Germans therefore are now preparing to fight as hard as they can in the traditional way, to defend their own ground and be ready to fall back slowly to prearranged lines in Belgium, Holland, and even France. This hypothetical strategy would exploit a known weakness of the Warsaw Pact armies. The megalomaniac number of armored divisions, the incredibly vast quantities of tanks, planes, vehicles, and weapons massed on the border, with only a limited number of roads, railroads, and pipelines to feed and supply them, presents prohibitive logistical problems. The Communists are therefore thought to be prepared mainly for a violent breakthrough and a rapid advance, with whatever supplies, fuel, ammunition, and food they can carry along with them. A long fight far from their bases is what they must absolutely try to avoid. NATO should therefore also plan for a strenuous resistance and an early counteroffensive, particularly a powerful counterthrust toward the enemy's rear areas. This new nonnuclear strategy would necessarily entail bigger and better nonnuclear forces than NATO possesses today and will probably possess in the near future.

Staff officers now have to work also on the presumption that a Soviet attack might come without warning at any moment. Pessimists notoriously believe it might come a few years from now, before the West will have completed the production and installation of new armaments, more modern and deadly than those of the Soviets. Soviet armaments are as up-to-date as is possible, but some were conceived, designed, and mass-produced one generation earlier. The old Kremlin leaders will by then have left their places to younger men, who will not have a firsthand experience of the horrors and hazards of war and who might think those years the last opportunity to destroy once and for all the military power of the capitalist West, before it is too late. Years ago Western staff officers were confident they could foresee the Soviets' intentions with days or weeks to spare, because they would have to assemble men, weapons, ammunitions, and stores in preparation. Such mass movements could not then have gone unobserved by satellites. The situation now is different. Everything on the Russian side is already in place, in battle formation, plans drawn up, units even too meticulously instructed, their objectives and schedules (like everything else in the USSR) bureaucratically predetermined and unchangeable. All it takes to start the war today is one code word telexed from the Kremlin.

In this hypothetical case, the Germans would have to face the massive surprise offensive in their sector practically alone at first. Nevertheless, they are reasonably confident. Their small army is considered the best, best trained, and most powerful in western Europe. The reserves can be mobilized and transported to the front in two days. Their weaponry is the best ("Better than what the Americans have," some say, and it may be true); their communication system is impeccable; the liaison between ground and air forces very efficient; the officers are back to traditional German standards; the men are well instructed, disciplined, and have the experience of several maneuvers a year; their morale is admittedly not what it was but still better than that of other allied armies; the tactics have been particularly designed to face what is known of the Russians' rigid, slow, and cumbersome technique. To be sure, all this is seldom mentioned in public, and never boasted about. There are no parades on national holidays. The army is less in evidence than the police or the fire brigade. It only appears briefly at the reception of foreign guests-of-state, and the obligatory wreath-laying ceremony at the war memorial in the Bonn *Stadtgarten*. Its own ceremonies, the great military reviews, are private affairs. The concerts of its military bands take place abroad. There is a widespread justified fear that young German leftists might stage antimilitarist riots at the first show of military pride. Nevertheless, in spite of all the careful staff studies, meticulous training and preparation, and wonder weapons, it is common knowledge that the Germans' conventional defenses could easily be overwhelmed by the vastly superior Soviet forces and their country overrun within days, before their NATO allies could come to their aid.

Most of the allies would need several days or weeks to get ready and reach the front lines, wherever the front lines might be at the moment. The French, of course, like to consider their country an island, keep themselves aloof, make believe they will decide autonomously at the proper time whether to join the fray and whether to launch one of their nuclear missiles or not. In reality, they know perfectly well they are part of a shrunken Europe and must defend their country as far as possible away from their borders. The best part of their army is already in Germany anyway. Their staff officers coordinate plans with other NATO countries and joint maneuvers are held regularly. On the other hand, a part of the Belgian and Dutch contingents are resting comfortably in their own countries. Half the men of all allied armies are absent in July and August. They go swimming. Belgian and Danish volunteer soldiers serve only forty hours a week. Their petty officers are on leave five months a year. It is calculated it will take between six and twelve hours to supply combat vehicles with ammunition and fuel. Part of the British contingent is on the spot, a few hours away from the front lines, but needs time for more men from home to reach the armored vehicles and the weapons already on German soil, for reserves to fill the empty places in incomplete divisions, and for more divisions to arrive from across the North Sea. The Italians have a precise task, the defense of their Alps and the "Lubjana Gap," which gives easy access to the Po Valley through Yugoslavia. The Americans are in Germany, of course, almost 300,000 of them, with their tactical and strategic new weapons. But they are peacetime volunteer soldiers, thought to be of dubious resolution and preparedness, commanded mostly by willing but inexperienced officers. The American presence is mostly symbolic anyway, like a hat left on a train seat, more political than military, a demonstration that the United States is earnestly involved in the defense of western Europe, which it considers almost part of its own territory, and will automatically be at war the moment the first American soldier is killed in action.

All this is highly unsatisfactory to German (and other) experts, but it is the best that can be arranged. The Germans know that the European peace cannot be defended in one small sector alone. War might perhaps be prevented if its possible causes were identified and neutralized in time by diplomatic negotiations or by other means, perhaps in distant lands and seas, years before a crisis. Intelligent and gradual political moves and coherent precautionary measures taken long in advance are essential. One cannot rely on improvised military action, dictated by anger or fear, decided upon at the last moment.

To preserve the peace, the Germans know that Europe should act as one nation as soon as possible, patiently weave a net of counterbalancing alliances or ententes to preserve the balance of power, act as one nation strong and authoritative enough to make Washington listen to its views and make the Soviets stop and think before they make a rash move. *Rebus sic stantibus*, the Germans can do little. They cannot build up their own armaments to the necessary level and train adequate parachute and marine divisions for emergency overseas employment. They are forbidden to construct nuclear weapons of their own, and at this point, do not want to, either. They were until recently also forbidden to build up their own navy. As a result they cannot conduct an energetic foreign policy proportionate to their economic power. This is why the country has been known for years as "an economic giant but a political dwarf." Helmut Schmidt once resignedly told a Swiss journalist: "For some years now our economic policy has been simultaneously our foreign policy." Nor can they openly assume the leadership of Europe. They do not dare to interfere visibly in other people's internal affairs. They cannot cajole, prod, push, or drive their allies. Sinister memories of the past are against them. They are aware they must be careful not to provoke, once again, diffidence, hostility, or fear among adversaries and friends. They know they must be very careful in order not to start that very war they want to prevent.

What other foreign policy could the hobbled Germans possibly have followed? The question is an idle one. They have never really been free to choose. The problem was settled weeks before the end of World War II, when the German armies facing the French, the British, and the Americans retreated practically without resisting while those facing the Soviets tried to slow their advance at all costs. Herds of disbanded soldiers marched toward the British and American armies to give themselves up rather than be captured by the Soviets, and millions of refugees walked west in the winter and early spring of 1945 so as not to be enclosed in the Soviet zone of occupation. The choice was not entirely a political and ideological one. It was known that the Russian soldiers were rough, primitive, brutal, and undisciplined, fought an old-fashioned war, raped women, massacred men on the spot or deported them to die on the road, ate the cattle, stole everything that was movable, preferably wristwatches, and set up subservient governments of unsavory, ignorant, and ruthless henchmen.

Close connection with the West was an irreversible fait accompli even before Dr. Adenauer became chancellor. Security and reconstruction then seemed more immediate problems than reunification. The Soviets had not demobilized and kept enough divisions on the frontier ready for what many Western experts thought could be an imminent war of conquest, a rush to the Atlantic. It was evident that only the power of the United States could intimidate the Russians. Furthermore, only the American cornucopia could feed the starving Germans and finance the reconstruction of their economy. Only the West as a whole could offer the credits, the technical know-how, and the rich markets without which the reconstructed German industries could not flourish. When politologues started meditating on German foreign policy alternatives and the possibilities of reunifying their country, they realized there were no alternatives.

Theoretically, of course, Germany could buy back its unity at any time by offering the Soviets its disarmed neutrality. Proteus could turn into a Finland or an Austria. It does not necessarily have to adopt the Soviet Marxist-Leninist model. It does not have to become a Soviet ally. Finland did not. All it has to do is accept Moscow's foreign policy directives and its military hegemony without a murmur. This prospect, inprobable but not impossible, which once frightened André François-Poncet and the U.S. State Department, frightens many people today. Germany would not only sacrifice its own independence, security, and prosperity, but also the independence, security, and prosperity of the rest of western Europe, automatically make the USSR the dominant power on the Continent, possibly in the world, isolate the United States on the other side of the Atlantic, and lose its (Germany's) own fragile identity and raison d'être. Their fragile identity and raison d'être are extremely precious to Germans; they are practically all they have left, all they have saved from the war.

What Germany did was simply what could be done. It clung, first of all, to its collaboration with the Americans, which later became an alliance. This was easy also because the Americans at the time discovered they liked and trusted the Germans best of all continental Europeans. So many Americans have German blood, admire the German virtues, and could not help honoring a valorous and worthy beaten enemy. Furthermore, as I pointed out, there was no choice: the security of Germany and the rest of western Europe could not be conceived without the U.S.A. To be sure, Americans have bizarre ideas and are often incomprehensible and unpredictable. "They are what they are," Helmut Schmidt once sighed. "I know, but they are the only Americans we have. . . ." Then the Germans did what they could to promote the unity of Europe. As Germany could not appear to be the leader, they did not push too hard or too visibly. They were afraid of awakening suspicions and provoking contrary reactions. Nevertheless, they were always at the head of the class, eager, willing, helpful, fertile with initiatives and suggestions. They had discovered the wisdom of what Bismarck had written more than one hundred years ago (in November 1876) in his diary: "Ich habe das Wort Europa im Munde derjenigen Politiker gefunden, die von anderen Maechten etwas verglanten, was sie in eigenem Namen nicht zu fordern wagten." (I have always heard politicians use the word "Europe" when they were making requests to other powers which they did not dare formulate in the name of their own country.) Then of course, as soon as they judged it possible, the Germans of the West began a tactful rapprochement with the Soviets. They visited them, brought them gifts, offered advice, pronounced noble toasts, and sold them technological secrets, trying to reassure them and to educate them to the elementary rules of today's international good behavior. They knew that the key to better and easier relations with the other Germany was in Moscow. At the same time, they cultivated their own Eastern brothers and managed gradually to acquire (or purchase) some small de facto advantages. East Germany is hungry for hard foreign currency.

The condition sine qua non of this difficult German balancing act between West and East was their strict collaboration with the French. This was formally set up long ago by Charles de Gaulle and Konrad Adenauer. It was at best a marriage of convenience. The French and the Germans do not really understand each other and do not always find each other's company attractive, in spite of the fact that (or because) almost half of the inhabitants of France are the descendants of Germanic tribes, the Franks, and in some of their eastern provinces, speak Germanic dialects. (In reality, these last, the Lorrains and the Alsatians, have greater difficulties than their compatriots in getting along with their Germanic cousins.) The marriage, however, was necessary and inevitable. Neither country could then afford to do without the advantages it offered. From the Germans' point of view, it allowed them to undertake in partnership many things they could not do alone. Together, they could, for one thing, gently drive their European partners toward desired goals. Evidently the French could do many things the Germans could not even dream of doing. The

French are founding members of the UN Security Council, are one of the four original occupying powers in Germany, and still retain remnants of their old wartime powers, particularly in Berlin. They could (but seldom do) talk sternly to the Russians, systematically disagree with the United States, drop parachute units in African trouble spots, often take the side of the Arabs against Israel. Franz-Joseph Strauss once enviously complained to Mario Luciolli, the Italian Ambassador in Bonn at the time: "Look at France. What can't the French do? They can get away with anything. They could almost hang four or five cardinals without troubling their relations with the Holy See."

Beyond the verbiage, the sentimental hopes, the official toasts, the ambiguous communiqués that try to save the lettuce, the goat, and the wolf; beyond the tropical proliferation of documents translated into ten or more languages; beyond the endless squabbles about wine, fish, sheep, wheat, chickens, butter, eggs, and cheese, and beyond the interminable disputes about Byzantine legalities, there was for years only one fixed *point de repère* in Europe, the French-German partnership. It is no longer, under Mitterand, proclaimed as solemnly and repeatedly. And yet, it could still be considered almost a directorate, the hard core of Europe. To be sure, the two countries do not always agree on policy; when they do, what they decide may not be accepted by all the others; but what France and Germany *do not* want never becomes common EEC policy. This was not foreseen by Europe's founding fathers or contemplated by the treaties of Paris and Rome. It was, however, a highly useful arrangement, dictated by necessity, even if vaguely *contro natura*. It scarcely provoked strong enthusiasm in either country. Too many memories worked against that. To be sure, there always were and still are French admirers of German culture, virtues, philosophy, thoroughness, strategy, and music, as there are German lovers of French literature, joie de vivre, wit, wines, vivaciousness, and cuisine, but they are small minorities of specialists. There are not enough of either kind to found a solid and long-lasting engagement that might one day become the fusion of the two peoples. In fact, the pale flames of Franco-German love must be artfully kept alive and fanned. The *président* and the *Bundeskanzler* must meet regularly. Under Giscard d'Estaing they met in suitable châteaus on alternate sides of the Rhine, together with flocks of experts and the best cooks available. Under Mitterand, they met in each other's middle-class summer villas. Sometimes in the past the two statesmen went shooting like nineteenth-century kings, sometimes (now) they more modestly play *pétanque*. There is a frequent exchange of art exhibitions (the self-absorbed French discovered what everybody had known for a long time, Expressionism, the Berlin of the 1920s, UFA films, and the Bauhaus), as well as exchanges of symphonic concerts, military bands, football teams, ballets, unexciting but impeccable theatrical performances of Goethe, Schiller, Molière, Corneille, and Racine, operas, circuses, acrobats, professors, and students. Foreign policies are coordinated as often and as far as possible; inoffensive and bland common communiqués are issued at the end of each meeting. Inevitably there are differences, dictated by the two people's characters, experiences, needs, industrial capacities, rates of inflation, per capita earnings, problems, and historic heritages. But the solidity of their partnership is assured, for the time being anyway, by the memory of past wars and the fear of what would happen if it did not exist. Each country knows that it would be doomed to impotence and frustration if it were alone.

To be sure, the future of Europe (and the world) has never really been determined by one nation alone, not even Germany. It takes a match to start a fire but the match alone is not enough. World War I, the rise of nazism, and World War II were the final results of an intricate tangle of everybody's miscalculations, provoked by complicated international rivalries, mutual fears, excessive precautions, political weaknesses, prejudices, myths, blind optimism, and each country's confused search for an impossible bombproof security at all costs. (All these factors are, incidentally, still present today.) Nevertheless, it is once again important to keep an eye on the German Proteus in an attempt to fathom the probable shape of things to come. What form will he assume next? After all, Germany is still *le coeur de l'Europe*. It is by far its EEC neighbors' best customer and supplier. Its economic weight influences them all. Its stability and glowing health in good times, or its despondency, internal strife, and emotional storms in bad times can spread like rings in water over the whole Continent. Its decisions could once again overwhelm Europe and the world. The fact to bear in mind is that, despite its economic vigor, it is dangerously vulnerable. Divided as it is between capitalism and Marxism, its redoubtable armies and its intellectuals spread in both camps, it is a small model of Europe (the greater Europe) as a whole. It is therefore once again a duty of responsible observers at this moment in history to focus their minds on the Germans. What are they, really (the eternal question)? What do they fancy they are? Where are they going, wittingly or unwittingly? Where *do they think* they are going? What is the significance of the mass meetings for neutralism and disarmament? How important are the clandestine terrorist organizations? What is the German mood? Are they happy, as happy as human beings can reasonably be? (It is when they are disconcerted and fretful that they can be most dangerous.)

Such questions cannot have definitive answers. There is as yet no reliable instrument to measure a people's level of contentment and reveal to them and to us their recondite hopes. What a veteran pragmatic observer can perceive is that the Germans of today are no longer the grateful citizens of Dr. Adenauer's republic, who, emerging from defeat, ruin, disgrace, hunger, despair, fear, and misery, tried to forget their immediate past, silence their remorse, and make believe they were back at the beginning of the century. Nor are they those of Professor Erhardt's era, who thought that an ever higher standard of living and a bigger GNP, a gradual unification of Europe, plus the protection of the United States, could solve all possible problems, military, political, social, and human. Germans no longer seem either to be wholly those of but a few years before, when first under Willy Brandt and later Helmut Schmidt, they believed *Ostpolitik*, détente, NATO, the redistribution of wealth, and improved social services were the answers and could achieve international and domestic stability once and for all.

Until yesterday, they looked superficially happy and untroubled by doubts, angst, and worries, at least most of them did, highly pleased with their unprecedented material conquests. They enjoyed their coquettish homes surrounded by well-curried tiny gardens, their electronic appliances, their pretty women, no longer fat but as blond and slim as Midwestern majorettes, their many gadgets, their fancy new clothes, their overloaded supermarket shelves, their flaxen-haired children, their draft beer, the exquisite domestic and imported wines. They filled the autobahnen with interminable corteges of large and fast cars, larger than anybody else's in Europe, almost as large as those of the Americans. They enjoyed their many festivities, the *Oktoberfest* in Munich, the *Dom* in Hamburg, the *Wurstmark* in Dürkheim, the *Karneval* in the Rhineland, and *Fasching* all over. They traveled incessantly, almost as much as the Japanese. In winter they invaded the Alpine skiing slopes or they flew to the West Indies, where they had built Teutonic hotels of their own, with a botanical label in Latin and German attached to every exotic shrub or tree for the guests' edification, and where they found ample supplies of beer and sausages. In the summer many of them crowded the Adriatic beaches, both Italian and Yugoslav, the Spanish and French seashore resorts, or the Greek islands. Families from West Germany met their East German relatives in Bulgarian and Rumanian seashore hotels, the easiest way for them to spend some time together. They also enjoyed less fleshly pleasures, to be sure. Every principal town had theaters and museums of its own; many financed opera and ballet companies, string quartets, symphonic orchestras, choirs, libraries, and held exhibitions of all kinds.

But then, when one observed the scene more attentively, one

realized that the ebullient joie de vivre was not quite all it seemed to be. Or, rather, that while the people appeared still relatively happy and contented, the *Bundesrepublik* as a whole was a morose land. "There is no night, now," worried John Vinocur in the *New York Times* in December 1981, "when television doesn't bring this message: too many burdens, too many risks; all the tensions, all the demands, all the threats—the Germans as victims. . . . One feels this sense of trouble, of dissatisfaction, of fatigue. . . . Germany seems agonized, enormously irritable, disoriented." And Johannes Gross wrote (*Encounter*, April 1981), "Whether you read daily papers or weeklies, whether you watch the television programs or listen to the radio, hear a sermon from the pulpit or listen in smoke-filled rooms to the prepackaged opinions of a political party, trade union, or club, you get the identical impression of inescapable desolation, the sensation that the present order is somehow doomed. This feeling is not accompanied by the fear or loathing or despair which should be there if all these black forebodings were all really serious. The widespread mood is rather a stultifying, mind-shattering boredom. . . . The German state celebrates more state funerals and national days of mourning than the rest of the inhabited world put together."

What does secretly perturb the mental peace of the affluent and jolly Germans? What obscure thoughts keep them, some of them anyway, like Heine, "awake at night"? To be sure, under the placid surface of life there always was dissatisfied restlessness ever since the end of the Allied occupation regime. The very foundation of Adenauer's *Bundesrepublik* had provoked mass meetings and violent polemics. Many people thought it was the tombstone over unified Germany, the resigned acceptance of an irremediable, definitive separation. Later there were bigger and more violent disorders against German rearmament and the inclusion of the new *Bundesrepublik* in the Atlantic alliance. "*Ohne mich*" (count me out), and "*Lieber rot als tod*" (better red than dead), cried many young people. Still later, small groups of terrorists organized themselves secretly with Germanic thoroughness. They kept close liaisons with similar groups in Europe and the

Middle East, acquired modern weapons and explosives, held up banks, kidnapped or murdered a few prominent people, and tried to kill one American general. When necessary they faced death like religious martyrs. All this without a visible coherent political design or the hope of a better world. They merely wished to destroy the *Bundesrepublik*, the Western world, and possibly contemporary civilization. They never were a real threat to the establishment. At the same time mass demonstrations, riots, and émeutes continued to grow more frequent, massive, and violent. Memorable was the monster riot that broke out unexpectedly at Bremen stadium in May 1980, at a military celebration attended by President Karl Carstens and Defense Minister Hans Apel. Two hundred and fifty-seven policemen, a dozen soldiers, and about fifty demonstrators were more or less seriously wounded. Or the mass demonstration for disarmament and peace held in Bonn October 10, 1981 (which *Le Monde* called "historic" the next day). Forty special trains and about three thousand buses brought 200,000 people to the park in front of the university. There were no casualties.

The people, most of them young, born after the war, and like the members of the terrorist groups, from well-to-do families, were against many of the things a large number of young people were against in the rest of the Western world: nuclear power plants, pollution, starvation in the underdeveloped countries, the consumer culture, the lack of jobs and housing for the young. But many of the things the Germans were against were particular to them and had to be interpreted strictly in the German context. They were against military preparations, the Atlantic Alliance, the installation of nuclear missiles on German soil, the presence of nuclear warheads in their country over which Bonn had no control. They wanted disarmament, unilateral disarmament if necessary, rigorous neutrality, and as close and friendly relations as possible with the Soviets and the East Germans. The central nucleus of their weltanschauung was hatred of the United States. The United States was, in their view, the Enemy, the cause of all evil. It imposed advanced industrialization which destroyed nature, polluted the air and the water, made workers into empty-headed robots, forced everybody to consume more and more, to acquire things they did not need, and destroyed what was left of European culture. It imposed its foreign policy, whether dangerously passive or dangerously aggressive. It kept the Germans divided and denied them a national identity.

These people's dream was, of course, the reunification and neutralization of their country. It coincided with the "Rapacki plan" which envisaged the withdrawal of all nuclear weapons from Europe. It was also practically identical with the note Stalin sent to Adenauer in 1952. Stalin had proposed the withdrawal from both Germanies of all foreign troops; the abolition of foreign bases; the limitation of German armed forces; and the withdrawal of both Germanies from the Warsaw Pact and NATO. Adenauer (and the Western allies) considered the proposal as a transparent ruse and rejected it because it would force the Americans to retire practically beyond the North Sea and the Atlantic with their weapons and supplies while the Soviets retreated only as far as the Polish border, and because it demanded that Germany ban "all organizations hostile to democracy and the cause of peace," which meant any party or newspaper or club or person the Soviets found uncomfortable.

Polls showed that active pacifist groups included about one-fifth of the population at the most and did not represent a real danger for the time being. It was rather the fanatic intensity of feeling animating the crowds and their bizarre composition that were alarming. The rage possessing them showed clearly that theirs was not a rational movement and that the slogans on their banners were mostly unconscious pretexts for something deeper. What they wanted was some vociferous expression for deep pent-up emotions, for their collective malaise, for their unhappiness. The heterogeneous formation of the groups was revelatory. Besides the young, there were more mature people. Some were clergymen, theologians, and their religious followers. The churches, which felt themselves gradually excluded from materialistic and hedonistic contemporary life, had finally found an honorable way to be back in the limelight. Was it not natural, anyway, for Christians to be against violence, bloodshed, nuclear weapons, and war? Others were the unwitting heirs to the Nazi philosophy. The Nazis were the first to identify the United States as the Enemy, the destroyer of the legends, the myths, and the archaic soul of Europe. Others were plain patriots. They resented the humiliation of their country, perpetually kept as it found itself at the end of the war, one part an American satellite, the other part a Soviet satellite, both sides bristling with nuclear weapons of all sizes, whose warheads were in the hands of the superpowers. They also resented the fact that, according to them, Germans were considered by the United States as self-paid mercenaries, hypothetically to be sacrificed at the very outbreak of a war, a war that would inevitably be a German civil war, with Germany destined for nuclear annihilation as the battlefield of the holocaust. These patriots also naturally wanted to save their country. The only way they could see was rapprochement with the Soviets and the purchase of reunification at the price of some sort of demilitarization and neutralization.

The nationalist element among all the pacifist groups, the desire to see Germany once more decide its own future and Europe's and the world's with an authority proportionate to its economic and cultural weight, by pacifism this time and not by war, by rattling olive branches and not swords, was so evident that some, *The Economist* among them, called the movement *Nationalpazifismus*. There is, among the pacifists and enemies of the industrial world, the growing party of ecologists, the "Greens." They have deep century-old roots going back to the pagan worship of trees, waters, sources, to the immoderate passion for nature of the nineteenth-century *Wandervogeln*, the hairy and bearded youths who wandered on foot over the wildest parts of their country.

To be sure, as long as the Germans could believe in the military supremacy of the United States and its capacity to intimidate the Soviets and preserve the peace, pacifists were few, cautious, and subdued. It was only after the Soviets surpassed the United States in conventional and nuclear armaments, that the movement grew. In reality, the deep emotion under all the political and religious and humanitarian arguments was the malaise provoked by their division and fear, fear above all.

Which is the shape of the German Proteus this morning? Which will be its shape tomorrow? Johannes Gross thinks his countrymen wear a mask. "But the day may come when someone lifts the mask," he wrote. "The face that appears may be less full-cheeked and rosy than today's. . . . So long as we wear the mask, we remain hidden and continue to conceal the situation even from ourselves. . . ." Is the German, as Nietzsche wrote, still "acquainted with the hidden paths to chaos?"

FOUR

The
Quarrelsome French

THE FRENCH WERE at first among the earliest and most determined champions of European unification. They saw in it, among other advantages, a way to solve most of their national problems at one fell swoop. It helped keep the Soviets on their side of the fence, pacified the Germans' ferocious instincts, and ended the recurrent bloody, costly, and senseless wars with the latter, which the French were not always sure they could win. At the same time, it would vastly widen the market for French industrial products, fashions, delicious foods, cheeses and wines, exquisite liqueurs, *les specialités de la maison,* all kinds of farm products, and with some sharp skill in negotiating, some polite blackmailing, and some government prodding and financing might give back to their country the economic and moral predominance, the great wealth, the radiance and the unquestioned prestige it had enjoyed before the First World War. Furthermore, the promoter of the project, the most probable George Washington of Europe, the future Father of our Common Country, whose monuments presumably would be erected one day in every capital, was a Frenchman, one of the best, Jean Monnet, a man of great international influence and authority. Finally it was tacitly understood that united Europe, created and inevitably led by France, would have its capital in Paris (or Versailles, as a *pis aller*). Where else?

Only a few years later, after Jean Monnet died, the same French turned into the most implacable opponents of the European idea. They managed to block all progress by skillful maneuvers and stubborn opposition. Three decisive decisions are worth remembering.

The first: they prevented the entry of the British for years and finally vetoed it on January 14, 1963. The British had applied only half-heartedly and much too late, anyway. Since Italy and West Germany, the guilty and defeated nations, had not yet regained moral parity and an appreciable political weight, France did not fear them. What alarmed it was the ghost of the mighty British Empire; the heroic island people who had stood their ground alone against the enemy when France collapsed, who had sheltered, financed, and rearmed de Gaulle, and destroyed the French fleet anchored at Dakar. British authority, political skill, financial tradition, and economic capacity, or what was left of them, and the partly imaginary "special relation" with the United States loomed like threats to France's tutelage of Europe. But could united Europe really exist without Britain?

The second decision: the French rejected the plan proposed by Walter Hallstein, then president of the European Commission, which would have assured clear sources of revenue to the Common Market and granted the European Parliament more powers to control the employment of funds. France then stopped sending its representative to the meetings. For seven months, June 1965 to January 1966, its chair was empty.

The third: in 1966 the French managed to postpone sine die the day fixed by the Treaty of Rome, which they too had signed and ratified, when all decisions would no longer be taken by unanimous vote but by a simple majority. This, of course, would eventually have turned a mere loose customs union riddled with loopholes into a compact confederation like Switzerland or the United States. This the French evidently feared.

They were reluctant to be included in a disciplined camp, among equals, in which their proudly egocentric freedom of action would have been hampered, the value of their currency and their very future determined by foreigners they might not always esteem or trust, and Paris might no longer be considered the one and only city worthy of being the capital. It must be honestly admitted that France was not the only country afraid of what would happen to it when imprisoned within rigid institutions. But the knowledge that

Paris would be sure to block all possible progress allowed the others at times, without great danger, to keep on advancing audacious proposals for greater and quicker integration and pass themselves off as champions of instant and thorough unification, without the fear of seeing anything happen and having to face unprecedented and unpredictable problems.

It is a common belief that one man, Charles de Gaulle, single-handedly swerved the French policy one hundred and eighty degrees from a wholehearted acceptance of unification to suspicion of the Monnet project and stubborn obstructionism. De Gaulle truly dominated the political scene for years, practically without a valid opposition. But can one man alone radically change overnight the beliefs and hopes of millions of people? He can, but only in one case, when his policy is not an arbitrary infatuation of his own but the expression of ancient irrational longings deep in the hearts of his countrymen, some of which longings may be reactions to their country's contemporary humiliations and impotence and some rooted in centuries-old beliefs and prejudices, the feelings, in this case, of *la France profonde*. That *la France profonde* was hostile to European political integration even before de Gaulle returned to power in 1958 is proved by the fact that its Parliament voted against the unified defense forces, EDC, or European Defense Community, in 1954, four years before he was called back to power. The EDC, of course, would have meant a common foreign policy as well, an idea repugnant to most Frenchmen.

This is why one of the answers, possibly the principal one, to the question why there is no integrated or united Europe today, when all right-thinking people believe it is essential for peace and the defense of civilization, has to be sought not merely in the French contemporary political scene but above all in the people's past and their character.

"France is the Gascogne of Europe," correspondent Heinrich Heine wrote from Paris to his German newspaper, the *Augsburger Allgemeine Zeitung*, in 1831 (*De la France*, sixth letter). This was thirteen years before Alexandre Dumas immortalized d'Artagnan, the Gascon musketeer, sixty-six years before Edmond Rostand made the Gascon character internationally famous with his *Cyrano de Bergerac*. Everybody is now aware that Gascons are proverbially chivalrous, prodigal, generous, recklessly brave, imaginative, irresistible to women, and above all vain and boastful. In Rostand's words, "free fighters, free lovers, free spenders, defenders of old homes, old names, and old splendors . . . bragging of crests and pedigrees." Almost inevitably, that most Gascon of all animals, the rooster, was chosen long ago as the national symbol of France. (The choice is fortuitous, of course, because of a Latin pun, *Gallus*, meaning both the courtyard animal and the inhabitant of Gaul. The English pun could probably be considered even more apt.) The brilliantly plumed cock is the first to announce the dawn of a new day to everybody, dominates his immediate world, seduces and fecundates all the unresisting hens, destroys his rivals, and crows triumphantly from the top of the dungheap.

There is, of course, much more to real France than Gasconnades. Both Frenchmen and France (like most human beings and countries) are notoriously complex, varied, multifaceted, often contradictory and baffling, difficult to imprison within neat definitions. What Heine was talking about was not France, but the Platonic idea of France, which is still deeply embedded in the hearts of its citizens and their leaders, an idea that fatally determines their behavior and decisions today as it did in the past, particularly when facing foreigners at crucial moments in history. In such circumstances the inhabitants of this only partly imaginary country try hard (at times too hard, as if they had secret doubts about themselves) to behave and to be recognized once again as the predominant nation in the poultry yard. They never hide their amused contempt of foreigners; force them, not always successfully, to speak and write French, while jealously protecting their own language from barbaric infiltrations.

In the Common Market they are reluctant to give and take.

They like to see everybody buy vast quantities of French produce and goods but are unwilling to open their borders to other people's. They refuse to allow the free importation of Italian wines and of Italian oysters (cultivated in controlled clean waters), British turkeys and lambs, German pigs, and many other products from partner countries. At the same time they complain bitterly about the Germans' regulations involving the quality of beer, which prevents the sale of Alsatian beers across the Rhine. (The Germans adhere to their own medieval rules, different from everybody else's, about what constitutes beer, what must go into it, how it is made, and how it is kept pure.) The French not only invent all kinds of cavils to prevent their European partners from selling anything to them (one instance: newlyweds get a state subsidy if all the furniture they buy is made in France), but above all, they do not allow anybody to forget the memory of their past grandeur. To be sure, they have many valid grounds for their pride. France is still one of the greatest countries in the world, one of the four predominant nations of Europe, indisputably the preeminent one in many fields. Its culture is still regarded as the polestar by many intellectuals everywhere; its language is a prodigious vestment to clothe precise thoughts, nebulous concepts, or subtle sentiments with clarity and elegance; its public administration and the schools training its civil servants and officials are the envy of the world; and surely there are few "old splendors" elsewhere more worth preserving and not many "new splendors" more worth envying and imitating. But why the irritating emphasis? Why the shrill persistent crowing? Why (as Horace Walpole wrote to Hannah More in 1787) "their insistent . . . airs of superiority"?

General Charles de Gaulle loved to repeat "la France est la lumière du monde" (France is the light of the world), thus extending to the whole country an attribute that had usually belonged to Paris alone, *la ville lumière*. "Son genie est d'illuminer l'Univers" (its destiny is to illuminate the Universe), he also said, widening the scope of the French *rayonnement* to infinity. The luminous metaphor, the country as everybody's beacon, is an old and curiously recurring one. Louis XIV, who thought with some reason *he* was France, found it natural to be compared to the sun. Centuries later, in 1981, François Mitterand said in his inaugural speech, "A just and generous France . . . can light the path of mankind." (He was more modest a few weeks later in his first press conference as president. He merely said, "France has a role to play for itself but also in Europe and in the world. Many people in this earth turn their eyes toward it. For many of them it represents hope.") A perennial idea is that the excellence of all things French is not to benefit France alone but the world (Montaigne wrote four centuries ago, "La gloire de la France est l'un des plus nobles ornements du monde" [the glory of France is one of the world's noblest ornaments]), the solar system, the whole universe, and perhaps, on occasion, even God himself. (The French crusaders thought His glory could be magnified by their heroic deeds. *Gloria Dei per Francos* was their motto.) This was eloquently summed up four centuries ago by Guillaume du Bartas (1542–90), poet and diplomat, who wrote these lines, which Charles de Gaulle might have copied in his diary and probably did:

> *O mille et mille fois terre heureuse et feconde!*
> *O perle de l'Europe! O paradis du monde!*
> *France, je te salue, ô mère des guerriers!*
> (O a thousand times happy land and fertile!
> O pearl of Europe! O this world's paradise!
> France, I salute you, mother of warriors!)

In Gustave Flaubert's *Dictionnaire des Idées reçues*, or *Collection of Common Beliefs*, after the term "French" there are the famous words: "Le premier peuple de l'univers" (the first people in the universe). Victor Hugo put the concept once and for all in a few words, "France, France, sans toi le monde serait seul" (the world would be alone without you), words which could have been written by a Chinese imperial court poet about his own country, the navel of the earth.

Surely this urge to set themselves up as the universal paragon, to consider all foreign things and people good or bad according to their resemblance to and admiration for French models, often helped the French to achieve perfection or, at times, a great and unique distinction in many fields. Surely also the history of the world and contemporary civilization could not be what it is without France. Its contributions were priceless and determinant. But its effort to force the world to acknowledge its supreme excellence in all things at all times, and to adopt its ways, ideas, styles, language, and tastes, its determination to ignore or fend off all foreign influences have often made its relations with foreigners sticky. They have almost always had to apologize for not being French, remember how touchy the French are on many subjects, and humor and flatter them in order to get anywhere with them. To be sure all this was easier in the past when France was almost exactly what the French believed it to be. Before the Revolution, and even after for quite a while, it actually was the leading nation of Europe and the world, known as *la Grande Nation*. It was very powerful, populous, rich, feared, adventurous, and often victorious. Its splendid achievements were sedulously imitated by all as a matter of course. Paris was the world's capital by *antonomasia*. All polite, cultivated, and civilized people from the Urals to Gibraltar, across the Channel and the Atlantic, not only spoke French but, whether they knew it or not, thought French thoughts. Many eighteenth-century princes tried to have a French philosopher resident in their courts, and all chic women copied the clothes worn by a doll shipped every year from Paris. French masters taught dancing to Europe and the United States. Practically all European nations owe their political foundations today to the ideas of the French Revolution. In those countries that are not yet governed by democratic institutions, the ideas inspire the revolutionary minority to heroic sacrifices. The French armies, Napoleon,

French literature and philosophy spread the concept of the nation, of the sovereignty of the people, of self-determination, of the citizens' army, of the rights of man, of freedom of conscience, opinion, the press, of the freedom to form political parties, and so on. (The fact that many people forgot that the Americans had proclaimed and established such rights several years earlier shows the great power of French moral domination.) Gradually, however, in the last two centuries, more uncouth countries began to rival France, at least in the grosser and more vulgar activities. Its vast cultural, moral, economic, industrial, scientific, financial, and military dimensions—but not its pride—slowly, almost imperceptibly shrank, generation after generation, until today, although preserving a strong afterglow of its unquestioned prestige, it is, materially speaking, an ordinary middle-sized power, the equal of (sometimes inferior to) others it rightly looks down on.

What makes relations with France today even more difficult is the fact that foreigners have to remind themselves they are not dealing with a country that really exists, a country many of them love, with its admirable past and its actual respectable achievements, potentials, and capacities, but with a country that most Frenchmen dream still exists. The gap between the two is a large one, but the French indefatigably try to ignore it or forget it. France strives hard to be a truly modern country, à la page in scientific and technological achievements, the first in the world in the construction of nuclear power plants, only one head behind the United States and Japan in some advanced fields and ahead of Great Britain and West Germany in others (fast railways, aircraft construction, armaments, electronics, nuclear applications, satellites, the Arianne rocket, and medical research). At the same time it must carry the heavy burden of its thousand-year heritage. It must preserve and protect the monuments of the past, its costly patriarchal agriculture, the *Académie*, *l'Institut*, the very expensive and excellent wines, the wonderful cheeses, the Sorbonne, the Comédie Française, the many châteaus and stately royal residences, the difficult and discriminating tastes, the famous restaurants, the stupendous literary traditions. Rival countries, of course, travel more lightly. They do not have as many "old splendors" to preserve, refurbish, and restore expensively.

The strain is sometimes evident. The insistent crowing from the dungheap, the demand that France be treated always as the foremost nation after the two superpowers, surely the first in Europe, the sometimes incoherent and contradictory foreign policy, complicate any relations with it as never before. Relations with it are further embroiled by the fact that it is admittedly true that it is still, in many ways, Numero Uno in continental Europe, whatever that may mean, and that Europe would be inconceivable without it. "France, France," as Victor Hugo almost said, "Europe would be alone without you."

Unfortunately, things were so arranged in the past (and might again be in the future, for all we know) that the only valid and indisputable proof of a people's greatness, glorious historic heritage, inner cohesion, virtues, and affluence, the only definitive demonstration of its superiority in all fields, the ultimate test, was an almost irrelevant one: the battlefield. To be sure, military capacity is not without some connections with the level of civilization and harmonious inner cohesion reached by a nation. Victory certainly depends largely on its capacity to discover, promote, and follow brilliant leaders; produce better weapons at the right time; inspire young men's patriotism, cultivate their bravery, and instruct them in the soldierly arts; invent devastating new plans both for the effective defense of its own borders and for the irresistible invasion of its neighbors'. And all these things are certainly done better in more advanced countries. Nevertheless, the fact that a nation must prove its worth by facing possible ruin and the extermination of many of its people, as well as by killing a vast number of foreigners both in uniform and civilian clothes, seems today, to thinking people anyway, as absurd and unreliable a method as the recourse to the "ordeal" or "God's judgment" was in the Middle Ages. Two contenders were then pitted against each other, not in front of a judge or referee, but heavily armed on a jousting field. God chose. The survivor, usually the stronger and younger of the two, was right. The victim was wrong. The dead, like the absent, as the Italians say, are always wrong anyway.

In older times, when enemy soldiers could see each other across the battlefield, wars did not clutter up vast regions, battles could still be decided by brilliant maneuvers and cavalry charges improvised on the spur of the moment, when impetuosity and individual heroism could carry the day, the French had excellent chances to defeat their opponents. They often did. They had the means and the men. France was, until the turn of the century, not only, as I said, the biggest, wealthiest, and the most populous nation on the Continent, but also the best administered by omnipotent and omnipresent officials, a centralized bureaucracy that went back without a break almost to the early Middle Ages and had been made by Jean-Baptiste Colbert (1619–83) and Napoleon into a relatively smooth and well-oiled machine. The people were mostly sturdy and patient illiterate peasants, devoted to their country, their king or emperor in the past, whoever he was, and their Church, resigned to suffering and tribulation, obedient, docile, and blindly loyal to their immediate leaders. They fought well and did not particularly mind dying. On the battlefield they were often possessed by a peculiar frenzy of their own that swept the best-drilled enemy battalions before it. It was known as *furia francese*, or "French fury," to the Italians, who were terrorized by it for the first time at Fornovo in 1495. Machiavelli speaks of it with envy and admiration. Von Clausewitz admired the mobile *voltigeurs* who did not fight in the rigid geometrical line formations of the regular Prussian soldiers but scattered here and there on the battlefield or appeared suddenly en masse where most needed. All this, the abundant war chest, the thorough capillary administration, the ample reserves of illiterate manhood, their loyalty, their patient acceptance of sacrifices, the efficiency of gunsmiths, artisans, shipwrights, and suppliers of all kinds, the occasionally brilliant generals, the brave and often impetuous soldiers made the French army and navy redoubtable instruments of policy for a very long time. They triumphed at Yorktown. The army was invincible in the hands of Napoleon almost to the end.

But as the nineteenth century advanced and turned into the twentieth century, as other nations learned some of the French military tricks (Napoleon, the old artillery officer, began to have serious difficulties as soon as his enemies adopted his way of massing and using guns), as weapons became more precise and deadlier at greater and greater distances, and wars more complicated and impersonal, the French somehow lagged behind. Their old virtues, impetuosity, heroism, improvisation, and *furia francese*, lost some of their decisive importance. They remained useful and terrifying only in small episodes and localized skirmishes. Strangely enough, in those same years the country did not lag behind in many other fields. Far from it. Between 1820 and 1900 it became richer and richer. Paris developed then into the dream city of all humanity; provincial cities became larger, more beautiful, and more commodious, connected by the best railway network of the age; modern factories grew everywhere; new mines were dug; immense department stores became legendary; the schools and universities were universally admired; agriculture and commerce grew more and more prosperous; restaurants provoked the world's envy; foreign tourists flocked to the Universal Exhibitions in Paris; French painting, music, fiction, poetry, the theaters, some of the sciences, elegance, and the exquisite amatory arts of the courtesans easily bedazzled Europe and the Americas. It produced a disproportionate number of eminent men, historians, theologians, philosophers, social scientists, constructors of utopias, phrenologists, physicists, biologists, surgeons. Young Sigmund Freud went to Paris to study under the neurologist Jean Charcot. The literature flourished almost without rivals. The meticulous technique of its great nineteenth-century novelists is still guiding writers today.

But for some reason, while still considering war as the only and ultimate test, France did not even try to bring its military establishment to the same level as everything else. Its generals were bemedaled, stodgy old men stubbornly attached to the strategies of their fathers' time; its weapons gradually grew obsolete, except for the breechloaded chassepot rifles. (Napoleon III tried in vain to make his army adopt the new-fangled machine gun.) Its defensive and offensive plans were nonexistent or chimerical, its mobilization arrangements slow and cumbersome. But the surprising thing is that nobody (with very few exceptions) was aware of or worried about the military shortcomings. Everybody in France (and abroad, for that matter) thought it had no need to make an effort as its army was invincible anyway. (This is something of a constant. It was as true before 1870 as before 1914 and before 1939. Repeating a reassuring opinion he had gathered in Paris from the highest authorities, Winston Churchill fervently exclaimed in the House of Commons in 1940, a few days before the debacle, "Thank God for the French Army!")

The reasons for the military decline in the nineteenth century were many, all connected with French history and the national inclinations. One was the rich record of France's past glories. What was good for Napoleon I seemed good enough for his successors for a long time. Even American generals on both sides in the Civil War had studied the emperor's strategy and tactics in the handbook of one of his generals, the Swiss Baron Henri Jomini. Why change? Don't handsome old ladies cling to the styles of their youthful years, of the times when their beauty was at its triumphant best? Another reason was that the *armée* was considered the ultimate perfect product which could not really be improved. It was, in fact, the very mirror of the ancient, slowly and reluctantly changing French society, the *France profonde* of peasants, artisans, ambitious greedy bourgeois, and reckless swashbuckling aristocrats, a society shaped down the centuries by the national character, traditions, mental habits, and natural inclinations. But what was perturbing was that, since France's pride and confidence were unimpaired, as well as its profound disdain of all other countries, its foreign policy was always based on the iron certainty that if things came to the worst, the army could always settle matters in a few weeks or months at the most. Somehow, France, once again like Imperial China, could not really believe that a nation that had been destined by God to dominate the Continent for so long, was preeminent in all things that really counted, an enviable, admirable, and lovable country, did not also, automatically and effortlessly, enjoy the same predominance in the military domain. This, of course, was the origin of many grievous miscalculations, mistakes, and catastrophic adventures.

In 1870 Napoleon III proudly declared war on Prussia, to defend the honor of his country and of the name he bore. He and his staff immediately set about studying, among other problems, grandiose plans for amphibious landings in the enemy's rear on the Baltic Sea coasts. Their preparation and execution would have taken months or years. Meanwhile, the mobilization of French reserves was taking an infinitely longer time than that of the Germans. Young Frenchmen were still unhurriedly traveling to their appointed stations to be dressed and armed when the Prussians were already crossing the frontier. Napoleon III took command of his army but had to go to the front on his train, as he was too sick to ride a horse. He suffered excruciating pains from a large stone in his bladder (somewhat like his uncle at Waterloo, who suffered from both cystitis and piles on that day and commanded the battle sitting on a borrowed farmhouse chair). Within a few weeks the old emperor was captured, the army encircled and defeated, and Paris besieged.

In 1914, the French, once again unprepared for the kind of war they were to fight (or prepared for another kind of war), saved themselves (and made the ultimate victory of the Allies possible) by the skin of their teeth, possibly by the intervention of some powerful national saint, Sainte Geneviève who saved Paris from the Huns, Saint Denis, the first bishop of the city beheaded on Montmartre, Jeanne d'Arc, or Louis IX. As the German armies were executing the perfect clockwork Schlieffen plan (the invasion of neutral Belgium, a run along the Channel coast beyond Paris, and a turn left to encircle the capital), one of their generals, Alexander von Kluck by name, decided on his own to turn left *before* Paris. Old and one-armed General Joseph Gallieni, commander of the city's garrison and not in charge of fighting troops, saw an opening. He sent all the men he could find north to the

Marne, mobilizing all vehicles, including the famous taxis, and allowed General (later Marshal) Joseph Joffre to attack the maneuvering Germans' flank. The battle was confused and uncertain but it stopped von Kluck. From then on the war settled down to the immobility of trench warfare, from the Swiss border to the sea, interrupted by murderous pendular offensives that killed millions of men for the temporary gain of a few kilometers one way or another.

In 1939 the French armed forces were once again years behind their probable enemy in material and theoretical preparations. Once again the high command had been slowed down, practically paralyzed by complacency. Once again the generals thought it impossible to improve perfection. Nobody could teach them anything anyway, not their own Lieutenant Colonel Charles de Gaulle, an eccentric and stubborn theoretician, a crank, and surely not foreigners like the British Captain B. H. Liddell Hart, General J. F. C. Fuller, or the German general, Hans Guderian. These men thought tanks should be used en masse on one point of the enemy line, the weakest point, to achieve a breakthrough. Then they should not waste time widening the breach but penetrate as quickly and as deeply behind the front as possible, to spread havoc, surprise unsuspecting units at dinner, in bed, or drunk (as George Washington surprised the Hessians at Trenton on Christmas night), destroy supply depots and communication centers, capture entire headquarters, occupy strategic points, and cut enemy forces from each other. All this was neither new nor secret. It was contained in books (including *Achtung-Panzer* by Guderian himself) which could have been bought for years in any bookstore on the boulevards, new at Galignani on Rue de Rivoli, or secondhand along the Seine. Nor was the theory as revolutionary as it seemed. It was the application to armor of what General Philip Sheridan's and General William Tecumseh Sherman's cavalry had done during the American Civil War. Any French staff officer who had seen the movie *Gone with the Wind* should have known how demoralizing and devastating the strategy could be on a small scale and how decisive it could be on a large scale.

The French general staff clung instead to the idea that tanks were nothing more than mobile artillery pieces, which could be useful only when scattered along the front lines to support infantry advances. They preferred horse-drawn guns anyway, which had done so well in all past wars. They therefore spread their armor and their available divisions thinly all along the front, from the Swiss border to the Maginot Line and Belgium, but particularly thinly in the Ardennes, where everybody had known for generations no enemy could mount an offensive, as the terrain was judged too impervious by experts. The French high command stuffed the Maginot Line (which years before General Fuller foresaw would turn into "the tombstone of France") with men and supplies and sent their own main body and their British allies north toward Belgium and Holland, where they expected the principal German thrust to take place, as in the previous war. (When a similar plan was proposed to Napoleon, a thin line of men and guns spread along the eastern border of France, he sneered, "What are you trying to do? Stop smuggling?" [Quoted by Alistaire Horne in *To Lose a Battle*, page 148].) Inevitably, the real German offensive came through the French's weakest point, the Ardennes, which were not after all as impervious as the French staff had imagined. A torrent of tanks, artillery, armored transport, infantry, fuel, ammunition, food, and other supplies poured through the gap, under a terrifying air cover, and spread out, guided by the ghost of William Tecumseh Sherman. They penetrated deeply and quickly into France, surrounded and neutralized the Maginot Line, reached the sea, and cut off the main body of the French army and the small British expeditionary force stranded in Belgium and Holland. The Germans reached Paris without great difficulties in a few days and won the war against France.

The defeat was not because of the lack of the proverbial French capacity to improvise brilliant maneuvers, or to the lack of the soldiers' heroism. Small units cornered in the open by the Germans fought valiantly to the last cartridge and loaf of bread.

Sorties from surrounded cities or forts caused great losses to the enemy. A few local offensives, hopelessly carried out by brave and intelligent officers (de Gaulle among them) who had rallied around them what armored vehicles and men they could find, provoked short-lived panics among the invaders. Nor was France lacking modern weapons because it was technically incapable of designing and producing airplanes, guns, and tanks as good as or better than the Germans'. Some excellent advanced models were on the drawing boards when the war broke out; splendid proto-types were being tested; a few were tentatively produced in small quantities and were beginning to reach the troops. The problem was that the rearmament program had been started much too late. It cannot be said, therefore, that the defeat was due to backward industrial capacity, the lack of technical knowledge, of the soldiers' courage, and of subalterns' initiatives on the battlefield.

The defeat had deeper ancient roots, besides the old excessive Gascon pride and the staunch belief that the *armée* was invincible anyway. Above all, it was caused by the people's ineradicable love of political squabbles. Weak coalitions of bickering parties fol-lowed each other in government like merry-go-round horses, too short-lived to conceive and carry out long-range projects. The left-wing *Front Populaire* government formed in 1936 (the alliance of Socialists and Communists) always felt a strong reluctance to strengthen the armed forces (the military being for them, by defi-nition, incorrigibly reactionary enemies of the working class plot-ting the overthrow of the Republic). The Socialists nobly but perhaps prematurely believed in disarmament, one-sided, if need be, in order to encourage that of other countries until it became universal; in an imminent change in human nature, when men-wolves would sleep with men-lambs; and in eternal peace consoli-dated by chains of sacred treaties. They persisted in these beliefs even after they came to power and were copiously informed for the first time about their country's weakness and vulnerability, the Germans' rearmament and aggressive intentions.

Curiously enough, the Left did not take Hitler at his word. They abhorred him, to be sure, but preferred to think he could not turn out to be as bad as he sounded. Possibly judging from their own oratory, they thought his insane screaming in public and his outlandish threats were mainly meant for internal consumption. The *Front Populaire* preferred to entrust the Ministry of War to unadventurous peace-loving men. In their turn the ministers promoted unadventurous peace-loving generals, possibly coming from nonfighting corps, such as the engineers, who would not bother them with catastrophic hypotheses and disturbing requests. All successive Center governments were also dominated by a natural bourgeois reluctance to spend a lot of money for a war that would probably never break out. Immense sums had already been allotted anyway to the construction of Pharaonic fortifications, the monster Maginot Line, which, like the Great Wall of China, was supposed to have solved the problem once and for all. The governments were also unwilling to waste more of the contributors' billions for ships, fleets of airplanes, tanks, supermodern self-propelled weapons, and motorized armored transport which might become obsolete without ever being employed. Furthermore, the politicians (like all politicians) going against French popular wisdom, "le pire est toujours certain" (the worst is always certain), were loath to base their policies, as the military must necessarily do, on the worst possible prognosis, and naturally wanted to shelter themselves and their electorate from ugly truths. Life in Paris was never as gay as in the last few years before the war. The lack of foresight, however, was not to be found only in the parties on the left (in power, or exerting great pressure on the transient moderate governments that later took their place). Conservatives of the right agreed with them for different reasons. They saw in Hitler a frightening phenomenon, to be sure, but also the Great Scourge of Bolshevism, the Archangel Defending Private Property, the inventor of a new efficient way to make the working class happy, disciplined, hard-working, and eager for sacrifices.

Once again, as before 1870 and 1914 and 1939, the foreign policy of France is today officially based on the comforting presumption (or the hope) that its armed forces and nuclear weapons are, or could rapidly become, a terrifying war machine, and that France is or should be such a hard nut to crack as to be practically invulnerable. It was believed in Paris for a long time in the past, and it is still firmly believed today, that the very threat of mobilization, military intervention, and, this time, the possible use of the French's own awesome *force de frappe*, would scare all ill-intentioned opponents into acquiescence. As in the past, French leaders of the Right, the Center, and the Left do not seriously believe in the threat from the East, naturally for different and sometimes opposite reasons. They still have the same difficulties in cutting their plans for the defense of their country to its actual size and power, and in coordinating their foreign policy with their objective military possibilities. It is evident, of course, that France cannot assure its own protection without the aid of the NATO allies, of the Germans first of all, who man the front line, and surely of the United States' nuclear arsenal. Yet the French withdrew from the NATO organizations and refused to fill a gap in the Western defenses with their troops when the West Germans asked them to. They treat their allies with their habitual disdain, consider the Americans with diffidence and apprehension and keep them at arm's length, those very naive and generous, if often clumsy, Americans without whom French liberty would not have survived two world wars and whose terrifying nuclear power has kept the precarious peace until today. The French pointedly show their dissension with the United States at every opportunity. "It is almost a French reflex to oppose what the United States wants, without feeling it necessary to propose anything different or better," sadly wrote an American expert (Theodore Draper, "The Western Misalliance," *The Quarterly Review*, Winter 1981). Evidently the only way to propose to the Americans any different or better defense strategy and to have it accepted by them, the only way to intimidate the Soviets, would be to consolidate the European political union first, and to endow it with a common defense policy, integrated armed forces, and a common foreign policy. But the French have stubbornly blocked all attempts to turn Europe into a kind of third superpower, the second Western superpower, for almost thirty years. They want a full barrel and a drunken wife, as the Italians say, "la botte piena e la moglie ubbriaca." Strange.

In 1939 and the beginning of 1940 a young Italian journalist heard these words repeated with confidence in French railway carriages, bistros, newspaper offices, salons, bourgeois dinner tables, Palais Bourbon lobbies, and many other places: "La France sera toujours la France" (France will always be France). De Gaulle repeated them often during the war. Across the Channel, the British were saying almost the same thing with almost the same words in those same months: "There will always be an England." But the tone of the voices and the meaning were different. The British meant that whatever was to be the result of the war, no matter how poor and enfeebled their great country would be in the end, no matter how much of its wealth and manhood it had to sacrifice, or how much of the old Empire would be lost, there would always be the little island left, home, its people, their stubborn virtues, their friendly ways of life, their traditions, their courage. There was, in those words, pride for the disciplined acceptance of duty, but also acceptance of the price to pay for the preservation of liberty, their own and Europe's, resignation to the inevitable, and consolation for the possible eventual loss of status. The French, on the other hand, had no doubts whatever about their unchanging destiny. Whatever happened, theirs would always be *la Grande Nation* of old, shedding its light on the world. "C'est dans la nature des choses que nous soyons les premiers en Europe" (it is in the nature of things that we be first in Europe), de Gaulle wrote after the defeat. Rouget de Lisle, the amateur poet who composed the words of *La Marseillaise* at the end of the eighteenth century, thought it was not the nature of things but God's own will that determined the supremacy of France. He wrote:

> O *France, à tes destins Dieu lui-même a veillé!*
> O France, God himself watched over thy destiny!

Like most other people, the French are best led with consoling and inebriating half truths. "They must be led by dreams," wrote René de Chateaubriand in the *Mémoires d'Outre-tombe*, words dear to de Gaulle who quotes them in his own *Mémoires*. Dreams notoriously unify divided people and make the job of leading them infinitely easier. In dreams harsh reality is annulled, men walk safely on the brinks of precipices, fly without wings, win wars without preparing for them, invent brilliant plans, and all this without spending money and without really getting hurt. This partly explains why the French were always more shocked (like suddenly awakened somnambulists), deeply grieved, hurt, and plunged into despair by defeats than other people, surely more than the British or the Italians. Practically all the paintings in the British Imperial War Museum impassively immortalize appalling military disasters in wars against the Afghans, the Ashantis, the Mad Mahdi, the Zulus, the Boers, and others. The Italians too do not flinch when reminded of their military misfortunes. They take them lightly and smile sadly, seem in fact to savor them, and dedicate well-researched volumes of history to their mistakes. Count Carlo Sforza, Italian foreign minister, defined the difference between the Italians and the French after World War II. He said to me, "Simple. The Italians must forget a defeat. The French must invent a victory. Our task is infinitely easier. . . ."

It is because they believe that the battlefield is the only real ultimate test of a country's worth that the French naturally hate to be reminded of failure, obliterate its memory, often explain it away, or "invent," as Count Sforza said, "a victory." Their extreme touchiness evidently arises from, as I pointed out, their reluctance to admit and measure the widening gap between their nation's comparative weight in the contemporary world and what they want to believe it is, between its peacetime greatness and its wartime weakness. They consider the last debacle (when they think about it) a horrible unfair joke played on them by mocking and cheating gods, since France "for the last five hundred years has acquired the habit of being a great power," "l'habitude d'être une grande puissance," as de Gaulle patiently explained to the British National Defence Public Interest Committee, April 1, 1942, and see no reason why it should not keep its old habit. The fact that decadence may be common to all of Europe and the West, possibly one of the symptoms of the universal *Untergang des Abendlandes*, does by no means console the French. They think their own case is unique. They desperately clung to their colonies longer, could persuade themselves only with great difficulty that their colonial subjects did not love France more than their own countries, and mourned the loss of their overseas possessions more loudly than any other imperial nation. They refuse to believe their relative military weakness is possibly a disease fatally aggravated by their political conduct, determined by the national character, by their inevitable addiction to the *querelles gauloises*, and their history.

From time immemorial, since the dawn of history, the inhabitants of the land we call France have tended to separate into antagonistic irreconcilable groups, fighting each other rather than common enemies. This was known of old as love for "les querelles gauloises" (Gallic brawls), or as de Gaulle put it, "notre vieille propension gauloise aux divisions" (our old Gallic propensity for divisions). Some of these are as old as the people themselves. "Les Gaulois sont entrés dans l'histoire pour leur penchant à l'indiscipline et à la querelle" (Gauls entered history by their lack of discipline and inclinations for quarrels), wrote Alain Peyrefitte, seven times cabinet minister since 1962, in his bitter book, *La mal français* (page 423). This is the reason why Julius Caesar, an amateur general from a decayed patrician family, lawyer, ambitious politician, demagogue, a sometime homosexual, and an excellent writer, easily defeated and enslaved millions of divided Gauls with his small, tough, and disciplined army of veterans far from home. Tacitus wrote, "Galli si non dissenserint, vix vinci possint" (if they did not quarrel, Gauls could scarcely be defeated). The French still find it extremely difficult, when not facing an imminent catastrophe, and sometimes even then, to form a solid coalition, and act in unison. "Disputes of the past accumulate," writes Theodore Zeldin (*France 1848–1945*, volume I, page 366), "so that present issues are still debated in terms of historical precedents, and old allegiances produce permanent animosities. Religious, social, constitutional and regional divisions cut across politics in different ways, so that agreement is nearly always only partial."

Perhaps France would not have become the great, admirable, and endearing country it was, and still is, in many ways *la lumière du monde*, had it been inhabited by uniform, dull, and docile people. Undoubtedly, it is also the great country it is probably because it was molded down the centuries by antagonisms and tensions between tribes, clans, cliques, classes, coteries, guilds, camarillas, sects, parties, factions within the parties; regions— Occitanie, Brittany, and now Corsica—against the centralized state; the Midi against the North; the provinces against Paris, and in Paris, the Right Bank against the Left Bank, the center against *la banlieue*, the poor against the Two Hundred Families. There was always guerrilla warfare of sorts between rebellious barons and the sovereign, the nobility and the bourgeois, the bourgeois and *le peuple*; the tentacular bureaucracy and the citizens; farmers against town-dwellers, industrialists, and industrial workers; the *patrons* and their employees; the intellectuals against everybody else; the military against the civilians; the religious against the miscreants; the Catholics against the Huguenots and the atheists; the Christians (some, anyway) against the Jews; the monarchists against the republicans; the daring artistic avant-garde against the timorous conservatives, and so on. These groups in perpetual conflict may be as numerous as the many varieties of cheeses de Gaulle loved to quote as a symbol of the impossibility of making his people act as one. He used to say: "Que voulez vous, cher ami, on ne peut pas rassembler à froid un pays qui compte 265 specialités de fromage?" (My dear friend, how can you make a country that has 265 varieties of cheeses behave, in normal times, as one?) Cheeses of many flavors were, of course, the tastable and visible proof of each man's attachment to his little native corner of France and his own particular preferences.

In normal times the many separations, rivalries, and conflicts possibly created the climate in which the unique national genius blossomed in all its varieties, and the individual was encouraged to compete, dare, experiment, explore, sharpen his intelligence, maneuver subtly, occasionally create great masterpieces, and often open new vistas for all humanity. André Gide (1869–1951) proudly defended his country's propensity: "Il y a et il y aura toujours en France (si non sous le pressante menace d'un danger commun) divisions et partis," he wrote in his *Journal* (13 February 1943), "c'est à dire dialogue. Grâce à quoi le bel equilibre de notre culture, equilibre dans la diversité. Toujours, en regards d'un Pascal, un Montaigne, et, de nos jours, en face d'un Claudel, un Valéry. Parfois c'est une des deux voix qui l'emporte en force et magnificence. Mais malheur aux temps où l'autre sera reduit au silence!" (There was and will always be in France [except under the pressing menace of a common danger] parties and divisions, which mean dialogue. Thanks to that, the beautiful balance of our culture, balance in diversity. Always, facing a Pascal, a Montaigne, and, in our days, facing a Claudel, a Valéry. At times one of the two voices wins through force and magnificence. But unhappy would be the day in which the other voice will be reduced to silence!)

One would think the people were happy, enjoyed "avec delice et volupté" (with delight and voluptuousness), in de Gaulle's own words, the benefits of their fragmented turbulent national life. To be sure, they are not always unhappy. Maybe they only feel at ease and prosper in an atmosphere of discussions, controversies, contrasts, rivalries, enmities, and a certain amount of confusion in which each man finds his own private *liberté*. Perhaps it is their very innate restlessness, love of strife, and some disorder that made it necessary from the beginning to try to weave around them one of the most intricate webs of codes, laws, regulations, and norms in the world, in an effort to foresee and control every possible circumstance and contingency of life. Nevertheless, when life becomes difficult, the franc loses value, the state is paralyzed, the country defenseless in times of danger, *sous la menace d'un danger commun,* or threatened by economic collapse, unemployment, anarchy, revolution, and ruin, the French become violently discontented with their traditional ways, sickened by the precariousness of each coming day, frightened for their very life and property. Then they long to be unified and pacified, by force if necessary, led to harmony, saved from ruin, and made prosperous by one man, a man who can enforce law and order, bridge the gap between mediocre reality and their national dream, make their country happy and glorious in peacetime and victorious in time of war, once more supreme in Europe if not in the world. In such moments "les Français vont instinctivement au pouvoir" (the French are attracted by power), as René de Chateaubriand says in his *Mémoires d'Outre-tombe* (livre 24, chapter 6). Then "ils n'aiment point la liberté; l'égalité est leur idole. Or l'égalité et le despotisme ont des liaisons secrètes." (They do not love liberty; equality is their idol. But equality and despotism have secret connections.)

The men who, at turning points of history, managed to make the French behave as a great nation and sometimes led them to victory, to grandeur, and to prosperity, are the immortal heroes of French history. School children recite their names like those of saints in litanies. Among them are (as François Maurras said) "the Forty Kings who made France": Clovis, the king of the Franks, who gave the country its name and its religion, Hugh Capet, the first king, Philippe Auguste, Saint Louis, Henry IV, Louis XIV. . . . Added to them, there are a young peasant girl, Jeanne d'Arc, and one fanatical and meticulous organizer of bureaucracy (he and his men worked sixteen hours a day), centralizer of power, spinner of meticulously intricate legal nets, promoter of all kinds of state-owned or controlled industrial activities, founder of the merchant navy, reformer of taxation, creator of the *cadastre* (the register of all lands and their owners) and the Bibliothèque Nationale. He gave the Académie, of which he was a member, thirty-nine of its famous forty armchairs. (One rich *académicien* had brought his own from home.) This man was the previously mentioned Jean Baptiste Colbert. There were two such heroes in the last century alone, less than thirty-seven years apart, an uncle and his nephew of the same name, Napoleon, the former speaking French with a Corsican accent, the latter with a German accent, both raised to power by the fear of the people in moments of turmoil and danger. Philippe Pétain was the penultimate. De Gaulle, of course, was the last. At perilous times, the French look for, to mention some examples, a victorious general in the most recent war (Napoleon Bonaparte, Marshal Patrick Mac-Mahon, duke of Magenta, first president of the Third Republic, Pétain, the defender of Verdun); or a restorer of centralized administration and rigorous finance (the two Napoleons, Raymond Poincaré, Valery Giscard d'Estaing). In war they want a resolute, unflappable, and unstoppable leader like Georges Clemenceau or Charles de Gaulle. No such man is always available, to be sure, and at times public opinion pins its hopes, *faute de mieux*, on some picturesque character such as flash-in-the-pan Pierre Poujade, a shopkeeper who stirred up masses of protesting taxpayers in the 1950s, or the poor general, Georges Boulanger (1837–1891), on his white charger, who seemed for a while in the 1880s a serious threat to the Republic but soon lost his prestige, his followers, and his nerve, and pathetically killed himself on the tomb of his recently dead mistress, Marguerite Crouzet Vicomtesse de Bonnemain, in the cemetery of Ixelles in Belgium.

These heroes of French history are proudly remembered and universally worshipped only after their deaths. When alive they all had an appalling time. Their job was always an ungrateful and dangerous one. They had to collect taxes, levy reluctant soldiers, defend themselves from dastardly plots, avoid being murdered, suppress mutinies and rebellions, and often fight bloody civil wars. Some of them were killed by assassins. Few Frenchmen really like a stern ruler, just as few people like bitter medicines. Nobody likes the impartial application of the law. Colbert died cursed by everybody, hated by Louis XIV, the king he had made great and powerful, and had to be buried secretly, at night, to avoid hostile demonstrators who might have snatched his body from the coffin and torn it to pieces. Louis Philippe was dethroned by a revolution in 1848 and fled, because his prudent despotism, his love of the *juste milieu*, common sense, and the lack of imagination had enriched France but bored the bourgeoisie. Obviously the French (like most people) love their country to be great and glorious but are reluctant to pay the price. "Il faut payer pour être la France," de Gaulle pithily warned them in vain more than once. He had turned defeat into victory, assured France's position among the great victorious powers, restored the liberty of his people, and reestablished the Republic; his job done, he was turned out immediately to pasture but recalled twelve years later in a new time of danger, when the Fourth Republic could not get rid of the irksome Algerian problem and was on the verge of civil war. Like many of his predecessors, he united most of the people for a time, made them more or less serve the common good as he saw it and not always each man's, group's, or party's particular interest. He had to defend himself (like most great French sovereigns and leaders) from implacable opponents, slander, defamation, ridicule, satire, a few plots, mutinies, attempted murders, riots, and revolts. He finally died alone, self-exiled in his drab country house at Colombey-les-Deux Eglises. He is not buried in the Pantheon in Paris with other great Frenchmen or in the Invalides with Napoleon and his son, but in the village cemetery, where he has no competition.

When the danger vanishes, law and order are reasonably reestablished, public finances restored, anarchy is tamed, and the machinery of government functioning once more, the French are again devoured by ennui, restlessness, and the irresistible desire to free themselves from rigorous discipline and get comfortably back to their impotent governments and to their accustomed life of divisions and strife. Sooner or later (sometimes within a few years, as in 1852 after the revolution of 1848) they start once more looking for a new providential personage. This tidelike movement of French political life has not been unnoticed by scholars. Among them, François Guizot (1787–1874), historian and statesman (minister of foreign affairs under Louis Philippe), wrote in his *Essai sur l'Histoire de France*, "La France a subi, depuis quatorze siècles, les plus éclatantes alternatives d'anarchie et de despotisme, d'illusion et de mécompte; elle n'a jamais renoncé longtemps ni à l'ordre ni à la liberté." (France has undergone, during fourteen centuries, the most astounding alternatives between anarchy and despotism, between illusion and disappointment; it never gave up for long either order or liberty.)

This, then, is the eternal, almost hopeless French problem: how to preserve their precious diversities and at the same time make the people act more or less as one, even in normal times. It is now a European problem too, something for all Europeans to worry about. The only man who tried to solve it definitely, once and for all time, was de Gaulle. It is important to study what new shape the general gave France because it is still the France of today and possibly tomorrow. His constitution worked well enough for him. He not only had the stature, the prestige of his country's savior, a mass following (even among many of his opponents), and a stubborn character, but a unique point of view. He was (like François Mitterand) the son of very devout conservative parents. His father was a monarchist and a professor of history. (Mitterand's was a stationmaster and later the manager of a little family firm producing vinegar.) De Gaulle was a military historian himself and also taught history for a while. Having commanded French soldiers in the two world wars and in peacetime, he knew intimately not only his country's past but also his people's character. He was a soldier through and through, who, like most French career officers, considered the army, and himself in it, above political factions, exclusively in the service of France, in fact the very soul of France. He despised political parties and politicians. The deploring of parties which divide the people, corrupt the administration, and weaken the country is an old recurrent theme in France. In 1851, "Louis Napoleon, running for the presidency, made the criticism of parties one of the main planks in his platform; parties, he claimed, paralyzed reform and produced only agitation; against them he offered a return to order and union," writes Theodore Zeldin (*France 1848–1940*, Volume I, page 389), and, "Pétain in 1940 attacked the sterile quarrels of the parties of the Third Republic, which had encouraged the feverish unleashing of permanent ambitions and ideological passions." Like his old chief and later enemy, Pétain, de Gaulle too believed the decadence and the fall of France in 1940 had been principally caused by the constitution of the Third Republic, which enfeebled the executive and made Parliament a quicksand on which nothing solid could be built, surely not durable governments capable of carrying out long-range projects and serving the common good. He believed, with the philosopher Victor Cousin (1792–1827), that "la France n'est pas difficile à gouverner; elle ne renverse pas ses gouvernments; ce sont eux . . . qui conspirent contre aux mêmes." (France is not difficult to govern; it does not overthrow its governments; it is they . . . who plot against themselves.)

Finally, *le général*, like most great patriots in other countries and like Hitler in the end, held a dim view of his countrymen and of their republic. He privately always called them *veaux*. *Veaux* means calves, but also, metaphorically, lumps, louts, blunderers, fools. Nevertheless, he .was not a fervent unquestioning monarchist like his father. He could not believe the lifetime rule of one man could save his country, not even if the man turned out to be Charles de Gaulle himself. What he appreciated and missed of the ancien régime was not the unpredictable aleatory character of each successive king or emperor but the "organic" unifying consensus of the people, who loyally served their anointed and crowned or elected sovereign as children of old obeyed their fathers, while in reality they served France as a whole without bothering about parties, ideologies, classes, regions, and cliques. He did not delude himself that the French people would put up with an anachronistic restoration of a Bourbon king after more than a century. He believed any attempt to set up a new *royaume* would divide public opinion further, when he was desperately trying to unify it. He concluded that the Republic, possibly a new Republic, with a new constitution, which would avoid most of the defects of the old ones, was the only solution the times allowed.

While he had little confidence in his individual countrymen, he had always been deeply in love with them as a whole, en masse, inhabiting their beautiful country, *la douce France*. He saw France as an imaginary "fairy princess" (his own words) to whom he dedicated his heart as Petrarch did to Laura (whom he only saw briefly in his youth) or as Jaufré Rudel, troubadour and knight of the thirteenth century, did to Mélisande, countess of Tripoli in Syria, whom he had never laid his eyes on, not even in a portrait. (He died a few minutes after he had seen her for the first time.) De Gaulle described France as a "Madonna on frescoed walls, destined for an eminent and exceptional fate." (How a painted madonna could have an eminent and exceptional fate he did not say.) The historian Jules Michelet (1798–1874) had a somewhat similar idea. In *Tableau de la France* he had simply written: "France is a person." Napoleon, according to Hippolyte Taine, loved it "comme un cheval" (as one loves a horse). And, according to André Fontaine (*Le Monde*, 14 July 1982), "Fort d'hommes, qui n'étaient pas tous Français, l'ont aimée comme une femme, voyant en elle, selon le cas, leur mère, leur maîtresse, ou la dame de leurs pensées." (So many men, not all of them French, loved it like a woman, seeing in it, according to each case, their mother, their mistress, or the woman of their dreams.) In newspaper cartoons France is often a comely girl in her early twenties.

Le général knew that not all his countrymen fully shared his idea of *la Madonne* France and her destiny. More precisely, he was aware that the French liked grandeur almost as much as he did, which meant glory, victories, power, supremacy universally acknowledged, foreign emulation and admiration, and the predominance of the French language (and culture) over all others; they could not bear to be citizens of a second-rate power, forced to submit, like all other people, to occasional humiliating concessions. He knew that an uneventful existence bored them, even if compensated by affluence. "They cannot bear being bored," wrote

Alphonse de Lamartine, the poet and revolutionary statesman in 1847, one year before the people revolted, mostly out of boredom, and got rid of Louis Philippe. Nevertheless, they loved their quarrels more. They could not feel at ease without them.

Since early youth de Gaulle had been thinking of all these problems and their possible solutions, but only in 1958, after his triumphant return to power, had he managed to draw up a constitution based on his ideas. The constitution (the thirteenth since 1791) was approved by referendum, as was later, in 1962, the election of the president, to represent the whole nation, by universal suffrage. All presidents, he included, had to pay solemn homage to the unity of all Frenchmen. Giscard called it by an ugly technological neologism, *decrispation*. Mitterand said on his inauguration day: "I want to bring all Frenchmen together for the great causes that await us . . . to create in all circumstances the conditions of a real national community." De Gaulle preserved the Republic, its images of "Marianne" with her Phrygian cap on coins and stamps, her busts in every *mairie* and public office; preserved too most of the old republican institutions, titles, structures, the motto *Liberté, Egalité, Fraternité*, and the priceless sentimental and rhetorical heritage, *les immortels principes de 1789*. As a historian with a Latin and Greek cultural background he knew this was more or less what Julius Caesar and Augustus had done in republican Rome and Pericles in Athens. They had merely superimposed the omnipotent rule of one man over the venerable but feeble existing institutions. *Le général* curbed the powers of the Assembly, whose ever-changing moods had been the source of many evils, and of the parties. He made the governments difficult to topple and strengthened the executive to the point that many considered the president in reality a king of old elected for seven years. He probably remembered what Lucien Anatole Prévost-Paradol (journalist, diplomat, ambassador to Washington, who committed suicide in 1870 after the defeat) had written: "France is republican when it is under a monarchy, and it becomes royalist again when its constitution is republican." In short, de Gaulle gave the French the monarchy many of them longed for under every republic, and, at the same time, the republic many of them longed for under every monarchy.

His ingenious custom-made constitution worked reasonably well as long as the sovereign-president was Charles de Gaulle, a man who was unquestionably head and shoulders above his countrymen, both morally and physically. He did not have to play the king. He was the king. He had trained himself for the role since his youth. His authority was surely not determined by the popular vote. In fact, the popular vote merely put a stamp of approval on an existing indisputable situation. His constitution worked less well but well enough in the case of his successors, George Pompidou, Valery Giscard d'Estaing, and François Mitterand, worthy and capable men but lacking the mythical authority of the founder. Giscard d'Estaing, a bloodless upper-class economist, looking vaguely like a Protestant bishop, was not helped much in his effort to impersonate a princely president by encouraging the legend that he was a distant descendant of Admiral Charles Hector d'Estaing, who had fought in the French navy in the American War of Independence (a very tenuous connection, so tenuous as to be practically nonexistent), as well as the descendant of two illegitimate daughters of kings of France (difficult to prove). That the constitution of the Fifth Republic had really tried to create a crypto-monarchy was acknowledged by everybody, friends and enemies alike. Alain Duhamel, a well-informed and thoughtful journalist, wrote, "L'Elysée [at the time of Giscard d'Estaing] règne et gouverne dans un climat de révérence frondeuse" (The Elysée reigns and rules in a climate of semihostile reverence [*La République giscardienne*, page 13]), that semihostile reverence that was proof of Giscard's having almost, but not quite, reached the ideal of the republican king or royal president. Almost, because nobody seriously tried to murder him.

De Gaulle then devoted himself to the other century-old national problem, which Charlemagne, the forty kings, one premier consul, two emperors, and a few capable and energetic prime ministers had tried to solve: how to utilize the conduct of foreign and military affairs to flatter the people's pride and their desire for glory and grandeur, in order to obtain from them the enthusiastic consensus and obedience necessary for the peaceful solution of intricate domestic problems. Like most historians, like Gide, he knew that only when facing a national crisis, "sous le pressante menace d'un danger commun," and not always even then, or when embarked on an enterprise to affirm their country's proud supremacy, the people (most of them, anyway) forgot their contrasts and their Gallic love for disputes and controversies. At such times they rallied around the leader of the day and allowed him to take the unpleasant measures necessary for the common good, at least as long as he was successful and gave them the proud feeling of belonging again to a *grande nation*. This is the key to understanding some of de Gaulle's (and his successors') inexplicable and dangerous foreign policy decisions: the abandonment of NATO, the construction of France's own nuclear weapons, the repeated vetoing of Britain's entry into the Common Market, the obstruction against the entry of Spain and Portugal, the stubborn and systematic anti-American stands, and the sabotage of any progress toward European unity. They needed to restore to their countrymen a feeling of pride and a sense of national mission at any price.

Inevitably, after de Gaulle's death, practically all Frenchmen became Gaullists of sorts, as most of them had become Bonapartists after Napoleon's death. They were enraptured by the memory of the victorious emperor but especially by the liberal ideas he had expressed at St. Helena, in exile. They forgot he too had been a tyrant. The general's followers kept the faith, to be sure; but also those who had admired him with some reservations became his loyal supporters overnight, men who thought him (as one of his collaborators used to say) "a man of yesterday and after tomorrow" (evidently, like Alice's jam, not of today), an eccentric, stubborn, diffident, unpredictable character. But even those, like François Mitterand, who had feared and fought him when he was alive, suddenly discovered they could not help consider it sacrilegious to reject or betray his political heritage, his idea of France, *la princesse lointaine*, his detestation of United States leadership and of European unity. Whatever he had said in Parliament, in well-prepared speeches, or improvised at press conferences, but also privately, in absentminded, sarcastic, irate moments, his dinner table paradoxes or heavy officers' mess witticisms, diligently preserved, became holy writ, immutable, fixed for eternity, *aere perennius*. If he had lived longer, of course, he might have changed his mind about many things, European integration possibly, as he had always done, sometimes within a few days. He could not. The dead do not change their minds.

This is why French foreign policy is exceptionally awkward and rigid, sometimes contradictory and difficult to justify. Its main aim is to flatter the people's high opinion of their country and prod them to accept the necessary disciplines and sacrifices. For this de Gaulle needed to set up a "foreign threat," an enemy (as Mitterand also needed domestic enemies, the bankers and the rich). De Gaulle could not (like the men of the Third Republic) focus his countrymen's hatred on the Church or the Germans. He was too good a Catholic to wage war on the Church. He wanted to be sure the Boches would not again become a menace as in 1870, 1914, and 1939. He wanted them to be divided and harmless, as they had been for centuries. "La France," he said in a speech at Bar-le-Duc in 1948, "a le devoir de s'opposer que l'Allemagne redevienne l'Etat unifié et centralisé, le Reich, dont l'armature et l'impulsion furent toujours les conditions de ses entreprises belliqueuses." (France has the duty to see that Germany does not once again become the unified and centralized State, the Reich, whose armaments and expanding impulse were the conditions of its warlike initiatives.) After Eastern Prussia was cut off, as well as the lands bordering on Poland, the Sudetenland, and East Germany, and after Austria was reestablished as an independent republic, what was left was not yet puny and weak enough to reassure de Gaulle entirely. That he considered one more war with Germany a possibility he told friends and collaborators. He said it to Henry Kissinger. Having listened to the general's description of the Federal Republic's miraculous resurrection and restored power, Henry Kissinger, the secretary of state, said (I quote from *White House Years*), " 'Fascinating. But I do not know how the President [of France] will keep the Germany he has just described from dominating Europe.' De Gaulle was seized by profound melancholy at so much obtuseness, seemed to grow another inch as he contemplated me with the natural haughtiness of a snow capped Alpine peak toward a little foothill. '*Par le guerre*,' he said. 'Through war.' " Obviously he had to choose between a possible war and a close relationship, an alliance within the alliance, an embrace so close that it would control and paralyze Germany like a straitjacket. He naturally chose the latter. He invited Adenauer to visit him at the Château de Rambouillet on July 29, 1960. There was nothing else to do. Adenauer was surprised, incredulous, reluctant, and gloomy. He listened to the general's proposals, read a French top secret memorandum, and departed, reserving his answer. To a few close collaborators, de Gaulle brutally explained his point of view, "The unification of Europe will be performed by France and Germany, France being the coachman and Germany the horse."

Lacking Germany, de Gaulle had to define another target for the national enmity. He evidently could not choose the Soviets, who were NATO's and the Americans' number one opponents. This choice would have tightened France's bonds with the rest of Europe and the United States, which he did not want. He preferred what he called "the Anglosaxons." The term implied an intimate racial union between the British and the Americans that is unverifiable; even a harmonious coincidence of ideas and hopes between the two countries, which is temporary and fragile at best, as unreliable and fragile as, for instance, the sisterly feelings between France and Italy, "*les soeurs latines*" (the Latin sisters), which crops up only very briefly at long intervals when they are allied at war (in 1859 and in 1915–18) and is forgotten the rest of the time, particularly when the Italians dare to sell wine, shoes, furniture, automobiles, and oysters to the French. He was led to choose the "Anglosaxons" also because he craved revenge for the many humiliations he had been subjected to by both Britain and the United States during the war, when he had to convince the incredulous and diffident British and Americans he was not what he looked like, a tall, thin, long-nosed, scholarly, obscure brigadier general, without means and official status, who might theoretically be court-martialed and shot one day for desertion, but France itself, like Louis XIV, or a divinely inspired heroine, like Jeanne d'Arc (he proclaimed many times during the war without smiling, "I am Jeanne d'Arc!"). The term "Anglosaxons" was particularly useful as it helped deflect toward the United States part of the traditional enmity that had been directed since the early Middle Ages exclusively against England, the perfidious Albion whom the French had to fight in innumerable wars. "Vive le Roi de France et merde au Roi d'Angleterre, qui nous a declaré la guerre," goes an old song. Britain alone was evidently too feeble, disheartened, and impoverished to be the main target of his bitterness. Most of the *merde* could now be directed toward the United States.

He had many other reasons to choose the Americans. France owed its liberty, independence, and status as a great power to American intervention in two world wars, a humiliating fact to acknowledge, one more demonstration of the gap between French pretensions and reality. It also owed its recent reconstruction to American financial gifts. Nothing notoriously makes for bad blood between nations and individuals as an undeniable claim for gratitude. Furthermore, the United States was then a patient and reluctant superpower which could be attacked verbally without fear of consequences. It never boasted of its charitable donations to the touchy French, also because their collaboration had become vital to the defense of the West. Finally de Gaulle's dislike of the most advanced industrial country in the West was also that of many elderly nineteenth-century European gentlemen, imbued with a classical education, who despised economic facts and the modern industrialized business world, its abrupt and uncouth ways, its contempt for history, its cheap tastes, its love for infantile oversimplifications. The American politicians he had to deal with were as incomprehensible to him as Woodrow Wilson had been to Clemenceau at Versailles in 1919. Could one really depend on them?

What he needed above all and at once was to show his people their country could, under his guidance, and that of his successors, fully take care of itself. He said, "Je refuse d'admettre que le defense de la France dépende d'un général étranger. Nous ne tomberons pas au rang des sujets des Etats-Unis" (I refuse to accept the fact that the defense of France may depend on a foreign general. We will never descend to the level of American vassals [Raymond Tournou, Le feu et la cendre, page 137]). To be sure, privately he knew better than anybody else that those were empty words, because the power and the nuclear armaments of the United States as deterrents were absolutely essential to the defense of the West, France included, then and in the immediate future. He knew that France alone had not been able to assure her own security for generations. Furthermore, he could scarcely attempt to impress the Americans and deflect their conduct. But he (and his successors) refused to draw the necessary conclusions. He closed his eyes to the obvious fact that only a firmly united Europe, in which France would necessarily have a paramount if not predominant influence, could talk to Washington (and incidentally, Moscow too) with authority. He said he wanted a "Europe des états," which meant a fragile patchwork of weak, vulnerable, and self-centered nation-states, without authority, each blindly struggling to defend its own petty and immediate interests against everybody else. What he wanted was really a ramshackle coalition that would immediately crumble in times of crisis or depression, each country trying to save itself by its own mediocre means. De Gaulle (and his successors) could not admit even to themselves the simple self-evident fact that the two French policies (anti-America and anti-Europe) could not be reconciled. This was particularly bizarre on the part of Frenchmen, proud of the clarity and Cartesian logic of their rational thinking. Bizarre and frightening.

De Gaulle smothered the *querelles gauloises* under the blanket of his authority, prestige, and the stubbornness with which he pursued his course without listening to anybody else. It looked to outsiders as if the country had really found its unity. But the *querelles* were there all the time under the surface. They began to break out under his successors. The leftist opposition, seething with internal factions, wanting many different and irreconcilable things, grew in numbers under Pompidou and Giscard d'Estaing until it won the 1981 elections. It had found unity of sorts only for the time necessary to defeat the common enemy. Under François Mitterand the political panorama began to resemble what it had been under the Third and Fourth republics. It was even worse in some ways, because the rigidity of the Gaullist constitution prevented the frequent changes of governments that followed the changes in political moods. The steadfastness with which Mitterand tried to apply his party's and his allies' vague electoral program, the control of the country's economy in order to transform society, inevitably provoked resistance and rebelliousness among people of all classes as traditionally attached to property as to their own lives. This was aggravated by the fact that the laws nationalizing industries and banks (an obsolete formula) had not been worked out in detail before the elections and had to be improvised among the squabbling factions of his followers, nineteenth-century Marxists, moderates, gradualists, idealists, radicals, ecologists, and with an eye to their Communist allies. The uncertainty was such that many rich people emigrated, stopped investing money and hiring workers, and smuggled vast amounts of capital abroad, which they had prudently done for years anyway; the middle class placed its savings where they couldn't be traced by the tax men; the majority gradually repented of having voted for such an incoherent coalition of revolutionary-reformer-utopians; the workers sulked and struck, the peasants rioted occasionally, and the Communists plotted their revenge against the

Socialists. France was finding once more its ancient love for dissension and contrasts, strife and controversies, the condition in which, according to many authorities, the country's morale was at its best.

This, summing up what has preceded, is France. Alexis de Tocqueville wrote these words in *L'Ancien régime et la Révolution*: "La France est la plus brillante et la plus dangereuse des nations de l'Europe, et la mieux faite pour devenir tour à tour un objet d'admiration, de haine, de pitié, de terreur, mais jamais d'indifférence . . ." (France is the most brilliant and dangerous nation in Europe, best suited to become in turn an object of admiration, hatred, pity, terror, but never of indifference.) It still is all that, a unique, lively, inventive, restless, courageous, brilliant, and disquieting country. It is perpetually torn between its dream of a more just society and its reluctance to give up its old comfortable but inequitable ways, between its desire to be once again united under one rigorous man, in order to regain its rightful place in the world, and its old preference for a pleasurable life of divisions, dissensions, controversies, and confusion, which made France at times the victim of its more disciplined enemies. It wants to be recognized as the dominating power in Europe but refuses to acknowledge the fact that nation-states, even one as glorious and prosperous as France, have shrunk to mediocre dimensions, impotent when alone, no match for the superpowers. Three wars since 1870, all of them fought against Germany, cracked its comforting faith in its invincibility, and this is why France must now keep abreast of the Germans, keep them under surveillance, maintain the most intimate relations with them, and hold them in an embrace as close as a stranglehold. If France cannot dominate Europe alone, it hopes that maybe the two nations together might do so. These are the reasons why France must be studied constantly, as seismologists study the trembling of their needles on the white paper.

FIVE

The
Flexible Italians

ITALY IS UNIVERSALLY considered a particularly unpredictable and deceptive country. Some people even believe that this is the only absolutely certain thing about it. They are, of course, right some of the time, but also wrong as often. There are no sure guides to what Italy is and what it might do next. Italians themselves are almost always baffled by their own behavior. The only people who have no doubts and hold very definite and clear ideas about the country and its inhabitants are foreigners who streak through it in a few days, possibly for the first time in their lives. Everything around them confirms what they have always known about Italy and the Italians—their tastes, habits, cuisine (strictly olive oil, garlic, and tomato sauce), their governments (inefficient and short-lived), love life, talents (artistic), virtues (private), vices (public), and political inclinations. Foreigners who linger longer and those who come back begin at a certain point to be disturbed by vague doubts. They suspect that things and people may not always be what they appear to be, and Italian words may not invariably mean what the dictionary says. Those who settle here (journalists, businessmen, art historians, husbands or wives of Italians, affluent expatriates, opera singers, archeologists, retired diplomats) end by discovering that there are no hard-and-fast rules. One must be en garde all the time, learn the hard way to distinguish between when one must be wary and when one can relax. Above all, one must remind oneself to resist the seduction of the famous fatal beauty, of the all-pervading charm, and of the inevitable compassion that the poor people, so mistreated by fate, history, economic forces, ill fortune, and bad rulers, inspire. Some foreign residents realize at one point that many

Italians never and all Italians, given the right circumstances, do not behave like proverbial Italians. They can be as surprisingly honest, punctual, faithful, tidy, efficient, truthful, and courageous as highly esteemed people with a better international reputation. The only rule to follow, these foreign residents discover, is the old Italian proverb that says, "Fidarsi è bene, non fidarsi è meglio" (to trust is good, not to trust is better). An illustration of this bewildering quality of life was years ago put in a nutshell by a foreign correspondent. He said, "In Moscow one knows nothing but understands everything, in Rome one knows everything but understands nothing."

All this is, of course, true. It is not true, however, what many foreigners believe, that Italians enjoy and are at their best living precariously in a disorderly country ruled by inept and impotent, or arbitrary and corrupt governments. They never liked it. As Ignazio Silone wrote once, "There are no sadder people than those gay Italians." For centuries, since the early Middle Ages, they have dreamed the same impossible dream of being one day governed with freedom and justice, of being able to dedicate their energies solely to their work and not to the task of avoiding cramping and frustrating laws or defending themselves from dangerous and powerful enemies. They dreamed of living an honorable, transparent life in peace in an honorable, transparent country in which there should be no need to lie. The dream can be traced down the centuries in many documents, books, poems, and paintings, from Dante's *De Monarchia*, Machiavelli's *Il Principe*, Giuseppe Mazzini's and Vincenzo Gioberti's *Oeuvres*, down to a large number of contemporary essays, newspaper columns, and political programs. The visible symbols of all this are the fourteenth-century frescoes by Ambrogio Lorenzetti in the Palazzo Pubblico in Siena. They are called "Il Malgoverno" and "Il Buongoverno." The "bad government" is filled with battles, turmoil, ruins, corpses, and desolation. The "good government" shows farmers ploughing, craftsmen working, fat cattle, vineyards loaded with grapes, and beaming happy faces. Italian history could in fact be interpreted as a vain and sickening search for *Il Buongoverno* down the centuries.

This necessity to decipher the Italian puzzle is by no means a frivolous private problem. Sometimes it can be a matter of momentous importance for the whole world, the chance for ruinous miscalculations. Before the last world war, experts saw Italy as a solid, well-organized, disciplined country, and treated it gingerly as such, a country ready for war at the drop of a helmet under the leadership of a charismatic leader with a Napoleonic and Periclean mind, Benito Mussolini. Lenin, Churchill, and Adolf Hitler believed him to be one of the outstanding characters of the century and perhaps of all history. In reality Italy was demoralized and flabby, deluded by a flood of improbable propaganda, armed with ancient Austrian guns captured in 1918, a few fragile tanks, and a handful of planes. It had no radar. The Fascists were, in the words of Benedetto Croce, "men who thought themselves gifted because they were ignorant, and strong because they lacked the ancient love with which one's country should be treated." The infallible leader was in reality an incompetent self-taught elementary school teacher, catapulted to a position too high for his particular talents, a gifted rabble-rouser, completely isolated from reality in his last few years. He could not bear intelligent criticism and factual objective information that contradicted his own preconceived and unchangeable ideas. He listened only to brazen flatterers, the only people he saw and trusted. He believed only his own newspapers and radio. Like a visionary, he followed his intuitions blindly in a crisis. The final result is well known.

Should one then always disregard Italian warlike appearances and take for granted their military reluctance? Are Italians always bad soldiers? This could occasionally be as ruinous a mistake as the contrary approach. When, in October 1917, the Austrians burst through the Italian front at Caporetto and were pouring down the Alpine valleys toward the Venetian plains, the highest ranking Allied military minds, meeting at Peschiera on Lake Garda, peremptorily urged the Italians to abandon most of the Veneto, including Venice, and set up a new front, along the southern bank of the river Po and the right bank of the Mincio. This, of course, could eventually have brought Austrian and German divisions to the French Alpine border, possibly outflanking the whole Allied northern deployment from Switzerland to the North Sea. King Victor Emmanuel and his generals indignantly rejected the advice. Cavalry regiments charged machine gun nests at Pozzuolo del Friuli and slowed the enemy advance; the Italian high command hurriedly scraped together all available reserves, called eighteen-year-old boys to the colors, improvised a new line of defense on the right bank of the Piave, north of Venice, and blocked the Austrians. Factories miraculously produced in a few months an incredible amount of new guns to take the place of those lost. It was from this new position that the final offensive was launched one year later, which outmaneuvered and destroyed the enemy and ended the war for Italy. The armistice was signed on November 4, one week before the other Allies managed to do so on the French front.

Another military expert who thought one could count on the Italian soldiers always lacking determination and the will to win was the French general, Léon de Lamoricière. A glorious veteran of many victorious campaigns, he had been entrusted with the command of the Papal land forces in 1860. His job was to stop the Piedmontese army on its way south to join with Garibaldi and his redshirts, who had liberated the kingdom of Naples. Lamoricière chose a favorable spot near the town of Castelfidardo, deployed his men, drew up the plans, distributed tasks, and concluded contemptuously, "Les Italièns ne se battent pas" (the Italians don't fight anyway). (His men were not Italian, but Catholic volunteers from all over Europe.) The battle (a modest one, as battles go, but decisive for the survival of the Papal States and the unification of Italy) started at dawn on September 18, 1860, and ended three hours later with the complete defeat of Lamoricière. He fled the field dressed in peasant clothes and found safe refuge on a boat anchored in the port of Ancona. The Italians *did* fight that day, as later they fought on the Piave. There is obviously for them a time to fight, even against desperate odds, a time to die, and a time to play safe, but nobody, not even their generals, let alone foreign observers, can ever exactly foresee what they will do. Somehow, only they decide, without passing word, as if inspired from above or from inside their hearts.

Miscalculations, sometimes irreparable, are also constantly made by foreigners in their estimates of the Italian political and economic perspectives. Inevitably, cures for Italian ills based on authoritative diagnoses, cures that might be excellent for other countries, are disastrously wrong. In the late fifties and early sixties, when the Italian economy was enjoying a boom and political problems were being gradually solved, save one, the Communist threat, foreign specialists decided the only hope for the country was not what common sense would have recommended, the strengthening of the coalition of center parties, which, with American help, had rapidly reconstructed the country after the war (all efficient governments are, whatever they call themselves, center governments). Foreign experts thought that a new Center-Left government would be the right medicine, a coalition of Christian Democrats and Socialists. It must be honestly pointed out that, as usual, these foreigners were deceived by Italian words, which seldom mean exactly what they seem to say. Italian Socialists of that generation were not what these people imagined. They were also very dissimilar from the Italian Socialists of today. They were then incredibly behind the times. Most of them were verbal extremists. Many clung to the 1870 myths of *La Commune* and to the excessive impossible hopes of the beginning of this century, some were Anarcho-Syndicalists, others were pure anarchists and a few were terrorists at heart. They believed the economy was the only motor of history but knew almost nothing about economics. They were openly pro-Communist, resigned to accept Soviet leadership in international affairs, resigned also to see the Italian Communists take power, and worked strenuously to help them destroy what was left of the bourgeois liberal state. The secretary of the party, Francesco de Martino, repeatedly threatened, "We'll nationalize everything in the country except barber shops." (The odd exception was probably because Professor de Martino, being Neapolitan, presumably did not use a razor, but like most middle-aged southerners, was shaved every afternoon after the siesta by a friendly barber, whose autonomy from the state he was understandably determined to preserve for the safety of his own hirsute jowls.) Contemporary Italian Socialists are younger, more experienced, better read, and more up-to-date. While still tormented by a minority of incoherent enthusiastic extremists, they are now carefully approaching the political beliefs of the German and British Social Democrats. They are wary of doctrinaire abstractions, afraid of failure and of cutting themselves off from reality. They are now, for the first time, tentatively in favor of the bourgeois liberties, private initiative, and the market economy, as *pis-allers* anyway; in favor of NATO, the Italian armed forces, the Common Market, eventual European integration, and the West in general. They fight the Communists, their principal rivals, with determination, for each vote, and are preoccupied and frightened by the Soviet Union and its "Socialist" experiment but also regard it with derision and contempt.

The plan to form a Center-Left coalition was first conceived by Italian politicians for many different reasons of their own, but also custom-designed to seduce the Americans, without whose approval and backing the Italians curiously believed it could not be carried out. The Americans immediately saw in it a wonderful way to fulfill their double vocation: the pragmatic one of leaving no problem unsolved and their missionary obligation to spread democracy and improve everything in sight. They spared neither effort nor money to implement the plan as quickly as possible. They thought it was the only way to cure all the Italian ills at once, so why wait? It would strengthen the decaying state; check rampant corruption; generally enforce law and order; defeat the Mafia, the Camorra, and the emboldened unattached criminals;

discourage the class struggle; decrease the number of ruinous strikes; swell production and exports; slow down inflation; levitate the standard of living; and as a result, encourage domestic and foreign investments. Above all, they believed it to be a certain way to isolate and weaken the pro-Soviet Communists, by depriving them of their Socialist vassals, and free Italy once and for all from the menace of a totalitarian takeover. A Soviet-dominated peninsula cutting the Mediterranean in half obviously would have thrown all NATO plans and the security of the United States itself into disarray.

To be sure, many naive Italians also believed in the miraculous possibilities of the plan, or at least hoped it would work somehow. Others had more modest and realistic motives. The Christian Democrats thought it was a good way to consolidate their power. The Church, without whose consent they could not have allied themselves to irreligious radicals, thought it could be a first cautious step toward easier relations with Marxists on this side of the East-West border to begin with, and which could then possibly one day lead to easier relations between the Church and parties in the East. John XXIII was reported to have said, "It must be made clear that the Pope is not the chaplain of the Atlantic alliance." The Socialists favored the plan because they contemplated with horror the gradual shrinking of their electorate (left-wing voters were naturally more attracted to a severe, disciplined, efficient, and well-financed Marxist-Leninist party that produced results, than to a feeble, dubious, and disorderly imitation) and began to suspect they might have no future in the Communists' boa-constrictorlike embrace. The Socialists also believed there was somewhere a magic secret chamber they wanted to enter ("the chamber of buttons," Pietro Nenni, the Socialist leader, called it), from which all national activities had been controlled for almost a century by capitalistic bourgeois, strictly in the interests of their class, and from which the proletariat had been excluded. The room, of course, existed only in their imagination, and even if it had been real, it is doubtful it would have worked in Italy.

The plan might possibly have produced in some other country

all the wonderful effects the Americans expected. In unpredictable Italy it produced the exact contrary. It was estimated that in the end the plan cost as much as a lost war and retarded social and economic progress for at least one generation. Its failure also came from external circumstances, to be sure, the rise in the price of oil, the revolt of the young and the workers in the late sixties, and the incipient world economic depression, but was principally due to the wrong diagnosis. The state (what was left of it after twenty years of arbitrary dictatorship and a crushing military defeat) practically collapsed under the burden of a vastly enlarged number of new tasks, some of them admittedly useful and necessary, but with which the bureaucracy, such as it was, was absolutely unprepared to cope. Among them was the enforcement of some of the most ambitious and intricate legislation ever passed outside Byzantium. Furthermore, the Christian Democrats and the Socialists, who had considered with hostility the secular liberal democratic state since its inception in 1861, joyfully kept on dismantling it. Too late they realized it had become an indispensable tool, not only to govern in the ordinary way, but above all to carry out any left-wing policy, which notoriously relies on an ever-increasing state intervention in every sector of the economy. Corruption grew to Levantine proportions. The police were demoralized, paralyzed, and ordered not to use their weapons even when attacked.

Only after Aldo Moro was kidnapped and killed did the more responsible politicians in power begin to realize that the dismantling of law-enforcing agencies did not harm their "class enemies" alone but was detrimental for the whole country and could be mortally dangerous for each of them. Law and order were violated by everybody as a matter of course with impunity; even sedate elderly drivers allowed themselves to cross red lights. Bank robberies and kidnappings of well-to-do gentlemen proliferated. Terrorists dynamited trains, cars, and office buildings and murdered innocent people almost every day. Every request of the trade unions was immediately granted without discussion. The endemic riots, the perennial strikes, the occupation of factories, and the continuous threats of universal nationalizations discouraged new investments. Capital surreptitiously fled the country in vast quantities. Production slowed down and sometimes came unexpectedly, without a reason, to a standstill in many plants. The state deficit, incredibly, grew higher than that of the U.S. federal government, and the inflation rate threatened to reach South American levels. The "economic miracle" of the fifties became but a nostalgic memory, a lost golden age.

Finally the Communists, who, deprived of their Socialist vassals and isolated in their ghetto, were supposed to wither away, acquired instead an all-pervading tentacular influence they had never previously enjoyed or hoped for. They seduced or terrorized the intelligentsia, more or less controlled schools, universities, newspapers, magazines, publishing houses, all means of communications, and through the trade unions, the economic life of the country. They infiltrated the bench and the bureaucracy. Many Italians, who were not convinced Communists, possibly anti-Communists in their hearts, saw the way the wind was turning, and prudently, resignedly behaved as if they were true believers, naturally with the neophyte's fanatic zeal, somewhat as their fathers had done as Blackshirts. Democratic opponents to the Center-Left, who did not fully trust the government's programs and still thought the Communists a possible threat to freedom, somehow found themselves without jobs or occupying obscure positions inferior to their capacities. As a result many bright and ambitious young men emigrated to countries where advancement was based on merit and not political affiliation. One Italian writer I know changed language to make a living.

The Communists' source of power was principally their capacity to stage riots anywhere at any time. The party had money enough to organize noisy and turbulent mass meetings a few blocks from the seat of the government by concentrating hundreds of buses and dozens of special trains on Rome within days. It could also paralyze the whole country overnight by means of gen-

eral strikes, brutally enforced by strong-arm squads. Sometimes
the party did not have to do anything. Threats were enough, veiled
threats imbedded in *Unità* leading articles, in a speech in Parliament, or even unspoken threats. The saying went at the time
that the Christian Democrats could evidently do nothing that dis-
pleased the Socialists, the Socialists could do nothing that dis-
pleased the Communists, and, in the end, even if the Communists
did not always get all they wanted, nothing could be decided that
they did not like. Some of the most controversial laws were in fact
passed with their votes or thanks to their abstention. The idea that
the Center-Left coalition could defend the people's liberty from
the Communist menace was best criticized by Giovanni Malagodi,
parliamentary leader of the handful of democratic opposition
deputies, with these words, "You are making the same mistake the
Romans made at the end. They entrusted part of the defense of
the empire to Germanic tribes, related by blood, customs, and
religion to the Germanic tribes pressing on the border."

Specialists in Italian affairs (diplomats, journalists, and professors of international relations in the best universities) were
frightened by what they had helped to bring about. They concluded the country was hopelessly, incurably sick, as sick as Imperial China or the Ottoman Empire on their last legs, ready for
extreme unction. They saw it correctly as rudderless, irreparably
torn by irreconcilable social strife, led by weak, incompetent politicians, and drifting toward final bankruptcy and collapse, or at
best, a totalitarian police regime on the Soviet model. They had to
conclude that the Center-Left coalition, while inspired by the best
intentions and based on sound information, had been a costly
mistake that had produced more terrifying problems than it had
solved, possibly only because its aims were too high and because it
had been set up before the country was ready for it. The Italians
surprised them again. Like the soldiers at Castelfidardo and along
the Piave, they refused to lie down and die. To be sure, most of
the large basic industries and utilities, state-owned or controlled,

managed by political appointees, packed for electoral reasons with superfluous workers who could not be fired, lost enormous sums of money yearly, some of them larger sums than their capital.

To be sure the small and medium private industries could not really save the country forever, but they proliferated and flourished, for a few years anyway. They invented new products, improved old ones, and exported them all over the world. Many specialized dangerously in chic luxury goods—fashions, shoes, leather goods— which, being dispensable, could mean that their customers would vanish in a depression, but others managed to beat the competitors in manufacturing advanced necessary products that would sell well in all seasons. Italian design triumphed everywhere. The wines beat their French competitors in the United States. The more expensive handmade cars dominated the playboys' market. Films found a vast international public. Olivetti carved itself an honorable place in the world of electronic office machines. Italian companies, freed abroad from their legal entanglements, built dams, roads, bridges, airports, canals, ports, railroads, new cities, hospitals, hotels, and universities all over the Third World. One firm even won the bids for a section of the New York subway. One man I met on a plane told me he built museums dedicated to local art in many newly created African republics and filled their showcases with admirable wooden sculptures and textiles that were made in Florence at his direction. The genuine ancient local product, he discovered, was scarce and hard to find. Made of wood or ephemeral fibers, it deteriorated beyond repair. The Florentine artifacts were much more satisfactory.

As a result of the well-intentioned but suffocating new legislation and of the paralyzing, ill-informed pressure of trade unions, old-fashioned piece-work was revived. Naples exported five million pairs of gloves a year, in spite of the fact that there was not one glove factory in the city. Most of the shoe industry, which practically came to dominate the world, was similarly organized. The majority of these enterprises kept diligently within the law, and paid their taxes and social security contributions in full. The village of Castel Giubileo, near Mantua, which produced panty-hose at extremely low prices; Brescia, where iron rods for reinforced concrete works were made much more cheaply than anywhere else; and other similar towns were inspected by suspicious Common Market functionaries who found nothing amiss.

Another result of the doctrinaire restrictions regarding labor drove Italy to conquer a newly developed industry. By law workers to be hired could not be selected by an employer; they were assigned to each industry by a state agency from a list of unemployed, at random, according to priority. The character of workers, their suitability, professional skills, and political opinions could not be investigated; their work could not be controlled by closed-circuit television or any other mechanism (even the black box on airline planes was theoretically illegal); the unwilling or inept could not be fired, nor the good ones promoted. Workers' indexed wages rose automatically like the tide, all at the same time, higher than the inflation rate, in good years and bad; men could not be moved from one sector of the plant to another, from one industrial activity to another analogous one, or trained for jobs for which there was a demand in new flourishing industries. As they agitated, struck, and stayed home when they pleased, it was almost impossible for management to make plans, to estimate costs of production from one year to the next, in order to make binding contracts and meet deadlines. As a way out, the Italians developed one of the best lines of robots in Europe and exported them to most industrialized nations, occasionally including Japan. This naturally did not diminish unemployment. In their own mysterious way the Italians somehow also prevented the Communist takeover, which had looked absolutely inevitable only a few years before. Communist votes, which had increased ominously at every election until 1976, dwindled the following years.

The experts were astounded. Once again it seemed Italy had saved itself in its own inscrutable way, without any public explanation or scientific exegesis foreigners could study. There were no reliable statistics. In fact the only way economists could estimate the growth of the gross national product was by comparing the yearly figures for the consumption of electric power. They concluded once again that Italy was an unpredictable country sui generis, which reached the brink but then somehow always managed to avoid definitive ruin and national dissolution. How did the Italians do it? What was their secret?

I visited Francesco Saverio Nitti at the end of World War II, shortly after he had returned to Rome from exile. A democratic liberal, considered one of the more authoritative intellectual opponents of the Fascist regime, second only to Benedetto Croce and Antonio Gramsci, he had spent the years of banishment in Paris, on the Rive Gauche, reading, writing, and thinking. He was one of the wisest, most intelligent, clear-eyed, and skeptical Italians alive. He was a revered scholar, the author of important books on politics and economics, a professor of finance at the University of Naples. He had been prime minister during some of the bloodiest and most turbulent years after the first war, from June 1919 till June 1920. The Fascists hated him because he had kept his head, reorganized the forces of order, tried to enforce the law impartially and to strengthen the authority of the state. They contemptuously called him by a scatological nickname, "Cagoia," and depicted him as a fat pig in their cartoons. The real reason for this hostility was the character of the man. He did not allow mass emotions to dictate his decisions, never tried to please the crowd, did not share (or make believe he shared, as others did) the fanatical nationalist dreams that then flattered many people, consoled them in their misery, and assuaged their incoherent fears. Above all he seldom hesitated to call things by their ugly names and to announce unpleasant but necessary truths.

I went to see him because I hoped he, in his old age, had reached fundamental and definitive truths about Italian life, the laws governing it, and could explain to me why our countrymen, sober, cautious, and realistic in their private affairs, could at times join demented political mass movements (Fascist yesterday and Communist after the war) and sometimes seemed to rush blindly, like lemmings, towards collective catastrophe and annihilation. I wanted him to tell me whether it was possible to figure Italians out and whether there was hope for them, one day, to govern themselves undramatically, reasonably, diligently, economically, and prudently; why they so often preferred to be led by quacks; why so many of them were always looking for miraculous formulas, instant cures, and shortcuts; and why men like him were seldom entrusted with power and lost it quickly when they were.

Nitti was a small, round-bellied, bald man, not unlike, I must regretfully admit, the cartoonists' pig, so small a man his feet barely touched the ground when he was seated. His eyes were small and bright, as bright as gems. He shook with laughter at my questions. I remember his answer exactly. His was not, of course, an all-compassing answer, a panorama of Italian history, an essay on the people's psychology, which would have taken hours or days, but an epigram of only a few words, by which he probably invited me to explore on my own the many ancient causes of our national curse. This is what he said: "Gli italiani sono stati ubbriacati di bugie per cento cinquanta anni" (Italians have been made drunk with lies for one hundred and fifty years).

I thought I knew what he meant. First of all, he was a Southerner, born in Melfi in Basilicata in 1868, and his bitterness reflected the desperate disappointment of his countrymen from the old kingdom of Naples, who had felt swindled by history, deceived by "lies." After the unification, in 1861, they had seen most of their hopes of cultural, social, and economic advancement shattered. The South had been shamefully neglected, they thought, had sunk into even more dismal poverty, lost the small dignity of its independence and proud local traditions without finding a suitable role in the new nation. Thousands of its rebellious peasants, led by fanatical legitimists, had been summarily slaughtered after the unification by the new Italian army, in a war of Vendean ruthlessness; millions more had been driven by hunger and despair to emigrate. At the same time, the North had begun timidly to develop industries and had known a modest prosperity.

The figure "one hundred and fifty," while slightly inexact (it should have been "one hundred and forty-seven") was also revealing. It evidently referred to the unfortunate short-lived republic, the Parthenopean Republic, set up in Naples by a small educated elite of liberal "patriots" (as they called themselves, loyal, that is, to their country and not to their sovereign), based on the principles of the American and French revolutions. Its weakness was the fact that it had been created, or rather, imposed on the people with the help of the French revolutionary army which had invaded the kingdom. The people, peasants, priests, soldiers, landowners, aristocrats, and cautious bourgeois, considered it the invention of the devil, a sacrilegious foreign importation, and fought it as they had fought the invaders. The idealistic founders were tried for treason and hanged by the Bourbon king as soon as he had been brought back to Naples from Sicily by the English fleet. Which were the "lies" at the time, I wondered, the radiant but premature delusions of the "patriots" or the anachronistic myths that surrounded the Neapolitan monarchy and preserved it for another sixty-one years?

"Lies" presumably also were the grandiose expectations aroused by the Risorgimento, which, like the Center-Left coalition a century later, was supposed to cure all Italian ills, solve all problems, produce wealth, spread literacy, transform all the people into democratic and well-behaved North Europeans, and open the road to national greatness and prosperity. United Italy turned out not to be exactly what many people had imagined, the people who had conspired, suffered jail and exile, fought and died. The final result was a rickety, divided, shabby, impoverished and backward nation, yet one that wasted its miserable resources trying to impersonate one of the world's great powers. Among the victims of such "lies" (which surely were not lies for them) had been the good Italian citizens, a minority, Nitti among them. Their Italy, the country they loved and served, tried with some success to prod its reluctant inhabitants toward the modern world, democracy, incipient industrialization, progress in many fields, and also managed to win the First World War. But this Italy was also one of Nitti's "lies," a thin papier-mâché structure, the eggshell holding the national Humpty-Dumpty together, a make-believe country that never obtained the complete wholehearted support of all its incredulous citizens.

The biggest of Nitti's "lies" surely were the myths of Fascist propaganda. The regime had created an imaginary Spartan country, in which all men had to make believe they were heroic soldiers, all women Roman matrons, all children Balilla (the Genoa street urchin who started a revolt against the Austrian garrison in 1746 by throwing one stone). This was done by means of slogans, flags, stirring speeches from balconies, military music, mass meetings, parades, dashing uniforms, medals, hoaxes, and constant distortions of reality. The Italians woke up too late from their artificial dream, those still alive, that is, hungry, desperate, discredited, the object of derision, *cornuti e mazziati,* or "cuckolded and beaten up," governed as in the past by contemptuous foreigners in a country of smoking ruins and decaying corpses, in which most things detachable had been stolen and women raped. But why were lies so necessary in Italian life? That, of course, was the problem. Nitti did not even try to explain.

Giorgio Bocca, one of Italy's best journalists, a Socialist, an acute and severe observer of Italian reality, begins his recent book *In cosa credono gli Italiani?* (*What do the Italians believe?*) with these words: "They surely believe in public lies and private truths. Do they believe in public lies because they are really convinced that other Italians believe them? Of course not. They think the only expedient way to live in public is to lie or to keep silent. They compensate for this by preserving their own private truths. . . . The humble lie by necessity, the powerful by cunning and arrogance." In an interview commenting on his book, he gave some contemporary examples: "Most newspapers, even many which were not on the left, refrained from attacking the Soviet Union. They were afraid to proclaim what even Karl Marx had admitted, that the capitalist system worked and had produced the best results. Even the moderate democratic leftist press refused to criticize Communist or Communist-dominated countries, Hungary,

Cuba, Vietnam, Cambodia, Chile. No analysis of the many mistakes made by Allende was published." (The largest Italian newspaper, the *Corriere della Sera*, ignored for years the existence of left-wing terrorists, when everybody knew they were numerous, disciplined, well organized, well financed, well trained, and supplied with armaments of all kinds, mostly from abroad, and when they killed with impunity all kinds of political opponents. The *Corriere* asserted they were at most only a handful of "naughty boys," because the only dangerous terrorists were right-wing. Anybody suggesting that some could also be from the opposite side, the offspring of an earlier and primitive aspect of the Communist party, was then branded a Fascist. The use of the expression "*opposti estremisti*" [opposed extremists] provoked intimidating attacks. Years later, when it was discovered by the Israeli army in Lebanon that Italians were being trained in PLO camps [a certain number were made prisoners] and armed mostly with Soviet weapons, the *Corriere* did not think the news interesting enough for its readers.) "Fascism?" Bocca said. "It was a case of collective amnesia. Most people made believe it had never existed. As a result, when an exhibition was organized in Milan in 1982 reconstructing Italian life in the thirties, all were dumbfounded to discover that Fascism had not been generated by monsters. The myth of the existence of a 'working-class culture' was likewise sacred. It is now easily admitted, as a matter of course, that there was never such a thing." Evidently Bocca one day discovered with horror that, after having been the happy victim of Fascist propaganda in his adolescence, he had just as easily been the victim of Marxist distortions a few years later, "public lies" all.

Why are Italians addicted to "public lies"? Will they ever get rid of them? Can one understand how the country really functions? To be sure, the picture of any country, reacting to day-by-day vicissitudes, accepting the ideological vogues of the moment can be distorted and misleading. Mistaken estimates can be reached if one believes, as some Americans seem to, that the world can be thoroughly understood and decisions taken on the basis of the morning newspaper alone. Events also have notoriously deep historical roots. Folk memories, religious attachments, past catastrophes, half-forgotten mental habits, some going back to the dawn of history, are sometimes just as important. What Bocca and Nitti and many others refused to admit is that Italy, whose precise borders you can contemplate on maps, a nation recognized by all other nations, with its own flag, armed forces, embassies, stamps, and currency, is a fragile construction, at times held together mainly because almost all its citizens play in public the role necessary to preserve its identity. Even the Italian language is a recent invention. It was, until one or two generations ago, a written literary creation, as artificial as Gaelic and Hebrew. Many still use their native dialect at home and pure Italian only in public or on paper. However, the Italians' public role is not always entirely play-acting. Most of them are unaware of their double life. They think it natural. They are sincere, or hope that what they pretend to believe in public may be true. What they are really trying surreptitiously to do is to preserve as much as possible their own private beliefs and customs; behind the façade, to cling to what is left of their ancient and well-tested ways of conducting their lives, dealing with problems, and managing their affairs, ways that do not always coincide with the approved official and legal codes of behavior.

This, of course, is not an exclusive Italian vice. It is true of many more countries than Nitti or Bocca imagined, perhaps more or less of all countries at one time or another. It was true of nations occupied and governed by a foreign imperial power, as the Irish were in past centuries; it was true of the Poles under the Czars, and still is true of the Armenians, the Georgians, the Kurds, and many other nations without their own independent states, who speak their own language at home and the foreign oppressor's in public. It is even truer today of all peripheral nationalities in the Soviet Union and of all Warsaw Pact republics, where the foreign domination is justified by an elaborate ideology that must be treated in public as sacred dogma, "public lies," and that only a few heroes dare challenge. In the Soviet Union itself, as in China and other Communist countries, the individual art of survival, avoiding banishment, jail, concentration camp, and the firing squad, getting a job, an apartment, enough to eat, a television set, a washing machine, a bicycle, and for the very smart, an automobile, requires the gifts of a Machiavellian chameleon and has little to do with the official rituals laid down in the law books or the propaganda texts. Fidel Castro surely does not repeat to his intimates or to himself what he says on television. The dichotomy between "public lies and private truths" can be equally detected in non-Marxist countries. It rules in Latin American republics dominated by a junta after a coup d'état. There, an entrenched elite has only one goal, which is never mentioned and has little directly to do with the public good: the preservation of its own power at all costs and by any means whatever, including the omnipotent secret police and the suppression of all human rights.

Almost always it is the process of forced modernization that provokes the dichotomy. In countries where an impatient foreign-educated leader—the late shah of Iran (who had studied in Switzerland) or Kemal Pasha in Turkey (who had studied in Germany)—brutally tries to push his countrymen into the twentieth century within a few years, the people must learn to live a double life. This is also inevitable in countries where a well-meaning intellectual minority manages somehow to seize power after a revolution, tries to set up an instant utopia, and works hard to change human nature and the laws of the economy overnight. The reforms it launches and the laws it passes and tries to enforce may be noble in intention but possibly also premature and ill understood. Such a government inevitably obliges the people to play in public the roles expected of them.

Very often such daring experiments provoke automatic rejection, a reign of terror, the extermination of the people who resent being forced to live a life they do not understand. In a way, this has been, for many decades, also the complaint of France where the experts distinguished the existence of two separate Frances occupying the same geographic space and inhabited by the same people, *le pays officiel* and *le pays réel*. In a few countries, the dislocation is almost imperceptible, merely a hairline crack, because the new ways have been generated spontaneously and painlessly by the old ways. In other countries (or in the same country at other times) it may be a wide-open, gaping abyss, which cannot be easily bridged by lies, make believe and play-acting, and threatens the very existence of the state.

The process of forced modernization is almost always brought on by the discovery, dramatically made at a certain point in a people's history, perhaps because of a humiliating defeat (China invaded by the Japanese in 1895, Spain defeated by the United States in 1900) or the fear of one, that it must become modern at all costs and as fast as possible in order to protect itself from arrogant, overbearing industrialized countries, infinitely more powerful and wealthier but seldom more tactful and civilized. An old and noble nation then finds the ancient poverty of its lethargic people suddenly unacceptable, its musical-comedy army inadequate, its state organization a useless antique. It feels it must also change its image, which has somehow become unbearably humiliating, from that of a picturesque, possibly lovable, but ridiculous and contemptible country, a tourists' paradise, to one that should be taken seriously, treated with respect, and possibly even feared. To be feared often seems the most desirable achievement.

This has always been a long, arduous, and almost impossible task. The Japanese seem to have been the only ones to achieve the transformation, though not without tension, struggles, and anguish. In all such countries the efforts are obstructed first by the obstinate reluctance of the people to abandon their dear old traditions, the taste of their food, the pleasure of their customs, the security of their patriarchal ways, even at the cost of perpetuating their starvation-level poverty; by their refusal to accept the dreary discipline of industry and of the scientific culture, to adopt hated foreign models, and to abandon their pride in their legendary past.

(Every nation cherishes the memory of some legendary past that consoles the people for their present weakness and misery.) The travail goes on for decades, forces people to live a double life in order to save their private peace, and often produces a variety of social dislocations, disorders, endemic civil wars, aborted revolutions, xenophobic revolts, the emergence of demented ideologies and fanatical mass parties, repeated coups d'état, the decay of the state, the proliferation of criminals, the formation of fanatical terrorists' groups.

The people are despondent, anguished, and frightened. The old ways they trusted and relied on, forced into clandestinity, are officially discredited and, being clandestine, inevitably become corrupted. The new ways are often but a flimsy show. The search for a charismatic personality of the Right or Left then becomes frenzied, a man who would cut Gordian knots, reestablish discipline, order, and somehow provoke international admiration, respect, awe, and possibly fear. He emerges almost always. He usually preserves his emotional hold on the people by magnifying the threat of foreign enemies or by launching easy wars of conquest. The only way for the people to survive under the tyrant is to submit, or feign submission, while carrying on their private lives as best as they can, ignoring laws when possible or necessary. In the end, they find themselves more or less living the public life of an imitation modern country and the private life of familiar subterfuges.

Like most countries in similar circumstances, Italy found it an extremely long and anguishing experience to turn itself into a moderately modern, adequately prosperous, reasonably well-governed, orderly, reliable, punctual, and internationally respected country, and to do all this in order to defend its recently acquired independence and fragile unity. In fact, for a number of reasons, the process has been longer and more tempestuous than in most other western European nations. Even today, the aggressively up-to-date appearance of some nonvital aspects of contemporary life, the enthusiastic acceptance of "progressive" political theories and way-out art forms should not deceive strangers. After more than a century the country is not yet thoroughly modern. Its heart is still largely in the past. This is not entirely a disadvantage. In fact it is the reason why Italy attracts and charms so many visitors. It is still a refuge from the impersonal discipline and the boredom of life in their well-organized, predictable countries.

Almost all Italians, of course, realized at the time, a century ago, that the transformation was not only inevitable but highly desirable too, a way to acquire *"Il Buongoverno."* They dreamed of basking one day in its beneficent results, but with one proviso. Each of them wanted all his countrymen to obey the law and to behave in a responsible, restrained, and orderly way, so that trains would run on time, the mail be delivered punctually, the streets swept clean, thieves locked safely in jail, and power entrusted only to capable men of integrity, all his countrymen, that is, with one exception, himself. This, of course, slowed down the process to a snail's pace. Perhaps it was only in China that the tensions, ordeals, and troubles, the schizophrenic split in society and within each individual soul, the rise of charismatic leaders (the war lords) were more evident, lasted longer, and produced more catastrophes.

Some particular Italian factors aggravated the normal difficulties. The country is a thousand-year-old society and a very recent state based on foreign models. One of the obstacles was the people's just pride in their glorious past when they had been masters of or teachers to the world. (The mementos of its glorious past are everywhere. It cannot be forgotten.) This made the adoption of what seemed gross and oversimplistic foreign ways exceptionally repugnant. Italians clung to the finesse of their ancient manners, rituals that made life pleasurable but wasted time and often induced paralysis. Another obstacle was the Italians' century-old ineradicable suspicion and mistrust of all governments, laws, regulations, and official authorities, with which they went on considering also their recently founded national government. In fact, the individual Italian only obeys the rules that he has privately decided are just and useful. Signs on trains categorically forbid, in French and German, leaning out of the windows: *Il est défendu de se pencher en dehors* and *Nicht hinauslehnen.* (In older days the German sign even said it was *Polizeilich verboten.*) The Italian sign is a mere courteous suggestion. It leaves each man free to decide whether to lean out or not. It says, *E' pericoloso sporgersi,* or, "It is dangerous to lean out." The reader has been warned. Let him do as he prefers. Let him die if he wishes.

This ancient habit of disobedience or flexible selective obedience may be also due to the fact that, with but a few glorious exceptions, Italian provinces had been conquered and governed by foreigners or dominated by their influence since the fall of the Roman Empire. Some had been ruled by the Byzantines, the German emperors, the Arabs (Sicily), the Normans, the French, the Spanish, the Austrians, and even, for a short time, the English (Sicily again, during the Napoleonic wars). (Why most Italians, as well as a few other European nations, should have been endlessly oppressed by foreigners, and only here and there managed to govern themselves, is a moot question debated by scholars. There are many theories. Machiavelli thought the Church had always prevented the liberation and unification of Italy. Cynics believe, with Rousseau, that "l'esclavage est une condition voulue par l'esclave" [slavery is an institution wanted by slaves].) Rapacious foreign rulers, who knew little of local customs and whom the Italians despised, brutally collected taxes, enforced absurd laws and decrees alien to the local *spiritus.* They could, however, be pacified with tributes and adulation, and almost always easily deceived. A Milanese economist and historian, professor Armando Frumento, told me recently, "We Milanese behave toward Rome today as we did toward Madrid and Vienna in past centuries. We welcome their representatives with applause, feasts, and flattery, but we see to it that they know nothing of what we are doing lest they interfere with our life."

This was one of the reasons why most Italians preferred to go on relying, for the conduct of their lives and the solution of problems, as they still do, on their own ancient private way, which inevitably robbed public institutions of their validity. This, in short, is what their ancient private way, perfected through many centuries and vicissitudes, is all about. It is largely based on the family, a term that in southern Italy often includes distant cousins, kinsmen, *clientes*, and close friends. It is a safe refuge, a bulwark against the hostile environment, a lifeboat in the storms and possible shipwrecks of life, an insurance company, an employment agency. Like most other things, it is, to be sure, no longer what it was; still, even today, there are families who go broke to pay the debts of a relative and save him from the humiliation of the bankruptcy court and a possible jail sentence. They still see to it that each member rises as rapidly as possible in his career and defeats his competitors and rivals. In order to do this, the head of the family (usually the father, the oldest or the most successful brother, as in the case of the very Italianate Bonaparte family) must cultivate all forms of power at his level in society. He must artfully acquire allies, friends, accomplices, and protectors, with favors, services rendered, gifts, or flattery, and suitable marriages. (The young men who court a cabinet minister or a powerful professor, carry his briefcase, and obsequiously hold his overcoat when he puts it on are known as *portaborse*.) Then he must enclose his humble or high-ranking kinsmen within the fortified enclave of a camarilla, a close-knit group, a political party, or a secret society, not necessarily always an illegal, clandestine, and disreputable one.

This technique, like the conduct of foreign affairs, aims at preserving peace by achieving the balance of power. Like statesmen and expert diplomats, the single plebeian or eminent Italian has to exercise great prudence in order to survive; some of them must be ready to employ subterfuges, deception, mystification, secretiveness; and, relatively rarely, mostly in Naples and western Sicily, they must have the power to eliminate dangerous opponents physically. Official institutions (the police, the courts, the civil and penal codes, the powerful personages) are not entirely neglected. They are considered obstacles to be reckoned with on the obstacle course of life, insuperable only for the timid and the weak, and utilized whenever possible to one's advantage. This necessity of conducting one's affairs, no matter how insignificant, with the sagacity of a statesman develops a man's intelligence, watchful-ness, resourcefulness, flexibility, energy, and his canine tail-wagging capacity to be simpatico at all times to everybody, above the level necessary in better-ordered countries. This is why, as Stendhal said, "In Italy the plant man grows more vigorous than elsewhere," and why the country has been compared at times to a fragile wall that weak winds can easily knock down but which is built with excellent and exceptionally solid stones, a wall without mortar, technically known as *muro a secco*.

After the unification, Italy not only had to tackle the arduous task of material and moral modernization but it had to do it along with other and even more frightening tasks, often confused and intertwined with the first. One was that of amalgamating all kinds of different Italians into a more or less uniform model, making them accept one culture, one language, and one law, something other European nations had done in the late Middle Ages under powerful monarchies. The nongeographical divisions among the people were deep and irreconcilable. They lived next door to each other, called themselves Italians, but were almost as different as inhabitants of foreign countries. Most of them seemed to be in-habiting their own personal imaginary Italies and to be trying to promote or perpetuate their existences. Some of the dividing lines often split the very heart of each individual, who felt at times on one side or other of the barricade, and often on both sides. Among the many divisions, one was between liberals in love with liberty and the future, and the nostalgic *laudatores temporis acti*; others between liberals and members of totalitarian mass parties; the Catholics, still loyal to the all-pervasive political power of the Church, a state within the state, still tenaciously hostile to the new unified secular Italy and the patriots; the monarchists and the republicans; the *Mitteleuropean* North and the Mediterranean South; the cities and the countryside; the middle class, fighting on two fronts against the aristocracy and the lower class; the rich and the poor; the Right and the Left.

The result was for a century and more utter and incomprehensible confusion, in which for many the only way to survive was again to trust a number of different sets of "public lies and private truths." A minority of all classes solved the problem by behaving as if Italy had already been transformed into an exemplary modern European nation. They fully accepted their duties, educated their children well, worked hard, kept their word, saved money, did not lie unless necessary, and paid their taxes. They were the patriots, the officers and men who died in the wars, the stern educators, the explorers who planted the flag on deserted and sterile African lands, the lonely scholars, the scientists, the inventors, the public-spirited bureaucrats, the stern administrators, the good farmers, the skillful craftsmen, the creators of industries, the organizers of early trade unions, the builders of railroads, roads, bridges, and Alpine dams, the carabinieri, the inflexible judges. Without them Italy could not have survived (and could not survive today), nevertheless nobody admired and thanked them. They were and are known as *fessi*, the dolts or damned fools. They seldom reach positions of power and leadership. Another part frequently behaved the same way as often as it was possible and safe, but knew how fragile and how fictitious this Italy was. They were always prepared to resort to the "ancient way" described above. A third part relied exclusively on it, as if the state had but a shadowy existence, or was just a convenient fiction.

In the confusion, most people naturally always felt unhappy, defenseless, insecure, baffled, frustrated, and frightened. Like many other people in comparable circumstances, they were perennially in search of a magic formula, a political panacea, or philosopher's stone, which would liberate them from the national nightmare and solve all problems overnight, or a larger than life personality, a Moses who would lead them all out of the Egypt of chaos to the Promised Land of progress, order, security, prosperity, domestic peace, international good repute, and the respect of foreign neighbors. They hoped the formula and the man would relieve them from the burden of working hard, facing the risk of failure or defeat, studying, and thinking. This gave rise, at the turn of the century, to the formation of demented and suicidal mass movements of the Left and Right, the distorted irrational caricatures of legitimate political parties. Frustrated men uprooted from the patriarchal life they knew and catapulted into a modern life they did not feel at ease in were recruited. They were inevitably led by unbalanced and colorful personalities who knew only how to whip up the crowd's emotions. Some of these mass movements are still with us today.

Both those on the extreme Left and the extreme Right wanted to establish dictatorships and abolish democracy and the rule of law. The former believed confusedly that all problems would be solved by general strikes, a bomb or two in a crowded theater, the burning of crops, the murder of the king of Italy (or the king of any other country, an emperor, an empress, or a president), a revolution, a bloodbath, the expropriation and possible extermination of the middle class, and the transfer of the property of all means of production, as well as all power of decision, to the bureaucracy, in a country where the bureaucracy, not especially known for its rapidity, energy, or efficiency, was barely adequate for its old normal tasks. The latter thought regeneration of Italy could be brought about, first of all, by the extermination of the Left, and then by waging expensive wars and conquering colonies, which was an odd program, at the time, for a country without the resources indispensable for simple survival and a people who had never shown particular eagerness to fight wars they did not think necessary.

Inevitable and monotonous were the vitriolic polemics and recurrent riots between the extremists, which kept the country in turmoil. The Left terrorized the conservatives, the reactionary Right kept masses of workers in a perennially mutinous state. The endemic conflict finally turned into bloody civil war in 1919–22. What was worse, the extravagant extremists discredited by their folly the very ideas they thought they were promoting and took all strength away from the moderate parties of the Left and Right which were essential for progress. Nevertheless, as usual, the country once again surprised all observers by gradually and slowly advancing in all fields, in the midst of disorders, in spite of the most pessimistic predictions. This was, as usual, the work of the same plodding, industrious, dull, and public-spirited Italians. Their number grew slowly in every generation, but if there were enough of them somehow to goad unwilling Italy toward North European standards, there were never enough of them to wield political power. Their reasonable parties, whose programs were based not on wild dreams of holocausts but on a skeptical knowledge of local possibilities and the experiences of other countries in analogous circumstances, attracted only themselves. (This, of course, is still as true today as it was in the past.)

The moment of glory and power for these serious and uninspiring Italians was short. They governed the country for about twelve years before 1915, when one of them, the best, Giovanni Giolitti, was prime minister. He resorted to disreputable tricks in order to win elections in hostile constituencies and to other disreputable tricks to maintain a steady majority in Parliament (he was violently attacked for this by honorable people who did not understand what he was doing), not for disreputable purposes or for his personal aggrandizement (he was a modest, disinterested, and unglamorous man), but to pursue necessary policies in the sole interest of the country. He promoted its welfare, advanced reforms (railroads were nationalized in 1906, national social insurance for sickness and old age was founded in 1911), launched overdue programs of public works, passed essential legislation, encouraged the foundation of needed basic industries. He justified his occasionally dubious behavior by saying, "I consider myself a tailor making a coat for a hunchback. In order for it really to fit, I must make it with a hump in the back, no?" Hunchbacked Italy flourished under his guidance. His work ended when the country unwisely entered the First World War against his opinion (he believed it was not solid enough for such a test) and his entreaties.

Other earnest Italians were similarly obliged to resort (some times unconsciously) to many subterfuges to promote the country's welfare, as if to promote one's country's welfare by the only means available was a heinous crime. They kept a low profile and carried on their work in obscurity, avoiding publicity and public controversies. They treated Rome as the Milanese had treated Madrid and Vienna. Some of them infiltrated one of the emotional mass parties, repeated its nonideas, shouted its slogans, wore the uniforms (after the First World War, red bandanas and armbands with hammer and sickle for one, black shirts and discarded army uniforms for the other), and gained the leaders' confidence. They tried to moderate the party's calamitous excesses, managed to promote some badly wanted reforms, and sought to prevent the country's ultimate ruin in either direction. Many of them were second-rank Fascists until the last war, some are members of the Communist party and trade union organizers as well as Christian Democrats today. All this, the moderate and sensible masquerading as insane extremists, produced one more set of "public lies and private truths" which, added to the normal bewildering chaos of Italian existence and to the desperate feeling of insecurity of most people, made life even more intolerable and incomprehensible.

The present situation is exceptionally confusing even for Italy. At the end of the last war the ominous presence of a dangerously powerful mass party, the Communist party, which had heroically fought in the resistance, well organized, disciplined, abundantly financed at the time by the Soviet Union, offering an instant workers' paradise, frightened most Italians out of their wits. The Communist party was then still openly in favor of setting up a totalitarian Marxist regime on the Soviet model. It was vociferously against bourgeois freedoms, the idea of European integration, the Marshall Plan, and an alliance with the United States. Terrified Italians turned for their defense to the Church, the only powerful institution in the country that could defend them, and to its secular arm, the Christian Democratic party. This was by no means a politically homogenous formation. It displayed a vast range of vague ideologies and programs from right to left. Alcide de Gasperi, its most distinguished and capable leader, defined it as "a center party moving gradually toward the left," whatever that meant. In reality, it was one more emotional irrational mass movement. Some of the elite were undoubtedly inspired by moralistic, more or less religious, ideals. The majority of the voters were inspired by fear. However, it was definitely anti-Communist, pro-West (the Church having been for centuries in the Middle Ages, and lately against Fascist and Nazi dictatorships, the fortress defending Western values), and what was more important controlled a century-old electoral machine, the network of parish priests, religious orders, publishing houses, newspapers, magazines, clubs, Catholic universities, and a group of influential intellectuals.

A large number of Italians, a majority in fact, voted for the party in 1948, including many who were not particularly in favor of the Vatican's meddling in political affairs, some actually in fear of it. Even Jews and Protestants voted for it. Liberty and democracy were saved. Italy remained in the West's camp. The Communists licked their wounds, regrouped, and started a slow and prudent examination of their conscience, which is still going on, in order to discover why, in all free countries, the party always scared people out of their wits, evoked vast formations of enemies, and was the cause of its own defeat. They began studying how to change their image to survive in democratic surroundings and to do it very gradually and ambiguously not to lose the indispensable Soviet backing and the fanatic loyalty of millions of their unreasoning followers. This was the origin of Euro-communism. The reappraisal is still going on. This was also helped by the fact that the word *comunismo* never really meant exactly what it means in other languages and does not correspond to its definition in any Italian dictionary. But the Christian Democrats, who evidently had what was necessary to save Italian liberty and to reconstruct the country, or, some say, allow the country to reconstruct itself, did not have all the qualifications necessary to run a difficult nation in the modern world. By its very nature, for reasons that go back to the medieval struggles between the Church and the empire and to the Italian Risorgimento, the party did not hold the Italian state in sufficient consideration. Christian Democrats do not respect man-made laws as they do, or should do, the God-given ones. They were too skeptical, lax, indulgent, compassionate, charitable, too afraid not to be sufficiently up-to-date, and too resigned to the immutability of human frailty, to administer the *republica* with rigor and impartiality.

Furthermore, a number of them believed with Weber that liberalism, capitalism, private initiative, and the market economy had been generated by Protestantism, a heresy and a schism notoriously contrived by the powers of darkness for the damnation of man, and had to be eliminated and destroyed because they were the causes of all the injustices and the ills of the modern world. They dreamed of a return to an immobile society regulated by guilds. For unfathomable reasons they ignored the existence of Renaissance bankers, merchants, and craftsmen, good Catholics all, with but a few notable Jewish exceptions, who had really started modern capitalism.

The party also understandably lacked good experienced men in sufficient numbers (it had only a few exemplary ones) for the many posts it had to fill once the Fascists were kicked out, and inevitably was infiltrated by intriguers, astute rogues, wheeler-dealers, adventurers, and men without scruples who exploited the impotence of the state and manipulated public affairs in their private interest. Not having one ideal model of its own for the future of the country, the party utilized in turn the model most pleasing to its allies of the moment, that of the small Center parties right after the war, with great success, and of the proto-Socialists later with ruinous results. Added to these shortcomings was the Christian Democrats' arrogant feeling of immunity, the assumption they would never be punished by the electorate for their shortcomings and mistakes, because their defeat would have meant a Communist victory, which was unthinkable. And in effect, people, in the words of Indro Montanelli, the most brilliant

Italian journalist and historian, kept on voting for them "while holding their noses." They had no choice.

It was noted by attentive observers of the Italian political scene that the party, which called itself the "dike against communism," in reality did nothing much to check the Communists' growth, their vast financial means (the party earned a percentage on every deal with a Warsaw Pact country), and the power they wielded in the omnipotent trade unions, which really determined or conditioned the governments' economic policies. Evidently the Christian Democratic elite was conscious of the fact that should the Communist menace wane or vanish, they would inevitably lose votes and power. One of the party's secretary-generals, Guido Gonella, wittily told me, years ago, "It is obvious that, should the disease disappear, there would no longer be need for the doctor." At the same time the Communists were fully aware that they could flourish only as long as their opponents continued to govern Italy in their own slovenly and wasteful way, not particularly caring for the common good, for public interest, and for the solution of urgent problems, but mainly in order to acquire *clientes*, enrich friends, and to consolidate their own power at all levels. There was therefore, all along, an occult, unmentioned, subterranean, objective alliance, a connivance, or rather, a converging of interests that united the two mass parties like Siamese twins, both working hard to preserve the status quo. The strength of each depended mainly on the existence of the other. This, of course, faced the voters with a very embarrassing choice between two political programs, both in a way preindustrial, both unsuited to govern the country and ease its way toward affluence and social progress. Both the Gospels and the collected works of Marx, Lenin, and Gramsci were no guides for the complex contemporary economic world of competition and strict interdependence.

All this came to a head in the seventies and early eighties. The doctors at Italy's bedside were of two opinions. Some thought it was definitely on its deathbed and some were sure it was already irremediably dead, returned to its natural condition once defined by Metternich as that of a mere "geographical expression." They were, of course, thinking of Italy the recently unified state and the young Republic, surely not of Italy the very ancient people who were very much alive, as active, energetic, inventive, resourceful, and spirited as they had always been, bent on surviving at all costs and by any means, sometimes despite the uncertain laws. In fact it was their very tireless, antlike search for ways to preserve their lives and prosper that weakened the legal Italy further and made it even more ineffectual. Some studious foreign observers even developed the theory that the reason why the various governments had been feeble was because the Italians unconsciously wanted them and did all they could to keep them that way. Why did they persistently elect inadequate, inexperienced, and easily frightened men?

Each government solved most problems (as many other governments did in other countries in those years) by printing vast quantities of paper money and borrowing immense sums from banks and the public which not even the great-grandsons could hope to pay back one day. Italian financial institutions, most of which are state-owned, could scarcely refuse a government request. All these billions were usually indiscriminately distributed to buy social peace for a while, a few weeks or months, and to assure very expensively the ministers' own tranquil sleep at night. It was also thought the people unconsciously wanted feeble governments because their impotence preserved what most Italians conceived as liberty, the liberty from overambitious laws and excessive taxes which, if applied, would have gummed up all activities. Luigi Einaudi himself, one of Europe's great traditional economists, and the exemplary first president of the new Republic, said repeatedly, "If all the taxes in the books were collected, the state would easily absorb 150 percent of the national revenue." The frenzied activity of the people and the partial paralysis of the governments were once compared by one pessimistic observer to "the liveliness of worms on a dead body."

In the early eighties it was evident something had to be done to avoid final ruin. The uncoordinated activities of single Italians could no longer save Italy, in a world in which, all economic activities having slowed down, all countries were fighting the universal depression, unemployment, and inflation. There were not, in responsible positions, the men, the legal structures, the political will, the knowledge, and the rigor necessary to tackle even the simple housekeeping problems on whose solutions everybody agreed (privately). Too many laws on the books made recovery practically impossible. There was no way to ask the people for serious sacrifices, to begin repaying the massive debts from shrinking revenues, force the state-owned basic industries (steel, chemicals, energy, petroleum, and communications) to earn some money instead of merrily losing lots of it, no way to reform the bizarre method of indexing wages, which, running as they did way ahead of inflation, made it uncontrollable. There was no way either to make the bureaucracy really work, prevent the government parties from squabbling, and stop the state social insurance from paying out unmerited pensions. (In some places invalidism or old-age pensions were handed out to everybody like cigars.) In other words, the Italians realized, as many other people did at the same time, that the ideal of everybody living at public expense without an adequate number of them working and producing wealth was unreachable.

That the country did not have the unity, the capacity, and the desire to solve its one problem—that of encouraging (and not obstructing) the increase in the production of wealth by private or state-owned industries, in order to support a higher standard of living, economic, moral, cultural, and social progress, and an adequate welfare organization—was evident to Alcide de Gasperi, the best Italian statesman since the war. I once walked down a Roman street with him, one summer afternoon in the late forties after lunch, and asked him why he was so keen on achieving quick European unification. I shared his enthusiasm and his impatient hopes for sentimental and cultural reasons. I always thought of myself as a European and had always longed for a European fatherland without frontiers. I knew he did too. He was born in

Trento, a subject of Franz Joseph, an Italian-speaking citizen of Austria-Hungary until 1918, a member of the Vienna polyglot Parliament before that, and therefore conditioned to thinking not in the narrow terms of a nation but in terms of a vast, multilingual, multiracial, political conglomerate held together by the Crown and by one of the most intelligent and enlightened bureaucracies Europe had ever seen. He was furthermore a pious observant Catholic, accustomed to thinking also in terms of a supernatural empire spiritually hovering over each single nation, the Church. He was undoubtedly a good patriotic Italian, but by no means a blind nationalist. All this I knew, but what I wanted him to tell me that hot day were the practical political reasons by which he justified his desire to see Europe unified soon, tomorrow morning if possible. In other words, how did he believe the United States of Europe would lighten his almost impossible burden as Italian prime minister in a dramatic moment of the country's history? He stopped, looked at me with his patient brown eyes, as if I had asked a tiresomely obvious question. His drooping jowls made him look vaguely like a hunting dog. Waving his briefcase in the air to emphasize each word, he said, "I must have a united Europe to absorb in her vast bosom three problems we Italians alone will never be able to solve and on which our future depends. One is the presence of the Church among us, a state within the state, oil and water. It has interfered with Italian internal affairs since the unification and made the creation of a well-governed and law-abiding nation more difficult." (This would have seemed to a non-Catholic a strange thesis from a Catholic statesman, if one did not remember, as I did, the difficulties he had always had with the Curia. He tried to do his best to serve and to reconstruct Italy, guided by his religious ideals. The Curia rightly thought only in terms of the Church's immediate welfare and future development. They seldom agreed.) He went on, "Two. We want to hand over to Europe our two million chronic unemployed and God knows how many of our underemployed." (Nobody else had so many at the time. Unemployment in normal prosperous years results from a scarcity of capital and an excessive abundance of available labor. We then had the willing labor and needed the capital and know-how of richer neighbors.) "In the larger context of Europe, the percentage of our unemployed would become insignificant. Three, the percentage of the Communist votes, dangerously high here, would reassuringly decrease in a United Europe until they would no longer represent a frightening menace." We resumed walking in silence under the sun. Understandably, he did not need to mention one more reason that was then in the minds of most Italians, including his and mine. We needed a united Europe also to hide in it, make other people forget the Fascists' shabby and dishonorable conduct of foreign affairs and our disreputable defeat.

In other words his Europe was one more magic remedy for Italy's persistent and probably incurable disease, the *ingovernabilità*. Would the people more easily obey European laws and respect European authorities than their own? Possibly. They sometimes behave noticeably better when foreigners observe them. Cities where many tourists go or where foreigners choose to reside are usually cleaner, less noisy, and more orderly than the obscure ones that no strangers visit. Italians behaved impeccably in the old Austrian provinces, Venetia, Lombardy, Istria, and de Gasperi's own Trentino, where the paternal authorities (Italians all) were awesome and inflexible and the laws could not easily be circumvented. They are exemplary administrators today in the Swiss canton, Ticino, where their French and German countrymen keep them under observation and where they proudly want to show they are as good as all other Swiss. They are among the best officials and bureaucrats in the EEC organizations in Brussels. Europe, for de Gasperi, as for many other people and possibly for me too, was evidently the contemporary form of the ancient dream, that of *Il Buongoverno*. And these are among the reasons why the Italians of all parties were and are among the most fervent champions not merely of the integration of Europe but of its unification, its setting up in business as a third superpower. This is why the creation of the Treaty of Rome was initiated by Gaetano Martino, the foreign minister, at the Messina meeting in 1955 when all hopes seemed lost, and signed symbolically in 1957 in the

Roman Campidoglio. This is why the Italian ministers in Brussels do not make waves, often accept decisions unfavorable to their country without complaining, and act as arbitrators and pacifiers between contending parties. As a result the EEC favored the French, German, and Dutch agricultures and penalized the Mediterranean products (olive oil, wine, tomatoes, citrus fruits). Italians think all sacrifices are acceptable if they help the unification of Europe to advance even an imperceptible forward step. They hope to rid themselves and their countrymen of the century-old Italian nightmare, the chaotic conditions that make the dichotomy between "public lies and private truths" inevitable.

SIX

The
Careful Dutch

AFTER SOME INITIAL hesitation, natural on the part of people who by nature never plunged impulsively into complex new deals, the Dutch, the Belgians, and the Luxembourgers were among the most enthusiastic and impatient early champions of whatever European system of economic and political integration could be realistically worked out. Paul-Henri Spaak, Belgian foreign minister, J. W. Beyen, the Dutch foreign minister, and their Luxembourg colleague were among the most ardent and fervent early apostles of the unification.

The problem was not entirely new to them. A monetary and tariff union had tied Luxembourg to Belgium since 1921. The two governments had decided, even before the end of the war, when they were still in exile in London, to enlarge the arrangement as soon as possible to include the Netherlands and try to function in the economic sphere almost as if they were one country. They founded on paper what they were to call Benelux in 1944, and later, after the defeat of Germany, discovered it worked well in practice and produced abundant results. The idea evidently found its right season. It was so successful, in fact, it was admired and envied by other Europeans. The French envisaged the addition of their own country and Italy to Benelux, the result to be called Fritalux, an unfortunate name suggestive of fried potatoes (*les frites*) and an inexpensive soap curiously used by affluent movie stars (Lux). Probably to avoid such pointless and unwanted commercial echoes, the Belgians proposed instead to call the same *combinazione* Finebel, more attractively evoking the beauty (*bel*) of a glass of cognac (*fine* in French). The eventual addition of Germany would have created something called Gerbenelux.

In everybody's mind then was the urge to prevent one more irresistible surprise invasion by Germany. There is notoriously always a locker room feeling among military and political experts after a war. Like all players at the end of the game, they go on interminably discussing mistakes made and opportunities missed, play again the various phases of the encounter, and draw retrospective conclusions. Napoleon in St. Helena fought Waterloo in his head practically every day. In the early forties, before the Atlantic Alliance was signed, the Dutch, the Belgians, and the Luxembourgers, whose thoughts turned preferably to international trade and finance, believed the best way to stop one more German attempt to dominate Europe was to enlarge their own economic and customs union to Germany itself, to France, and as many other European nations as cared to join. This would have tied up Germany, or whatever was left of it, in such an inextricable web of international economic bonds as to render it incapable, like Gulliver, of making an independent move. The plan's other advantages understandably seduced the Benelux people. It widened the market to American size; gave frail provincial industries the chance to grow to continental proportions, lowered costs of production, and competed victoriously with the rest of the world. The new prosperity, generated by the large market and by the opportunity to invest heavily in industry and agriculture the resources that would otherwise go for armaments, would allow the creation of efficient welfare states and surely prevent social unrest, the mutiny of the working class, and the rise of revolutionary movements, which notoriously follow all disastrous wars. At the same time social peace plus vaguely Keynesian management of the economy could encourage the prosperity to grow indefinitely without disturbing interruptions. All wars, and not just a German aggression, would also be made impossible by the terrifying progress in armament technology. The new nuclear weapons were so devastating that they could possibly prevent a conflict by their very existence. What was even more attractive to economy-minded statesmen, they were, in the end, also cheaper than conventional armaments, cheaper than recruiting, dressing, training, feeding, and arming many divisions, especially since the United States, at first the only country that could build and deploy nuclear missiles, would have to foot the bill. As the Americans said, they produced "a bigger bang for a dollar."

Bearing in mind that German power came from the coal mines and the steelworks conveniently placed near them (Krupp had been the symbol of this since 1870), another project was launched successfully in 1950, designed to stop a new war between France and Germany. Jean Monnet and Robert Schuman proposed the immediate creation of a Coal and Steel Community, with some supernational power. Schuman was backed by two colleagues, friends and collaborators, and almost accomplices, Alcide de Gasperi, prime minister of Italy, and Konrad Adenauer, West Germany's chancellor. The three must have been put on earth at the same dramatic time and in a powerful almost omnipotent position by divine intervention. They were bordermen in their own countries, fervent Catholics, founders and leaders of their respective Christian Democratic mass parties. Since Schuman, born a German citizen, had studied in Munich, and de Gasperi, born an Austrian citizen, had studied in Innsbruck, the three elderly gentlemen understood each other, conversed easily without completing sentences, and joked in German as if they were still students. All three wanted to preserve their countries once and for all, not only from their incomprehensible, unpredictable, insane, and ruinous addiction to wars, not only to break the fatal historical chain by which one European war generated another, and so forth, endlessly, but also to free the world from the ups and downs of economic booms and crises. They probably had a final model in their minds (Protestants accused them of having it, anyway) to recreate one day a modern version of Christendom or the spiritual union of the West under the aegis of the Church. They thought they could begin safely with the Coal and Steel Community, a down-to-earth economic organization that would shackle the Germans' mines and industries. Later they would go on to unify other sectors when the going was good. As a first successive step, they also envisaged a close customs union along the Benelux lines, which fortunately was not to be called Franitalgerbenelux, or later still, Franbritdaniregerbenelux, but more simply the European Economic Community. (The Coal and Steel Community worked well enough when there was no need for it, when prices were high and buyers eager for more coal and steel. Well enough, but not perfectly, even then. Italy, one of the signatories, paid no attention to it and kept on buying cheaper coal from the United States. And when the market became tighter, no member nation obeyed the supposed supernational decisions of the community and its High Court of Justice.)

These ideas of the Benelux people and those of Monnet, de Gasperi, Schuman, and Adenauer are respectable, honorable, and noble. They might have worked and preserved peace and prosperity if man were the rational *homo oeconomicus* the economists imagined. As he is that only part of the time and with only part of himself, these ideas may be dangerous delusions, the eternal delusions of people who, like Karl Marx and some orthodox conservative economists, believe economy is the principal motor of history, the real cause of wars. They are, however, attractive ideas, willingly accepted by the middle class of all countries, by bankers, merchants, shipowners, insurance underwriters, brokers, and industrialists. They are more easily accepted because they are not new ideas. Even before 1914 reassuring books were published that demonstrated war was a thing of the past for two reasons: one, because the close economic integration of each nation to the rest of the world made it materially impossible; and two, because the new weapons, so destructive, terrifying, and deadly, made it unthinkable.

Benelux worked wonders in spite or because of the fact that three economies (in reality only two) had become competitive and were no longer as complementary as they had been in the past, when Belgium was more industrial than agricultural and Holland the other way around. Competition, in fact, accelerated economic growth in both countries and the increased production for a larger market lowered costs. The success was also due to the fact that the people of each country more or less shared similar fundamental beliefs, ideals, hopes, and aims. To be sure, there are differences between them. Approximately half the Belgians are imbued with French culture and speak French with an accent the French think extremely funny. It is parodied by comedians even on television that the Belgians see. The other half speak Dutch with an accent the Dutch do not think particularly funny. What they think funny are all Belgians in general, whatever language they speak. Jokes about them, similar to Polish jokes elsewhere, are very popular. (The Amsterdam control tower to a Belgian pilot: "What is your position exactly?" The Belgian pilot: "I'm sitting in the cockpit.") To be sure, the Belgians are predominantly Catholic and the Dutch are, or were, predominantly Protestant, before their own Catholics raced ahead to produce more and more children; the Belgians have more coal and iron ore mines and boast of some of the highest hills in the region, one of them reaching 600 meters in height, while the Dutch have fewer mines and no hills to speak of. From the start, the Belgians were artisans, miners, industrialists, and not particularly attracted by the sea, while the Dutch were farmers, merchants, and seamen, who had traveled to the ends of the earth since the Middle Ages in search of gain. The Dutch cuisine is by no means remarkable while the Belgians proudly boast of theirs, which is rich, varied, hearty, and extremely elaborate. Finally, Holland has been for centuries a nation of sorts and the Dutch were consciously proud of it (though their patriotism was weaker than that of the British or the French), while Belgium is a recent construction made possible by nineteenth-century diplomats around a table in London. The Belgians can feel Belgian only in life-or-death crises, as they did during the First World War under their legendary King Albert. At all other times they feel like Walloons or Flemings. The Dutch, whether they speak Dutch, Limburger, or Frisian, know at all times they are Dutch.

Nevertheless, they have a lot in common. When considered by

other Europeans, particularly from the South, the differences between them seem less conspicuous than those between some inhabitants of the same country, as, for instance, between Normans and Provençals, Sicilians and Piedmontese, Hamburgers and Bavarians. Their long history has been shaped, for one thing, along similar lines by their peculiar geography. They have been united for centuries, nominally at least, collectively known as the Low Countries, under the rule of the dukes of Burgundy, the kings of Spain, the Austrian emperors, later the French revolutionary republic and Napoleon, and were still united from 1816 till 1830 under the Dutch King William I of Orange-Nassau. To be sure, the wilful Dutch, jealous of their liberties, gained de facto and later de jure autonomy, under the name of the United Provinces, long before the Belgians, who, dominated by the Church, adapted themselves to the comforting rule and the protection of Catholic governors, Spanish and Austrian and Napoleonic French. Nevertheless, the consciousness of an existence of their own and the defense of their rich cultural Burgundian heritage had also given them an identity, pride in their achievements, and a particular love of their own corner of Europe, long before they had become an independent kingdom.

The encroaching seas, which had to be fought relentlessly, had tempered the character and the ingenuity of both nations, of the Dutch more than the Belgians, as they (the Dutch) have more flat coasts below sea level. They both are stolid people, hard-working, parsimonious, earnest, unimaginative, methodical, meticulous, slow-thinking, and self-reliant. They were naturally conditioned by bourgeois capitalistic ideologies (free trade, market economy, private initiative, cautious risk taking, the rule of law, and liberty) centuries before the terms had been invented, praised, or deplored by political thinkers. Both respected the law and considered all contracts sacred, feared wars and thought them a deplorable waste of lives and money. The incessant rains and the maritime climate, worse than the British and the Irish weather, made their plains fertile, their farmers, nurserymen, and cattle breeders among the best in the world. Before trucks were invented, all heavy hauling in Europe was done by Zeeland or Belgian horses. The best cows are still the descendants of the Dutch breed. The vast estuaries of the large rivers, coming from the heart of the Continent, and the capacious natural ports made them both (especially the Dutch) the natural suppliers and exporters of goods for half of Europe. The many rivers and canals, as well as the absence of mountain chains, made communications easy and cheap even before the Belgians built the first railway on the Continent in 1832. The mines and the quarries have furnished fuel, raw material, and marble for industry (especially in Belgium) since the Middle Ages. (The only black marble in Europe, the most expensive lace, and the best linen cloth came from Belgium. They still do.)

The geography that had made both people patient, industrious, adventurous, and rich unfortunately also made them the perennial victims of other people's wars. The Low Countries (somewhat like the Po Valley for similar reasons) were for many centuries the most convenient battleground for foreign armies. To be sure the Dutch and the Belgians sometimes had to fight on their own account, to defend themselves and their liberties, and once against each other, in 1830, but most of the time they had to see their lands being ravaged by powerful foreign armies vying for European supremacy. These foreign armies violated existing treaties, crossed the borders or landed from the sea without a by-your-leave, destroyed what fortifications they found on their way, pushed aside or slaughtered the feeble local armed forces, ruined business, stopped trade, sacked the wealthy cities, requisitioned the food and the fodder, emptied cellars and safes, deported the men or put them to work building fortifications, raped the women, maneuvered infantry and cavalry divisions all over the impeccable green pasture land and the tidy and carefully cultivated fields. Michelet wrote: "C'est là, en Belgique, le coin de l'Europe, le rendezvous des guerres. Voilà pourquoi elles sont si grasses, ces plaines; le sang n'a pas le temps d'y sécher." (It is there, in Belgium, that corner of Europe, the meeting place of wars. That's why those plains are so fertile; blood does not have the time to dry.) In fact many of the most famous battles in history bear the names of previously obscure and undistinguished Flemish villages.

The memory of the last two world wars surely could not be forgotten by the Dutch and the Belgians. In the first, the Dutch were spared the fighting and flourished, but in humiliating vassalage to the Germans. They hated themselves for it. The Belgians suffered famine, poverty, and the ruin of their economy; their army defended heroically the southwestern corner of Flanders till the end, while the rest of their country was exposed to the deliberate *Schrecklichkeit* of the German occupiers. The latter killed and deported thousands of civilians, set fire to the priceless library of Louvain, incited the rebellion of the Flemings against the French-speaking Walloons in order to break up the people's solidarity; exploited mines and industries, and starved the population. In the second war both countries were invaded. The Dutch resisted five days, the Belgians eighteen. Both had to endure even worse conditions than the Belgians did in the first war. The deportation included almost all the Jews, most of whom never returned.

Naturally enough, the Dutch and the Belgians enthusiastically favored a political design that would tie all European nations together in such an inextricable snakes' nest that wars fought on Belgian and Dutch soil (a nuclear war, this time) would almost become inconceivable. They were tired of invading armies, of other people's historic battles fought on their soil, of seeing their people massacred and their economies go bankrupt, and of being liberated in the end by friendly armies which could be as destructive as those that had conquered them in the first place. A European political union, the natural outgrowth of a customs union, seemed to be the obvious answer to all this. As the years went by, however, the situation changed. The sense of urgency and imminent danger grew dim. Germany, mutilated and democratic, was in no condition to attack anybody. The massively armed Soviets had not moved when they could have conquered Europe in a few days and were not moving even after the West had started rearming.

The men who had lived through the previous war retired or died. As each disenchanted European nation turned more and more to its own business, the dream slowly faded. The simple and generous ideas of yesterday became hazy and contradictory. Slowly, with regret for some and relief for others, the Dutch and the Belgians realistically cut the grand design of a United States of Europe down to more modest and practical dimensions, those they could more easily appreciate, shaped as they were by history and their own character. What they did not want was to see Europe become some sort of a third superpower. There was the danger it could find itself crushed like a nut in a nutcracker by the other two hostile superpowers. And what could the Dutch and the Belgians do if a united Europe went bankrupt or decided to start a preventive war? They feared to see their future decided by foreigners, their money squandered in armaments which had to be renewed every few years without ever being used as they became obsolete, and to see a large part of their young manpower dedicated to the unproductive job of sitting in uniform in barracks, or buried in underground fortifications, playing cards. All they wanted was to have business improve year by year, trade expand, wealth accumulate and generate compound interest, wealth that they wanted to distribute more and more equably, and to finance the best welfare states in the world. To achieve this, a loose Common Market, as large as possible, was all they really needed, even if occasionally made ineffectual by squabbles and the many built-in loopholes.

The after-war prosperity did not last long. Belgium, a few generations ago one of the richest model countries in the world, where the economy flourished and everything functioned almost impeccably, is now confused, depressed, and partly paralyzed by inflation, social strife, and the racial and language separation between the Walloons and the Flemings, as isolated from each other now as two different hostile nations. Governments, which used to be solid and long-lasting, are now as short-lived as the postwar Italian or the French under the Third Republic. Walloons and Flemings are so distinct they can often be recognized at first sight by their looks and clothes. The Flemings dress like Germans and the Walloons like the French. They seldom intermarry. "I have nothing against my son marrying a Flemish girl," a Walloon father told me recently. "It is, however, an abstract problem. My son will never have the opportunity to meet her." Proverbially opulent Belgium was impoverished after the war by the loss of its fabulously rich Congo colony. It is now even more impoverished (like other countries similarly vulnerable) by the steel crisis. Most of its plants, spared by the Germans during the war for their own purposes, are now obsolete and produce more expensively than recently built ones in other countries, particularly the German plants that had to be constructed *ex novo*. Then there were the factors common to the whole West, the rise in the price of oil, the slowdown of international trade, the competition of Japan and emerging Third-World countries, inflation, social unrest, strikes, and unemployment. The currency had to be devalued several times. State deficits grew alarmingly. To assuage some of these ills, the Belgians like the Italians dreamed of submerging their problems in the European cauldron, the bigger the cauldron the better. Nevertheless, they, like the Dutch and other European nations, recoil from too many automatic responsibilities. In fact, their military enthusiasm is noticeably tepid. While other NATO contingents are ready on West German soil to fight within hours in case of a Soviet attack, the reluctant Belgians are at home, in their comfortable barracks, sleeping in good beds at night, and could theoretically join the fray only within a week or a fortnight at the earliest, which might be too late. They are prudent people.

The roots of Dutch foreign policy are buried deep in history. Holland is a tiny placid country surrounded by three strong, restless, well-armed, populous, ambitious, and occasionally dangerous nations: France, Britain, and Germany. Holland was inevitably shaped by all three. It is Germanic by race and language, but it is not really a thoroughly Germanic country. The sea brought it closer to the British (and to the Hanseatic people and the Scan-

dinavians, who were also influenced by the sea and the British).
English is the second language of the country. France irresistibly
attracted the Dutch in many ways, by its culture, elegance, *art de
vivre*, philosophy, and, since the end of the eighteenth century, its
political ideas. The Dutch also share with the French middle class
and peasants a religious respect for profits, the compulsion to
pinch pennies and to make shrewd investments. Furthermore,
they, like the Venetians and the British for analogous moral but
also mercantile and sea-going reasons, cultivated the cult of liberty
and toleration, dear to the heart of Christians and progressive
liberal thinkers but also essential for the free flow of commerce.
This opened the country at all times to refugees from everywhere:
Spanish and Portuguese Jews escaping the Inquisition, Russian
and Polish Jews escaping pogroms, German Jews escaping Nazis,
Protestants from Catholic countries, Catholics from Protestant
countries, Belgian, French, and German merchants and bankers
fleeing the paralyzing shackles of mercantilistic control. Books
forbidden in other countries were printed in Amsterdam (or Brussels) and smuggled across the borders. This tradition enriched the
Dutch morally, culturally, and financially. (It encouraged, among
other things, their bankers to finance the American Revolution.)
They accepted and respected all points of view and all races. The
early symbol of this praiseworthy national trait was Erasmus, a
native of Rotterdam, to whom *nihil humanum* was *alienum*. Privately, of course, the Dutch were and are strict Bible-reading
Calvinists. Even Jews, Catholics, and atheists are influenced by
Calvinistic ethics in their country. This I realized when I flew over
the flooded countryside, in 1953, on a relief helicopter, as a correspondent covering the immense disaster. The pilot would lower
his craft over the isolated farmhouses, besieged by the rising
waters, on whose roofs some farmers' families had been living for
days, and would ask through an electric megaphone what they
needed more urgently, food, blankets, medications, or drinking
water. The answer was very often "a Bible." Calvinism is evidently connected with the commercial vocation. It is not clear to
an Italian, however, whether Calvinists, driven by their stern reli-

gious code, become the best merchants, or whether merchants become Calvinists because Calvinism is a superior guide for the successful conduct of business.

Inevitably the sea made the Dutch among the best shipwrights and sailors in Europe and the world. (Czar Peter the Great went to Holland to learn how to build ships.) They were such good sailors that Carlo Cipolla, professor of economic history in Italy and the United States, believes the competition with their merchant fleet was one of the decisive causes of the decline of Venice. Dutch ships went to the Levant and returned several times while the Venetian ships managed only one trip. This passion for the sea drove them to conquer not neighboring provinces, in order to become one of Europe's great nations, as Prussia and France had done, but to set up distant trading points all over the world. (This Dutch historians now regret, because if the Dutch and the Belgians had never separated, and if they had formed a large, wealthy, well-armed, and cautious Netherlands between France and Germany, the history of Europe would surely not have been the same.) They settled in New Amsterdam, a vast natural port, cluttered with flat sandy islands large and small, at the mouth of a big river, which evidently reminded them of home; in South Africa, Japan, Formosa, Brazil, Ceylon, Indonesia, the West Indies, and many other profitable places.

In the old days they fought whenever necessary for liberty on the seas and land: for their own liberties, liberty to trade and sail, not to be taxed without their consent, to pursue their own chosen religion, and to govern themselves, their guilds, towns, cities, provinces, as they saw fit, according to their traditions. As soon, however, as they had consolidated the complex structure of their economic prosperity in the seventeenth century, they avoided military adventures, which they disliked, and concentrated on preserving the peace of Europe. They became universal peacemakers. They considered peace indispensable also for the defense and consolidation of their affluence, which could vanish overnight in other people's wars. They were not always successful. The visible expression of this concentration on simple material things, the enjoyment of their private opulence, the contempt for glory and fame, the praise of the democratic associations and groups that ran their placid lives, the pleased contemplation of the ruddy, well-fed, happy faces of women, children, and men at rest or busy at simple chores, and of the pleasure of their flat watery land, is their seventeenth-century painting, one of the great glories of Europe, in which, curiously enough, there is no trace of Calvinistic self-torture and commercial greed. It contemplates wide and tranquil landscapes, the animated life of markets and city streets, fleets under sail, the coziness of simple private homes, and lovingly lingers on the tools of everyday work, on plain food, fruit, fish, and game. The landscapes are dominated by horizontal distant views, soft lines, hazy and tenuous colors, still waters or slowly flowing peaceful canals. Clouds acquire a deep significance; loaded ships and grazing cattle are affectionately depicted. In indoor scenes, the dim light evokes silences, sweet dear words whispered, and half-formed thoughts. The portraits are accurately honest but respectful. There is nothing pompous or rhetorical about Dutch paintings, no triumphant celebration of power, glory, and grandeur as there is in Venetian paintings of the same period, but the delighted and proud description of the intimate industrious life of the people.

The Peace of Münster (1648), which recognized the independence of the United Provinces, more or less the Holland we know, codified the policy of noninvolvement that still dominates Dutch thinking today, a policy of "seeking friendly relations and maritime and commercial treaties with all, but alignment with none," as the Dutch scholar Joris J. C. Voorhoeve writes in *Peace, Profits, and Principles* (page 25). "Every time the European balance of power tilted, the Dutch interest in peace, quiet and stability was threatened. . . . They tried to set things straight but their diplomacy was not very firm and decisive," Voorhoeve says. The moment their foreign policy consisted solely in the search for peace and profit at any price the nation fatally declined, as Venice did at the same time for the same reasons. Even the profits, for which all other ambitions had been sacrificed, diminished when England and France surpassed Holland in international trade. "Later, in the XIXth century, non-alignment, non-participation in international politics, and strict neutrality became obsessions," according to Voorhoeve. "The country turned away from power politics and from then on occupied itself exclusively with domestic reform, colonial affairs, and international trade and finance. When, for instance, the Dutch foreign minister denounced the Russian government in 1863 for the ruthless suppression of the Polish rebels, he was attacked vehemently in Parliament for this departure from absolute neutrality. When he dared accept an invitation from Napoleon III to attend a conference on the Polish question, he was forced to resign. When, ten years later, the government again strayed from its course and reproached the Turks for the inhumane behaviour during the Russo-Turkish war, this display of concern was criticized sharply in Parliament" (ibid., page 31). And less than a century later, before the last war, the Dutch refrained from criticizing Adolf Hitler's appalling behavior too openly for about the same reasons, while of course they privately considered him as deplorable as Attila or Genghis Khan.

Naturally, all initiatives encouraging perpetual peace—the outlawing of war as an instrument of national policy, the formulation of laws to protect neutrals and their sea traffic, and to make wars more humane, disarmament, or arbitration—found at all times enthusiastic champions among the Dutch. It was only natural that Czar Nicholas II, anxious to improve diplomatic relations and his country's image, and to slow down the armament race, should ask Holland to host a European conference. It was convened in The Hague in 1899 and reconvened in 1907. It generated the Permanent Court of Arbitration with its seat in The Hague which still dozes undisturbed in the same place today.

These scrupulous pursuits did not pay in the end. Pacifism has been shown not to be the surest way of defending peace. Claude

Cheysson, the French foreign minister, once said, "Pacifism is not a policy. It is a headache." For one thing, in Holland, it encouraged and justified a further decline in military pride, a weakening in national sentiment, and a resigned defeatist attitude. True, another policy than neutralism was probably impossible for the Dutch to pursue, particularly in the thirties, when France and Britain also consoled themselves with wishful thinking, were incredulous of Hitler's so evidently insane intentions, and were therefore reluctant to spend money on armaments. It is also true that even if Holland had burned with a patriotic flame, had armed itself to the teeth, signed secret alliance treaties with France, Belgium, Britain, and Luxembourg, the German invasion would have been inevitable and the defeat probably retarded by only a few days.

To all this one must add the particular Dutch form of Protestantism, which also preached pacifism, disarmament, and the brotherhood of man. (Other countries' Protestants considered armaments and wars inevitable evils and did all they could to win them.) This religious compulsion has been intensified since the last century by the Socialists, who, in many ways, had inherited more or less the same noble hopes in a secular era, in which the churches were gradually losing influence and socialism was slowly gaining a mass following. Furthermore, the Calvinist or ex-Calvinist Dutch, conditioned to a way of life guided by rigorous rules, were putting the same great trust in legal agreements and treaties that they had always put in all sorts of commercial contracts. Treaties, of course, may not always be *chiffons de papier*. They are often respected. It is to be wished that they be considered inviolable. They are the best defense of weak countries. Nevertheless, it sometimes happens that they are ignored whenever they stand in the way of some powerful nation's imperial interests. One must be prepared for that eventuality. This trust in other people's respect for covenants, this blind passion for pacifism, the defense of human rights, and for the sacredness of neutralism were ennobled by the Dutch. They saw themselves not as a weak nation trying to survive somehow in troubled times among bellicose neighbors, but as "the only sane people in an insane world" (which they surely were, with disastrous results), "an island of sanity amidst the folly of humanity," or "a lighthouse in the darkness of the world." They believed their historic mission was "not to be carried away by the passions of war and to guard the higher ethical values for mankind and, in particular, Europe."

Given all this, it is not surprising to see the Dutch at the end of the Second World War join with enthusiasm all possible international organizations, attempt to preserve the peace, and enlarge markets. "From the outset, however, the Netherlands government was less enthusiastic about the political unification of Europe," writes Voorhoeve. "For the Dutch, politics had to follow economics as opposed to, e.g., the view of the French government at the time, the Fourth Republic, which subordinated economic integration to foreign policy." J. W. Beyen, Dutch foreign minister, was the man who proposed to Gaetano Martino, the Italian foreign minister, a meeting of their colleagues, simply to set up a Common Market, when the plan to create a unified European defense organization (the EDC) had failed, blackballed by the French. This was, after all, what the Dutch really understood and preferred. They saw Europe as a big Holland, threatened, as Holland always was, by bellicose unpredictable rivals. Just as Holland had been protected by Britain, Europe was to be protected just as inexpensively by one of the two superpowers, but in reality, by their rivalry, by the balance of power. In the meantime, the Dutch thought Europe should, as they had always done, keep excellent relations with everybody and look after its business while bestowing lessons in correct behavior to all, defend all moral causes, finance the development of the underdeveloped world, chastise violators of the rights of man in distant countries (particularly their relatives in South Africa, who had drawn curiously opposite lessons from their common Calvinism), and exercise a high moral authority in international relations. The rest of Europe eagerly accepted their economic proposals but did not fully accept their crusading moral stand. Since then the mood of Europe, mollified by affluence, trying to avoid complications, and dreaming of eternal peace, has come very close to the Dutch mood since the Peace of Münster.

The Dutch formula (Europe as a big Holland) worked well as long as nobody, including the Soviets, questioned the military supremacy of the United States. As Holland had prospered in the past, leaving the peace of the world in the hands of the British, Europe prospered for years under the American nuclear umbrella, without worrying overmuch about military appropriations. Gradually, however, trust in the power of the United States began to be corroded by doubts. Its omnipotence and invincibility looked less reliable, the wisdom of its statesmen less evident, the continuity of its foreign-policy aims more difficult to detect. When the Soviets acquired an awesome nuclear arsenal and one of the biggest navies the world had seen, the Dutch (as well as the rest of western Europe) became apprehensive. They began to doubt the Americans would really launch the first nuclear weapon in case of an attack on Europe. They surely would not want to sacrifice one of their great cities with millions of inhabitants, which would be destroyed in retaliation by the Soviets, for the sake of their allies. This, of course, was stated clearly by Henry Kissinger, among others. If the first strike became unbelievable, the whole defense strategy of the West had to be reconsidered. More and more Europeans realized they had to rely once again on themselves and conventional armaments. The Dutch set up the best armed forces they ever had, small but as good and as well trained and armed as those of West Germany, and one of the best navies in Europe. Naval prowess has always been one of their few military traditions. But conventional armaments are infinitely more expensive than somebody else's nuclear missiles and more difficult to sell to the electorate.

Not surprisingly, a vast pacifist movement sprang up among the Dutch (at least among many of them, the most vociferous part of the population). They instinctively found refuge from the fear of a nuclear holocaust in the century-old Dutch dream of universal and perpetual peace and a world governed by reason. The pacifists wanted a civilian, neutral, disarmed Europe, which would defend itself by passive resistance against an invading army "as Denmark faced the Nazi aggression." They wanted universal nuclear disarmament, unilateral if need be, to set an irresistible example for others to follow. The movement filled many squares and parks with enthusiastic young people and spread to neighboring countries. A delegation went to Moscow to persuade the Soviets to disarm and renounce nuclear weapons. (The Soviets were not persuaded.) The money for all this was contributed by an autonomous "interchurch Peace Council" (not directly by the churches themselves), by worried wealthy people of good will, by the young, and (very little and inconspicuously) by the Communists.

From talks with Dutch pacifists it is clear they do not face the real problems connected with their campaign. They evidently can worry European governments, the State Department, the Pentagon, Western public opinion, and the president of the United States. They possibly can modify or attenuate American policy. But they are impotent as far as influencing the Kremlin. They do not take into consideration (or try to forget) the fact that in the Soviet Union there is no political liberty and no public opinion, without which there is no way to change policy. They also reject the only possible way to influence both the White House and the Kremlin and lead the world toward the kind of peace they seem to hope for. It is evident that only if western Europe acquires adequate conventional armaments, a unified foreign policy, and some sort of political cohesion, almost a supernational government, it will be listened to with respect and might influence the course of history. The Dutch pacifists are adamantly against all this for excellent century-old Dutch reasons. This is how State Secretary L. J. Brinkhorst described the national view of the future of Europe in the *Netherlands Foreign Ministry Yearbook* (1973–74):

"Europe would participate in world affairs by means of constructive policies in the field of trade and development aid to underdeveloped countries, by assisting the world in the wise management of its resources, by an exemplary advancement of the quality of life, by a happy compromise between society's demands of freedom and equality, for social justice and individual opportunity. It is for this Europe, which will have an unmistakable identity of its own but will remain linked to the nations on the other side of the North Atlantic, that we opt. . . . Only this Europe will be an additional force for stability and progress in the world, instead of a new factor of uncertainty, disruption, and discord."

SEVEN

The
Baffling Americans

$\mathbf{F}$EAR, OF COURSE, was and still is the prime mover toward European integration, or, more precisely, many fears. At first it was only the fear of the Soviet armed forces massed on the eastern border of western Germany, ready to pounce at any moment. Later it was also the fear of the precariousness of the international situation, based on a very unstable "balance of terror," the fear of the two superpowers snarling at each other over the Europeans' heads. Henry Kissinger wrote: "[They] often behave like two heavily armed blind men feeling their way around a room, each believing himself in mortal peril from the other, whom he assumes to have perfect vision. Each side should know that frequently uncertainty, compromise, and incoherence are the essence of policy making. Yet each tends to ascribe to the other side a consistency, foresight, and coherence that its own experience belies. Of course, over time even two armed blind men in a room can do enormous damage to each other, not to speak of the room" (*The White House Years*). Both superpowers are dangerous enough (each in its own totally different way) but probably not as dangerous as each is depicted by its adversaries, according to a law I worked out and which, I hope, might one day bear my name. I developed it years ago when living, working, and meditating in a weak, underdeveloped, disorganized, totalitarian country, my own, and, at the same time, reading about it—its far-seeing dictator, terrifying armaments, and awesome disciplined power—in the foreign press. My law states that nations, organizations, institutions, bodies, or single human beings are never as powerful, intelligent, far-seeing, efficient, and dangerous as they seem to their enemies. The Vatican (to name a few examples) is by no means the collection of sagacious and sleepless Machiavellian monsignori that atheists and fanatical Protestants imagine; Wall Street is far from being the omnipotent, omniscient, and tentacular conspiracy the Marxists believe it is; and the British Intelligence Service was laughably inferior to the diabolical iniquitous network Hitler, Stalin, and Mussolini thought it was.

What is particularly disturbing about the two superpowers from a strictly European point of view is, first of all, the apparent disproportion between their capacity to destroy each other, Europe, as well as the rest of the world, and their evidently inadequate wisdom. This, of course, is not because of an innate and irremediable incapacity. Facing the terrifying dangers of the present with contemporary destructive capacity, any other country would also have to improvise new-fangled policies and strategies without the comfort of accumulated historical experiences and precedents. Of this necessity, to invent brand-new solutions for brand-new problems, Europeans are not fully aware. Many of them tenaciously cling to the belief that most situations, no matter how unprecedented, can be better understood, and problems solved, if reduced to terms familiar to their own great-grand-fathers. One of Italy's brightest foreign relations experts says, "I always translate contemporary problems into the language Metternich would have used, before I tackle them." Henry Kissinger would probably agree with him. Whether Europeans are right or wrong is immaterial. What is to be borne in mind is that they understandably long for a vanished familiar world and would prefer to entrust their deaths, if die they must, to their own time-tested expedients, artifices, machinations (the "balance of power," for instance, a juggling act that Lorenzo il Magnifico invented to keep peace among rival Italian principalities in the fifteenth century, but which has always been considered a cynical, corrupt, and immoral subterfuge by the Americans), or to prudent stealthy attempts at conciliation and compromise, rather than submit to the blunt white or black decisions of others.

To be sure, the superpowers also often surreptitiously follow the ancient rules of statecraft, speak the traditional language of diplomats and foreign relations experts. They are, most of the time, flexible enough, but not always. In moments of crisis and imminent catastrophe they sometimes become incomprehensible, rigid, dangerously so, deaf to outside warnings and advice. It is evident at such times that they cannot maneuver easily, because they cannot follow courses that may differ from their respective national mystiques. This, of course, is nothing new. Two disastrous world wars were started because kings, emperors, dictators, prime ministers, and generals could not betray their own mystiques and their rigid codes, could not contradict their past utterances, could not renege on their word, could not show themselves and their countries as cowardly, and had to defend at all cost their countries' military honor. But this time, in the case of the two superpowers, things are disturbingly different.

To be sure, the vast majority of Europeans, both openly in the West and secretly in the East, are definitely on the side of only one of the two national ideologies, that of the United States. The American ideals and hopes are part of the common moral heritage of all men. Theirs is the Athenian point of view as described in Pericles' famous speech in Thucydides. But the problem haunting the Europeans is not only that of the comparative worth of the two philosophies, two conceptions of man, politics, and international coexistence. The problem is that of the rigidity of both superpowers in dangerous times, when procrastination, silence, evasion, ambiguity, and flexibility would probably postpone a showdown in a crisis and find some solution, perhaps unsatisfactory but better than no solution at all. There are several reasons for this lack of elasticity. The main one is that both superpowers are partially (or see themselves as) intellectual constructs, abstract philosophic experiments born of glorious revolutions, both in opposite ways determined to modify and improve the life of man on earth, based (the experiments) on two partially artificial conceptions of history and human nature.

Each sees itself as the ultimate model for humanity. Each believes it is exclusively in possession of the ultimate truth. The ideal of each, therefore, is a world shaped according to its beliefs. (Not the whole world, perhaps. Soviet Communists have been earnestly repeating for years, "When all nations will be Marxist-Leninist Democratic Republics, we must keep Italy as it is, so that we may go there on vacation and relax.") Both try to convince men to accept their way of life, by persuasion if possible, occasionally by force. One superpower is a noble experiment famously based on the ideas of Scottish, English, and French philosophers of the *siècle des lumières*. The other is notoriously a primitive and brutal adaptation to semi-Asiatic conditions of oversimplified Marxism-Leninism. As a result both superpowers are obliged to live and act at times in partly imaginary worlds. They then see man, man's nature, and man's motives through ideological lenses, ignore history and past experiences, and try to force humanity onto a Procrustean bed of prefabricated concepts, stretching what is short and trimming what is long.

To be sure, this moral, almost religious compulsion to transform and improve the world is not without precedents. It was the ancient Romans' compulsion; it was the Spaniards', in their wars to free their country from the Arabs and their conquest of Latin America; it was the Venetians', who fought the infidel for centuries and built little Venices and Saint Mark's belfries all over their Ionian domains. It animated the Crusaders' many expeditions to the Levant. It was also one of the ostensible motives of the British and other more recent colonial powers. The British nobly abolished slavery and the slave trade almost half a century before Lincoln emancipated the blacks; abolished polygamy among their Moslem subjects, as well as the burning of widows in India; spread Christianity, literacy, cleanliness, the rule of law, sanitation, parliamentary rules, and good table manners everywhere. The Italians conquered Ethiopia allegedly to wipe out slavery. Hitler himself dreamed of a nazified world, perfected and pacified for a thousand years. Nevertheless, there is a fundamental difference between these countries' older urges to force their religions, cultures, ways of life, and conceptions of politics on reluctant foreigners, and the compulsive sense of mission of the two superpowers today. The ancient nations could, when necessary, forgo spreading their beneficent influence on distant lands with difficulty but without real damage to their identity. There was no drama. On the other hand, the United States' and the Soviet Union's sense of historical mission is their principal raison d'être. In fact, when they occasionally try to betray their heritage, they risk not mere loss of prestige and foreign followers, but above all internal demoralization, disintegration, and possibly dissolution. The United States, born of an anticolonial revolution, endangers national unity whenever it fights what look like colonial wars, as it did in the Philippines at the start of the century, in San Domingo and Nicaragua in later years, or in Vietnam; the Soviet Union seriously endangered its power, prestige, and internal cohesion, as well as the loyalty of many foreign Communists, when it allied itself to Hitler or when it invaded Afghanistan; it risks eventual collapse if it tolerates a minimum of elementary liberties in its satellites (or at home).

The fear of the Soviet Union is, of course, paramount. What larval European union exists today was created after the war not only by the threat of a Soviet invasion, but also by their encouraging (and financing) menacing revolutionary parties and underground terrorists wherever possible in the West. The second fear, of course, is seldom mentioned in official society, in books, magazines, or newspapers. It is the Europeans' fear of themselves. They have fought so many senseless wars, started so many ruinous revolutions, tried so many experiments, provoked so many catastrophes, were swept by so many demented mass emotions, believed so many myths, followed blindly so many spuriously charismatic leaders that they are always uneasy when considering their own future. They know anything might happen in Europe because everything has happened.

The third fear is of the United States. Fear, of course, is not the right word—anxiety, apprehension, doubts, uneasiness may be more accurate terms. (What follows is not the author's idea of the United States but an approximate sketch of how it has baffled

Europeans in the past and still baffles them.) This perplexity has grown alarmingly in the last few years. Right after the last war Europeans finally felt secure. They could always rely on the United States, on its immense power, terrifying scientific weaponry, and noble intentions. It was the richest, most disinterested, disciplined, advanced, best-organized, and most invincible country, not only of the day but of all time. It was always ready (almost always, anyway) to defend with its young men and its wealth what was dearest to Western man. Europeans had no doubts that the United States would be able to keep the peace all over the world forever as surely as Britain had kept it in the past, and that they had nothing to worry about. These convictions were fortified by their incredible misconceptions of American reality, shaped mainly by what they wanted to believe. The fear (perplexity, anxiety, apprehension, bafflement, doubts, uneasiness) recurs, in fact, every time the real America does not behave exactly as the imaginary America of Europeans' dreams is expected to.

Once the Italian foreign minister, Amintore Fanfani at the time, both an authoritative and shrewd university professor of economic history and a skillful politician, told me he had deduced the Americans' plans for the immediate future. "These," he said, "are their intentions." General X had made a speech, he enumerated, the New York Times had published an editorial, Columnist Y had leaked a secret, the secretary of state had issued a communiqué, the president had answered a particular question at a press conference, Senator Z had given an interview, the Italian ambassador had had a hunch. As in those children's games in which, when each numbered spot in connected with a line, an unexpected figure appears, he had connected all these declarations, statements, hunches, leaks, and articles and had come up with a tidy answer. "This is their grand design," he concluded, beaming. When he saw the incredulity on my face, "Don't you believe it?" he asked. I explained that, yes, he could be right, but he also could be entirely wrong, because there wasn't always the strict coordination he imagined in the United States between all the various branches of the executive, the legislative, the judiciary, and the most authoritative newspapers; and this because the United States was not Louis XIV's France, Metternich's Austria, Bismarck's Reich, nor any other ancient European imperial nation-state, but something entirely sui generis.

I explained that one could not deny there were coherence and cohesion of sorts in America, without which the country could not play its part in international affairs, but they were often produced by the people's mysterious and unpredictable capacity to conceive the same ideas at the same time, to react the same way to external threats, to be swept by the same emotional storm or dominated by identical moods from ocean to ocean. Not all the people, of course, maybe not the same people in differing circumstances, but a large majority, which varied in composition according to the problem facing it. I could see I was hurting Fanfani's feelings as I demolished his well-ordered and logical academic construct. But then how could he know how America worked and what America was when many eminent European observers, some of whom had lived years in the country, had always reached deformed conclusions, for instance, Georges Clemenceau, who had been a doctor, a teacher of French and of horseback riding in New York and for a while had been married to a girl, Mary Plummer, from Stamford, Connecticut. He liked to say this about the United States: "Americans have no capacity for abstract thought and make bad coffee." He was entirely wrong, of course. Americans, whether they know it or not, are eighteenth-century philosophes at heart. Their bad coffee can at times be surprisingly excellent, surely better at its worst than French coffee.

European ideas of America (as well as American ideas of Europe), on which mutual relations and the common future and the world's peace ultimately depend, are predictably superannuated (clichés having a way of lagging far behind reality), erroneous, based on insufficient and distorted information, on myths, idées reçues, rhetorical exaggerations, wishful thinking, travelers' tales, cheap novels, and the cinema. Some of these indestructible, obsolete stereotypes go back to the beginning of the century—Theodore Roosevelt's "I took Panama," "Speak softly but carry a big stick"; Admiral Alfred Thayer Mahan's theories. It was believed to be a virile, proud, unafraid country led by a conservative, moneyed, Protestant oligarchy of gentlemen who lovingly followed British examples of the previous century, handled the economy with skill, were addicted to monopolies, and adored the almighty dollar, all of which was more or less true before World War I. This antiquated family-album view should not be dismissed. It is still very much alive in Europe. European monarchists, conservatives, pro-Soviet Communists, Marxists, many (political) Catholics, socialists, democrats, anti-American revolutionaries, terrorists, pacifists, ecologists, and populists in general cling to it tenaciously today. Some of them (like Jean Jacques Servan-Schreiber) fear the *défi Américain* as Wilhelm II and many others once feared the "yellow peril." To be sure, some of the terminology has been brought up to date. Old-fashioned American patriots are now called neocolonialists, and the monopolies or trusts of old are now called multinationals.

Then there are, superimposed like layers of successive snowfalls, World War I America (a young, naïve, generous, heroic country on its way to becoming a benevolent empire—"Lafayette, we are here," Woodrow Wilson at Versailles, "open covenants openly arrived at," Herbert Hoover feeding the hungry) and World War II America (the immense industrial capacity that within weeks could place vast armies, fleets, air forces, with diabolical weapons and all their stores, including ice cream for the troops, anywhere in the world, led by rough but efficient generals and admirals who were always capable of destroying the enemy, any enemy). Truman's America follows (the Marshall Plan, the Atlantic Pact, the Korean War, the defense of liberty, anybody's liberty), and then contemporary America, a country apparently full of doubts and controversies, in which outlandish new ideas and experiments are always being tested, foreign policy meanders incomprehensibly from time to time, cults and crackpots pullulate, but in which all the past Americas are still very much alive, in perennial debate among themselves, debates that are not, as they would be in other countries, a cause of disruption, decadence, and weakness, but of eternally renewed vigor and progress. The United States is believed to be a healthy and hardy, if somewhat turbulent, country, which in the end always finds its way. One can count on it when the chips are down. You'll always find it on your side, on the side of the angels.

The depression of the thirties, the murder of JFK, race riots, the defeat in Southeast Asia, Watergate, Nixon's resignation, and many other unfortunate vicissitudes that left their mark on Americans did not greatly modify the reassuring European image of the United States. Europeans knew that similar (or worse) mistakes and misfortunes happened in the best of countries. Most of them, in fact, could be considered beneficial, healthy pauses or alarm signals necessary to review and correct past errors and delusions. Ancient wisdom welcomed scandals: "Oportet ut scandala eveniant," says the Bible. Scandals never really changed the character of a people; in particular, they could not change the fundamental character of the American people, who were, as one saw daily in Westerns or war movies, bigger than life-size, decent, plucky, resolute, truthful, brave, philanthropic, ruthless, successful, and lucky, always determined to destroy the villains, defend the underdog, see justice triumph, hang dishonest or corrupt men and horse thieves. In movies or paperbacks dedicated to the adventurous intrigues of secret agents, Americans were shown to be capable of covering the world with a fine diabolical net of dedicated and cunning men who invariably defeated the enemies of peace. So why worry?

What is the United States really? To find a reliable answer to this question has now become a matter of life and death for Europeans. Continental statesmen know their decisions in an eventual crisis depend on an exact estimate of probable American behavior. A wrong guess may spell disaster, as it did when Napoleon III sent Maximilian to Mexico in violation of the Monroe Doctrine; when Kaiser Wilhelm II and Hitler thought the United States would not fight a European war; or when the North Koreans believed the Americans would not defend South Korea.

There is, of course, not one answer to the question What is the United States? but many answers, most of them almost true, all of them demonstrably true, all of them confusing. The United States is as many things as there are vantage points, many sometimes in rapid succession, and often many at the same time, some of them puzzlingly contradictory and irreconcilable. The Americans themselves cannot always be depended upon for a reliable portrayal of their country. (One can rarely trust a son for an objective description of his mother.) For one thing, they never mention what to them are their obvious characteristics, not worth describing. Their definitions are inevitably deformed by love, hope, disappointment, or resentment. This, of course, is not unusual. All nations, as well as individual human beings, are multiform and incomprehensible. "How can we know others when we do not know ourselves?" somebody wrote. But nowadays, to define exactly what any nation other than the U. S. and the USSR really is, is a matter of little importance, whether it is one of the many small, ill-armed, dispirited, and impecunious European countries, or even one which sees itself (as France does) as wise, great, heroic, autonomous, a teacher of civilization to the world, and powerful. A reliable definition of the United States today is something else. Europe's destiny depends on it. It may be a matter of life or death.

Europeans who have been to the United States, met Americans in Europe, or consulted an encyclopedia or an almanac are certain it is a nation, a great nation, inhabited by people as typically what they are as the inhabitants of any other nation (British, Swedes, Hungarians, Chinese, Iranians, or Kurds), recognizable by their language, clothes, habits, tastes, and the food they eat. Now that the United States is an empire, a reluctant empire, Europeans also believe it is (and must conduct itself) more or less like previous empires. From this many, like Senator Fanfani, deduce that there must be, somewhere in Washington, a central command, a bunker, a *Kanzlei*, where all decisions—domestic, foreign, military, economic—are firmly taken, plans elaborated, orders given and obeyed, and initiatives of all kinds harmoniously coordinated, possibly with the aid of unerring computers: the ordering of armaments based on foreign policy lines, for instance, or foreign policy decisions based on the divisions and transport available. Europeans are certain somebody in Washington is perennially worried (as they would be) by the need to preserve the balance of power in the world. They imagine that the vast plan is constantly brought up to date by the teamwork of the Pentagon, the State Department, the White House, the National Security Council, CIA, and the Congress. All these institutions must impress a rigorous (even if not always detectable) continuity on foreign policy, direct secret intrigues, search for new wonder weapons, cunningly predispose the acquisition of allies and bases for eventual future use, and deploy armed forces throughout the world.

All this, of course, is almost true. The United States is definitely (among other things) a nation, a great nation. It always has, almost always, in a crisis behaved as one. It will probably do so again. But then no nation or empire, not even Napoleon's France or Hitler's Reich, has ever been entirely logical and coherent, and the United States is no exception. It often plunges European Americanologists and Americanophiles into despair, whenever, as Henry Kissinger wrote, its foreign policy fluctuates unexpectedly "between euphoria and panic." Why did the mighty and well-informed United States, these European observers ask, not conquer North Vietnam in a few weeks, as it had the means to, destroy Castro in time, foresee and prevent the revolution in Iran or the invasion of Afghanistan? Why did it lose control of the Horn of Africa and why did it not prearrange acceptable solutions for Nicaragua or San Salvador long before an emergency arose?

In reality, the United States can also be seen as an unpredictable loose conglomeration of heterogeneous people of different races, origins, cultures, religions, and values, further transformed and conditioned by the varied regional histories, environments, and even landscapes of their country—which range from Scandinavia (the North) to Italy (California) to the Alps (the Rockies) and the Sahara (the desert), Andalusia and North Africa (the

Southwest). These heterogeneous people are kept united mainly by their resolute beaverlike determination to construct a more rational and just society, possibly one day a perfect society, which, of course, like the cathedrals of old, may never be completed. Their vision of the future is paramount. It is what keeps them together. The United States can therefore be seen as a country always on the move from a shabby today, which many consider a betrayal of the Founding Fathers' designs and lofty hopes, to a radiant tomorrow. It has been compared to a man on a bicycle who falls if he stops pedaling and moving ahead. It surely is not like other and older nations, which are immutably what they are whether standing still, going backward, or advancing; whether prosperous or impoverished, victorious or defeated, independent or oppressed. Probably the Americans' moral necessity to justify their individual and national existence is their real patriotism, what they fight for in war, what unites them and makes them victorious and gives them strength and unity, as the magnet imposes a pattern to a random scattering of iron filings. The United States, in its relentless pursuit of ultimate and unreachable perfection, has been described as a daring experiment, one generation ahead of everybody else, the last word in modernity, the future that works, the next century. I remember the General Motors exhibition at the New York World's Fair in 1939, a vast miniature panorama, not of contemporary or past achievements, but of the imaginary wonders of the future, none of which exists today, for example, fruit trees were capped with plastic domes to accelerate the ripening of the fruit and isolate them from diseases and bugs, and rosaries of driverless automobiles ran along the highways.

One must not let the science-fiction appearance of many things American deceive one. The dream is not entirely modern. It is, as I said, partly an anachronistic experiment based on eighteenth-century anticipations. (Benjamin Franklin described his people's future achievements with astounding accuracy.) Like the dream, its symbols have also changed little. They are revealing. The style of Federal architecture, until at least a generation ago, the eagle still engraved on official stationery, on embassy plates and embassy matchboxes, the starred and striped flag, and the solemn prose of the presidents' inaugural addresses, all tenaciously preserve the fashions of Louis XVI and George III, particularly the flag whose design could serve (the stars) to upholster an elegant gilded sofa at Versailles or to make (the stripes) an *incroyable*'s fashionable waistcoat.

From the Americans' deep-seated awareness that they are entrusted with an experiment never before tried by man derive the national characteristics most baffling to Europeans. One is their apparent lack of respect for other people's precedents and experiences and the past in general. The great seal of the Republic on the back of every dollar bill bears the proud motto, "Novus ordo seclorum," more or less meaning, "The world and history begin with us." Many Americans seem to believe every problem is born that very morning. Europeans wonder why (to mention but one of the latest examples) the Americans did not bother to consult the French beforehand on Vietnam, a country they had conquered with some difficulty eighty years before, governed for decades, and knew well; or about the Vietnamese, whose language many of the French spoke fluently, a people they had fought on and off for a century with disastrous results.

Another corollary is the philanthropic and didactic urge that makes America see itself as the world's best hope, the mentor, preceptor, and example to all men. One of the moral justifications for the 1776 rebellion against the Mother Country, besides independence, was the hope of incorporating in the new nation all modern improvements, philosophic and juridical, not only for the Americans' own benefit, but also to help other countries, including England itself, to adopt and enjoy them. Until a few years ago, this conviction was freely, artlessly, proudly, and candidly advertised. "We saw ourselves moving benevolently," wrote George Kennan, "helpfully, among the waiting peoples of the world, our experience now finally recognized as relevant to a wider sphere of humanity, our virtues no longer just the virtues of the American frontier but the virtues of the world at large." This is no longer openly and wantonly proclaimed today. Americans know it somehow irritates more foreigners than it seduces and does not work miracles. It produced in the past unexpected catastrophes in many countries which, under the American influence, followed American teachings too faithfully and too quickly. There are now many people, even Americans, who are incredulous about the task assigned by history to the United States. They ask how, at the present moment, America can set itself up as a shining example to the world when it is itself haunted by unsolvable ghastly problems, some of them generated by the very attempted solutions of old problems. Nevertheless, one must always remember that, even if muted or left unsaid, what Henry Kissinger calls "the traditional sense of universal moral mission" is still one of the motivations (or, at times, indispensable rhetorical justifications) of American international behavior. It must never be disregarded (but never fully relied on) when dealing with the United States.

The success of the American model has been undeniable. To be sure, what non-Americans were more eager to adopt were the gross material aspects (the pursuit of a bigger and better GNP; brisk efficiency; American scientific discoveries and technological improvements; forced consumption of all kinds of goods made possible by widespread affluence; the training of specialists, omniscient world authorities in their tiny fields but dangerously naive and credulous in all others). More difficult (but not impossible) to imitate for distant people who did not share the American historical background and moral commitment were the political models (universal suffrage, the checks-and-balance act, a bicameral parliament, human rights, division of powers). Some Latin American nations anxiously put up almost credible parodies to please the United States: a neoclassical capitol surmounted by a dome; a constitution very much like the original Philadelphia document; a bicameral parliament, division of powers, and, in Brazil and Mexico, the separation of the land into separate states, and so on. Behind the façade, of course, life in those countries went on more or less in its own cruel, shabby, ancient, arbitrary, almost unalterable way.

The American model has been irresistible in many other ways. It dominates the world today in large and small matters, even in fads and fashions, newly invented sports and gadgets of all kinds. American films fill cinemas and TV programming everywhere. A few years ago, blue-jeaned and long-haired youths demonstrated, in imitation of American students, against the Vietnam War, which was scarcely their business. Now they all jog like the former president of the United States. Men all over the world automatically turn to the "American way" of doing anything, to the "American" solution of any problem, possibly only because the Americans were chronologically the first to face the problem. Such solutions are the handiest and easiest, and may, of course, be the best, but could occasionally be the worst in a different context and time. Evidently, to start from a clean slate, tabula rasa, and disregard past experiences has often been demonstrably the best way. The list of American achievements is indeed staggering. They have transformed and improved their own life, life in the Western world and in Europe, but also in many ways life in the most remote and primitive corners of the terraqueous globe. Most American ideas are sensible and practical, most of them the result of long experiments, trials, and errors. Some, to be sure, are European ideas transplanted, tested, acclimatized, and (as the labels on sundry food products, such as Ronzoni spaghetti, say, in the United States) "enriched." Admittedly most American hopes are more than American or European hopes; they are universal man's hopes, too.

There is no doubt (in my mind anyway, and in the mind of all reasonable people) that the world (including the United States) would be a better, more livable place if it were possible to transform it according to American ideals and precepts. It would be a duller and more boring world, to be sure, but prosperous, well fed, healthy, clean, law-abiding, literate, punctual, and at peace. Unfortunately, men are not as easily malleable as Americans believe, not even in the United States itself, and reality is as unpredictable as it always was. Men's behavior and mentality lag far behind the more rapid changes of society precipitated by industrialization, technology, mass communications, advanced political experiments, the power of nuclear weapons, and the shrinking of the world. Men en masse are seldom guided by reason, not yet anyway. Old evils and appalling habits are often more attractive to them than efficient and intelligent new ways. (When Naples was liberated and the Americans distributed cans of Spam to the starving population, Neapolitans exchanged them in the black market for the much less nourishing but much more satisfying traditional *maccheroni*.)

What few imitators have understood is that the secret of the United States' tremendous success was in reality not merely technology, know-how, the work ethic, the urge to succeed, or plain greed. It was a spiritual wind that drove the Americans irresistibly ahead from the beginning. What was behind their compulsion to improve man's lot was an all-pervading religious sense of duty, the submission to a God-given imperative, to a God-given code of personal behavior, the willing acceptance of all the necessary sacrifices, including death in battle. Few foreigners understand this, even today. The United States appears to them merely as the triumph of soulless materialism.

To be sure, the religious fervor and the Protestant ethic which were so blatantly evident a century ago are now less visible. But they are still there, even if few Americans mention them. The original Protestant sense of mission has also contaminated the Catholics and the Jews. They are feebler, discredited by intellectuals, corroded by the doubts of these impious times, but without them, or what is left of them, America would not be what it is. *Tout se tient.* One cannot look for new cures for old social ills, as the Americans do; one cannot promote justice, universal education, democracy, and liberty, defend international legality; one cannot be prepared to send armies at great expense all over the world to fight for democracy and possibly win, increase the GNP and distribute its bounties more widely; one cannot set oneself up as the universal model without a perception of right or wrong, without the presence of God, of Him by any other name, looking over every man's shoulder, breathing on the back of every man's neck, and pointing the way.

The conviction that one was obeying God's commands was also true, of course, of most previous empires. Charles Martel destroyed the Arab invaders at Poitiers in A.D. 732 in the name of Christ; the Venetians fought the Turks in the name of Mark the Evangelist; the Western allies who defeated the Ottoman fleet at Lepanto called themselves the Christian League; the Turks died for Muhammad; monks brandishing the crucifix went with the conquering Spanish armies in Central and South America to baptize and absolve Indios before they were massacred; the Anglican church was among the first buildings, together with the forts and the barracks and the club, to be erected by the British in every newly conquered colony. (George Orwell called British imperialism "forcible evangelizing.") The "Lord of Hosts" was invoked by the Bible and Kipling.

But there always was and still is something disturbingly unique in the American drive, something which must not be overlooked. A sacrilegious Promethean element is detectable, an impious challenge to God's will. It is as if, while zealously serving the Deity, Americans knew better than He and tried to improve His own inadequate and obsolete idea of the universe and man. They strove to annul Adam's curse, *la condition humaine*, man's predicament, at all costs, and partially succeeded: man's life has been prolonged beyond all hope, the ultimate target being to defeat God once and for all and make man immortal. (Frozen corpses are preserved in liquid nitrogen at Berkeley, waiting for science and not God to manage their resurrection on Judgment Day.) Man no longer earns his bread by the sweat of his brow, indeed less and less bread is consumed; air conditioning prevents perspiration; Americans only sweat at play; and by no means all women have to suffer pain when giving birth.

On the other hand, to consider uniquely (as some Europeans do) this American idea of themselves, the world's leader, while essential, can also be misleading, the source of dangerous mis-understandings and catastrophic miscalculations, because the philanthropy, the somewhat impractical knight-errant idealism, the compulsion to improve man and his surroundings must be understood in conjunction with another fundamental, ever-present, and sometimes contradictory American trait: prag-matism. The two things don't always go well together. Pragmatism is the belief that all problems can be solved, combined with the urge to solve all of them in the shortest time, get the job done, whatever the job, get it done well, but above all, quickly. Ameri-cans do not like to admit failure or defeat. This contrast between idealism and pragmatism is visible in the contradiction between their perennial fondness for issuing high-minded pronouncements, imparting severe lessons of correct democratic behavior, and the occasional propensity, when absolutely necessary and opportune, for sending expeditionary forces to foreign countries, corrupting foreign officials, financing unsavory tyrants and supplying them with a surfeit of weapons and "advisors."

To be sure, bribing dignitaries and propping up tyrants is part of normal imperial business, occasionally essential for the defense of a country's interests and the world's peace. These things have been done as a matter of course by other powerful nations throughout history but with this difference, those empires of the past knew what they were doing was wrong according to private morality, sometimes (not often) regretted it, but also knew it was unavoidable or politically right in a tight spot, and that the only test was effectiveness. (The USSR leaders, on the other hand, seem firmly to believe wrong is right. They suffered no visible qualms as they bribed, subverted, deported, imprisoned or exter-minated people, and at opportune times, incorporated directly or indirectly into their system unwilling foreign countries.) The Americans, on the other hand, a fundamentally decent people, suffer when accused of duplicity, hypocrisy, imposture, fraud, or lack of consistency between their declared principles and their actions. Such forms of cynicism and dishonesty they mostly attribute to corrupt Europeans. Christopher Newman, Henry James' *maschera* of this "new man" in *The American*, thought only Europe was "unscrupulous and impure." For this reason Americans are more reluctant than most people to admit to shoddy behavior. They are easily troubled by remorse. Theodore Roosevelt vigorously denied he had ever said, "I took Panama"; McKinley "prayed all night" and was absolved by God before deciding that the Philippines should become a ward of the United States; Lyndon Johnson desperately clung to the thesis that the Vietnam expedition had been in response to a liberty-loving ally who had cried for help when attacked by a foreign aggressor. He could not bear to think that his country had involved itself in what could be interpreted as an un-American war.

In fact this moral necessity to deceive himself paralyzed him. His generals could not afford to do to the North Vietnamese the harsh immoral Old World things Julius Caesar did to the Gauls, the Spaniards to the Dutch, Lord Wolseley to the Ashantis, Kitchener to the Fuzzy-Wuzzies, and the French to the Algerians. On the other hand, President Johnson could not pull out his expeditionary force and admit defeat. The Vietnamese problem could not be left unsolved. Liberty in Vietnam had to be saved and consolidated. A new and better country had to be set up on the ruins. The Americans' sense of mission and pride, their confidence in their power and invincibility, but above all, their pragmatism, the need to finish the job at all costs, prevented them, until it was too late, from admitting they had made a mistake and from packing up and leaving Vietnam to its tragic destiny. They tried to disentangle themselves in the end by non-American means, devious, "unscrupulous and impure" Machiavellian or Talleyrandian methods, secret diplomacy, the application of the balance of power, and the *raison d'Etat*. They did not like it. "We cannot," warned George Kennan, "when it comes to dealings between governments, assign to moral values the same significance we give them in personal life." No wonder when the Europeans have to guess which way the United States will jump, knowing that their own future and that of the whole world are at stake, they are frightened and cautious. Will Americans be pragmatic or idealistic tomorrow?

Nobody is, in reality, excessively perturbed by the Americans' contradictions, their public and official insistence on sincerity, purity, and virtue, their contempt of cynicism, their faith in their own excellence, in progress, in the endless perfectibility of man—all traits occasionally and embarrassingly in contrast with their behavior. Nobody is perturbed overmuch by their need tirelessly to tinker, improve everything and everybody, never leave anything alone, or by their belief that new is always better, that there is (or should be) magic power in treaties and legal documents and international organizations, or by their contemptuous disregard for history, for other people's precedents and errors. These are things one can live with. Even if they are ineradicable American characteristics, they are not exclusively American. Who does not want to see oppression, poverty, hunger, injustice defeated, treaties honored, and war really outlawed? What country's rhetoric is not at times in contrast with its conduct? What really frightens foreigners, Europeans in particular, and makes them worry about the future is something else, the one characteristic that really makes the United States a world apart, a truly different country, one that it is difficult to work with, risky to rely on and trust one's future to. This is America's impatience.

It could also be called impetuosity, ardor, eagerness to apply premature formulas and achieve rapid results. Its origins are obscure. For more than two centuries foreign visitors to the United States noticed with awe that the inhabitants were all anxiously rushing about, always in a great hurry, and many of them (like Thomas Jefferson) were tirelessly inventing time-saving devices. Whether Americans are really always in a hurry, more in a hurry than other industrialized people, say, more than the Germans or the Japanese, is, of course, debatable. Personally, I haven't made up my mind. American trains and waiters have always been much slower than European waiters and trains; American drivers surely do not go as fast as the Italians. In the absence of the results of a conclusive scientific survey, I'm merely interested, at this point, in the undeniable fact that travelers from abroad have invariably recorded and still record today the same impression. Why this American impatience? Where was and is the fire? What is the deadline each American is trying to beat? There are, of course, no satisfactory answers, merely a few hypothetical explanations of the phenomenon. Here's a European one. Perhaps the hurry arises because, as I said above, pragmatic Americans consider the very existence of problems intolerable and life with problems unacceptable. They believe, as I pointed out, that all problems not only *must* be solved, but also that they *can* be solved, and that in fact the main purpose of a man's life is the solution of problems. They also believe (or want to believe) that "a" solution, if not "the" solution, can always be discovered. "If there was a problem [he thought] there had to be a solution. He conveyed acute impatience and urgency," Arthur Schlesinger says of one American, Robert Kennedy, and he could have said the same thing of most of his countrymen, including himself. If each problem had a solution, why lose time, why not find it immediately and apply it now, today, tomorrow morning, next week, next month? Why wait? All it takes in most cases is the allocation of sufficient funds, the gathering in one barn, office building, or laboratory of the best minds in the country (sometimes one man of genius, Edison, or two, the Wright brothers, are enough), an assemblage or florilegium of eminent and talented specialists, scientists, and professors from the right universities, with enough money and time—not too much time, of course—and the answer will emerge.

This belief has been proved right so often that it is almost ineradicable. American feats have been spectacular, particularly in science, whenever teamwork and disciplined organization is essential, whenever data can be accurately gathered in sufficient quantity, measured statistically, and manipulated by computers, questions reduced to mathematical formulas, and the percentage of probable errors accurately foreseen. (The number of American Nobel Prize winners for scientific pursuits is infinitely larger than the number of those from the rest of the world.) The most fulgid example of this, the acme of course, is the Americans' conquest of the moon. On the other hand, their disappointments have also been proportionately numerous, particularly in fields in which exact data cannot be gathered, figures manipulated, and computers are useless; in which the solutions may be many, and all of them being more or less good enough, a choice is almost impossible; and whenever the human limitations (stubborn human vices and virtues) are a decisive obstacle.

The above distinctions, of course, should by no means be taken too seriously. Many of them are nothing more than Europeans' glib generalizations, flattering to their egos, rough attempts to isolate, magnify, and emphasize only the characteristics that seem to set Americans apart from them. Admittedly, Europeans too have been guilty of catastrophic mistakes, misjudgments, and have been victims of their lack of perception. Furthermore, they sometimes manage to beat the Americans in their own fields, science, mathematics, or technology. Non-American Albert Einstein revolutionized the conception of the universe, and Enrico Fermi developed the theoretical foundations of atomic fission. On the other hand, Americans have occasionally been more successful than Europeans in the arts, music, painting, architecture, poetry, literature, the theater, the ballet, and above all, the cinema, all of them intuitive activities whose success can scarcely be planned, controlled, and programmed. In the first decades of their independence, they also brilliantly handled intricate political and social problems whose wise solutions depended on a perceptive and skeptical knowledge of human nature and history. These exceptions merely prove the United States is more complex than Europeans believe, that the world is not as simple or things as clear-cut as journalists and scholars would like them to be.

The Americans' impatience may also have another source. (This is a second European hypothesis that cannot be confirmed or tested.) Most Americans believe (or seem to believe) that all achievements must be completely accomplished (and possibly enjoyed) within a person's lifetime. Life being a short voyage in the light between two interminable darknesses, the past and the future do not really count. What counts is the contemporary generation. A man must perform what he set out to do before he dies or consider his existence wasted. This is not so in Europe, at least it wasn't so until a few years ago. Each man in the Old World knew that he was merely a link in a chain between ancestors and descendants. Life for him was a relay race. Each man received the rod from his father or his teachers and passed it on to his sons or followers. Therefore the amount of time allowed to achieve any-thing—political reforms, scientific breakthroughs, personal success, fame, or the family's fortune—was longer and more leisurely in the Old World. If a man didn't make it, his sons or grandsons might. To be sure, with the gentle decay of the family, this is no longer as true in Europe as it used to be, although it is still the prevalent attitude, more prevalent in Europe than in the United States, and one of the reasons why Europeans are struck and puzzled by the Americans' alacrity and the eagerness with which they sometimes plunge much too soon into premature, untried, though almost always necessary, well-meaning, and noble projects, the impatience with which they sometimes push unprepared nations into political experiments (often slowing down or stopping the very progress they want to promote): half-baked agrarian re-forms, premature or dangerous alliances with left-wing parties, overnight democratizations. The record is long, from the coalition between Chiang Kai-shek and Mao; the early encouragement given to Fidel Castro, a simple "agrarian reformer" fighting in the mountains; to the founding of the Center-Left coalition in Italy, which put an end to the "economic miracle" and pushed the country toward bankruptcy.

One other perennial contradiction has always perplexed and often deceived Europeans. It now makes them extremely wary. Is the United States a fundamentally interventionist or a deter-minedly isolationist country? It is evidently important to know the answer in order to avoid grievous mistakes. When the Hungarians revolted in 1956 and the Czechs tried to in 1968, they felt sure of being helped by an American gesture, some demonstration of solidarity that would intimidate the Soviets. But the Americans were not in an interventionist mood at the time. All they had contributed were the stirring speeches on Radio Free Europe over the previous years. When in 1956 the French and the British tried to wrest the Suez Canal, which had been their property, from the Egyptians who had taken it over, they were stopped in their tracks by a few sharp words from John Foster Dulles, the secretary of state. They too had misinterpreted the American mood.

The truth perhaps (or a working hypothesis) is that the United States can be both things, isolationist and interventionist, but one never knows which it will be and when. Like other countries it would prefer to be a vast neutral Switzerland, keep itself free from foreign entanglements, and enjoy undisturbed, behind impregnable bastions, the pleasurable advantages of its ever-growing affluence and its own way of life, or in the words of Theodore Roosevelt (who deplored it vigorously) "the soft and easy enjoyment of material comforts." That is unfortunately not always possible. In order to enjoy peace, one must be sure that one's neighbors in the world condominium behave decently. Almost always they unfortunately don't. Some cling lovingly to obsolete barbaric ways, to unsanitary living conditions, to faulty diets, to idleness, to anthropophagy, to wasteful techniques of production, to ancient superstitions, miseries, injustices, and decrepit political ideas, ruinous to themselves and to their neighbors. Some play with outlandish and explosive new political theories. Some endanger everybody's peace by subverting other countries, financing and training terrorists, and instigating civil wars. There is a point at which the Americans' impatience plus their irresistible philanthropic instinct, their sense of mission, their pragmatism and love of order, logic, and tranquillity forces them to intervene against their nature. They cannot help it. They realize that the disturbers of the peace must be taught the correct way to behave, to govern themselves, to avoid unnecessary and wasteful revolutions and wars, work hard, make money, spread it among all classes, and mind their own business. At such times in the past cavalry divisions swept across the Mexican border, Marines landed in banana republics, and vast armies and fleets crossed both oceans to fight and win two world wars.

Some of these interventions provoked a number of miniwars, mostly in Central America and the Caribbean, which left behind an inheritance of ruinous political consequences, memories of hatred and hostility, and the ardent desire for revenge. Some of these interventions were successful, a few highly successful. The most felicitous textbook example is the chastising, reconstruction, and ultimate Americanization of Germany and Japan, countries that became such good pupils they soon surpassed their teacher. To be sure, the possibilities of armed intervention for therapeutic, surgical, and educational purposes have diminished in the contemporary world, for the time being anyway. But the urge is always present. At the time of a devastating increase in oil prices, in the summer of 1979, a Harvard professor, Theodore Levitt, published, aptly on July 4, these words in the most authoritative American newspaper, the *New York Times* (a *cri du coeur*, an echo from the past): "Swift decisive military action to control the supply and price of Persian Gulf oil is technically feasible. The fact that oil is 'owned' by others is beside the point. . . . OPEC has declared illegitimate war upon a world that, armed to the teeth, wrings its hands while its economies slip uncertainly to the brink of disaster. . . . Preventive action, discredited in Vietnam, is justified now because the silent rules of civility that bind the world have been broken . . . the United States has been the most charitable of nations. . . . To be charitable does not require one to be a sap, soft to the point of self-immolation. Charity today would be to halve, by whatever means, OPEC's open piracy against the world." Professor Levitt is an impatient isolationist.

The difficulty of determining with any degree of accuracy the tack on which the United States is sailing at a given moment and the tack it might be sailing on in the immediate future (intervention or isolation, concern or indifference, euphoria or panic, moralism or pragmatism) is aggravated by some uniquely American features of which only a few foreign specialists are aware. One is the elaborate routine for any decision to be taken in Washington. Another is the time-consuming process for the selection of a new president and the transfer of powers from his predecessor. In all European parliamentary democracies but France, the head of the government, the man responsible for all political decisions, is the prime minister. When he errs, he can be easily overthrown in a few hours, without trauma, by a vote of Parliament. All prime ministers are veteran parliamentarians. They have been marinated for decades in national and international politics, are well acquainted with all their political colleagues and rivals at home and abroad (they have grown old together), know all current problems intimately, and could answer questions about them in their sleep. They also have a thorough knowledge of their own bureaucratic and military organizations, their possibilities and limits. Prime ministers may not always be successful (success depends on more than one man's capacity and luck) but nobody can deny their skill and experience. When they are installed in their new offices they find themselves surrounded by complete up-to-date files and by a staff of permanent officials and experts, most of whom have been there a long time, who know the precedents and developments of all problems down to the preceding day.

To be sure, some of the newly elected presidents, such as Lyndon B. Johnson, have been in Congress for years and know many of the problems. But some come from peripheral posts. They have had little contact with the federal government and know little more about national or international affairs than what they read in newspapers, in their dossiers, and what experts have told them. They usually have been too busy, anyway, campaigning for months or years, and, after their victory, selecting heads of departments and a staff, to do any cramming. Even most vice-presidents who get the job at the death of the president have been kept from the knowledge of secret affairs. (Truman knew nothing of the atomic bomb project when Roosevelt died.) The day the newly elected President is installed in his office he finds no all-knowing permanent staff and no files. His predecessor's documents were once considered the private property of the previous president to be disposed of at his pleasure; some embarrassing ones could be burned, the rest were usually deposited in a provincial library for the use of future friendly historians. Now the files are to be removed as before but must be delivered to the National Archives. When the new president presses a bell button that first morning in his Oval Office in the empty White House only the butler and the chief usher answer. Everybody else has gone home. All he can get is a cup of coffee. In the following weeks and months he must install his own collaborators, as eager but often as insufficiently informed and inexperienced as he, in the office space available, and give them tasks and titles often invented from scratch. It takes some of them weeks to learn their duties. Even the scholarly experts sometimes recruited from universities are baffled as they discover the difference between problems seen at a distance in academic tranquillity and the contradictory confusion of day-by-day business.

It is not surprising that the laborious selection, election, and education of a new president can sometimes paralyze American initiatives for months and that nobody, no foreign ambassador relying on Georgetown gossip and no foreign minister far from the scene, can with any certainty guess which way the ship of state will veer next. The study of electoral promises is of little help. In the United States as elsewhere in the world they are made in order to gather uncertain votes or those of opponents, sometimes to correct evident defects of the previous administration (not a few of which turn out to be incorrigible). In the meantime Europeans can only wait and see, speculate, and cautiously hedge all bets. It is no wonder that seeing the supreme executive authority fade for months and the political line meander uncertainly, they are sometimes preoccupied.

It was easy for Truman and Eisenhower to please Europeans. In their days America was the mother hen of the Western world, the most prosperous, powerful, generous, and courageous country of all. It alone had the Bomb. Europe was broke, demoralized, afraid, troubled by remorse for past mistakes, and in ruins. It was grateful for any kind of help from Washington, for kind words of encouragement and promises of protection. It relished leadership. American presidents then looked like legendary heroes. Later, when the Soviets also acquired the Bomb and built a mighty fleet, when France and Britain proved that anybody, or almost anybody, could build a nuclear weapon, when the economy perked up for a few years anyway, when the Continent was reconstructed and the feared invasion from the East did not materialize, Europeans became nitpicking, critical, and difficult to please. Today it is almost impossible for any president to win the whole-hearted approval of all of them. When he happens to be, like Jimmy Carter, a sentimental humanitarian, a born-again Christian devoured by doubts, scruples, and retroactive remorse, or Ronald Reagan, who is nostalgic for the American dream, when the American armed forces seem to Europeans in danger of becoming a division of the YMCA in uniform or the Peace Corps with not enough guns, and American foreign policy appears to move uncertainly "from appeasement to panic" and back again, a substantial number of Europeans (including some of the leading statesmen, intellectuals, and commentators) are disconcerted. Some are downright frightened. They feel abandoned. They lament the fact that nobody leads the Western world any more. They suspect the United States is forgetting its global responsibilities, and entrusting the future to juvenile, deceptively optimistic, fairy-tale hopes. They fear Americans really believe what angels sang in Bethlehem one distant December night, *pax hominibus bonae voluntatis*, that peace will come to men of good will, and therefore that good will alone can somehow generate peace.

Europeans, then, suspect casual friendly American gestures toward the Soviets to be attempts to build a bridge between the superpowers over the head and at the expense of Europe. In self-defense, European politicians immediately embark on a policy of rapprochement to Moscow, possibly a closer rapprochement than that, if any, envisaged by the United States. Statesmen from all western European countries follow each other, hat in hand, to the Kremlin, friendly joint communiqués are issued, huge credits are extended, technical secrets freely made available, mountains of butter sold below market prices, gas pipelines planned from Siberia, ballet and opera companies exchanged. To be sure, these Europeans realize they may eventually have to pay a heavy price for Russian friendship (or a milder hostility). They know they might have one day implicitly to acknowledge Soviet predominance, consider their own unruly and uncomfortable Communist parties with indulgence. They must occasionally close their eyes to brutal violations of international law and common decency by the Soviets. But they also know that without American aid, only a docile and unwarlike Europe, merely symbolically armed, acquiescent to the Soviet will, could possibly survive quasi-intact and continue to enjoy the delightful perfections of its own decline. The temptation is strong. These people are realists.

On the other hand, when a new president firmly assumes the leadership of the free world with all its obligations, takes courageous decisions, follows an inflexible foreign policy based on a clean division between good guys and bad guys, promotes the construction of diabolical new weapons, and asks Congress for countless billions for defense, many Europeans, more or less the same substantial authoritative minority, are by no means reassured. They are even more disconcerted and perplexed. Some are downright frightened. They see America unwisely provoking the Soviet Union, making war ineluctable, a nuclear duel fought mainly on their own Continent, Europe. Once again, they embark on a policy of rapprochement with the Russians. Statesmen publicly deplore the American recklessness and reassure the Soviet leaders that Europe is not as firmly determined to resort to arms as the Americans seem to be. They are also reluctant to apply economic sanctions. They hope the war, if there must be a war, a nuclear war, could eventually be fought as far away as possible, the borders of Chinese Turkestan, the Himalayas, the Mongolian prairies, the Gobi Desert, the Aleutian Islands, Alaska, or the

North Pole, and if absolutely inevitable, limited to exchanges of nuclear missiles strictly between the United States and the Soviet Union. Hundreds of thousands of pacifists favorable to unilateral disarmament gather in Berlin, Bonn, Paris, London, and sometimes even in Rome. In Perugia, carrying red flags and holy images, led by Communist leaders and a few ill-informed priests, they once marched all the way to Assisi, Saint Francis' birthplace. Long-haired students riot in university cities all over the Continent. Bombs are exploded against American army barracks or airline offices. Missiles are thrown against the car of an American general in Frankfurt, American generals are kidnapped. Terrorists subvert law and order and murder policemen, judges, politicians, and journalists, all in the name of peace, and try to weaken and possibly topple pro-NATO governments.

In other words, no matter who the president is, whether he is well up on foreign affairs or not, whether he leads or forgets to lead the West, no matter how well or badly armed the American defense establishment is, and no matter what the American foreign policy is at the moment, hard or soft, a large number of Europeans will not be pleased. Some are directly or indirectly for peace at any price. The fact that mass peace movements are partly financed from abroad and helped by foreign experts to organize themselves efficiently, that their demonstrations obviously cost millions of dollars for special trains and buses, for flags, signs, sleeping bags, blankets, and meals, that their activities are ably directed toward predetermined goals, the fact also that some underground terrorists get weapons, money, and training abroad, should not deceive us. The movement is largely indigenous. While a large number of people in Europe are becoming European patriots, a large minority are reluctant to accept the hard responsibilities, the expense, and the dangers inherent in the defense of their own liberty and their civilization.

The Europeans who nervously rush to the Kremlin to placate and reassure Soviet leaders whenever the United States issues bellicose statements, adopts a sterner foreign policy, or launches ambitious rearmament programs inevitably provoke the Americans' resentment and suspicion. Then they express doubts about their allies' reliability, loyalty, and determination to save themselves. There is also talk in the air at such times of a possible withdrawal of all United States forces from Europe. All this is, of course, the result of ancient misunderstandings between the New and the Old World. The Europeans take the president's and the secretary of state's words at face value, not knowing any better, and begin to fear the United States is actually in danger of plunging itself and all of them into a final nuclear war of total extermination. At the same time the Americans suspect that the Europeans are so fainthearted they prefer ruinous compromises and demeaning submission to the Soviets to the firm virile stand that alone could prevent that ultimate nuclear Armageddon. There is then insistent talk of a terminal crisis in the Atlantic Alliance.

In reality the collaboration of NATO allies probably works best at such times, whether the Americans are aware of it or not. To get the Soviets listening, the Europeans need the Americans' vociferous, resolute, and threatening stand. They can then convince the Soviets to be more prudent, to behave more correctly, to make conciliatory gestures, and to refrain from invading other foreign countries, directly or through their satellites. At the same time, the Americans can freely give voice to frightening threats, including the dedication of trillions to new armaments, because the Europeans are keeping the Soviets calm and mollified. It is really an unconscious division of labor comparable to the antagonistic but parallel double roles of de Gaulle and Pétain during World War II, both working for the salvation of France.

Another serious cause for European apprehension and despondency at all times, a factor that always magnifies all other causes for apprehension and despondency, is the immense size, cornucopian fertility, and voraciousness of the United States. It is not surprising, to be sure, that momentous decisions (or nondecisions) of such a great nation should provoke world-shaking consequences. Americans are not always aware of this power of theirs. It is disturbing but understandable that an official state-ment, a confidential leak, a few words spoken or omitted (inten-tionally or absentmindedly) by a high official, the president him-self, the secretary of state, or an "unnamed source" make stock exchanges crash or levitate everywhere, settle a dispute between parties in a distant foreign country or embitter it, turn an election one way or another, disrupt or placate public order, spark or discourage military coups d'état or bloody popular revolts. Oc-casionally, the United States has unwittingly helped topple or con-solidate an unsavory dictator, brought to power a gang of well-meaning but dangerously inexperienced fanatics, provoked the random execution of scores of rebels, previous rulers, or simple bystanders, as well as the murder of an occasional American ambassador. It was enough, years ago (to quote a memorable example) for a secretary of state to *appear* to have said that the United States might not defend South Korea to start a bloody, expensive, and long-drawn-out war.

It is also disturbing that in such a vast and rich country small insignificant casual events, such as the absentminded directive of one multinational, flurries in the exchange, the rise and fall of the discount rate, a drought, a flood, labor unrest, a record or scarce harvest, a political decision taken for strictly local, sometimes electoral reasons (or no reason at all), the adoption of a new ersatz, a technological breakthrough, a teenagers' rage, a new health fad, a whim, or an advertising campaign—occurrences that cannot be foreseen or prevented by foreigners—revolutionize living conditions in other places, some of them thousands of miles away, send rings of concentric waves that reach in time the most remote corners of the world and alter the course of history.

Take the case of mahogany. It was for a very long time the symbol of bourgeois affluence and good taste. When it suddenly went out of fashion in the United States sixty or seventy years ago, prosperous and stable tropical countries that lived mainly on the export of that wood were ruined almost overnight. Rivers were blocked by masses of rotting tree trunks. Starving people rioted. Streets were strewn with corpses. Dictators took power. Foreign embassies bulged with political refugees. And what would happen the day American doctors decree (as they may) that bananas are carcinogenic? Or take the American discovery, a few years ago, of an obscure kitchen appliance made in limited quantities by a small factory in France. It did everything for the housewife except sweep the floor. The factory making it was transformed within months into a monster industry. A mushroom growth of competitors sprang into being. They (the original factory and its competitors) will just as easily (and quickly) wither and vanish the day their American clientele turns to some other wonder machine. Or take the miraculous overnight development, several years ago, of a few modest European mineral water bottling firms the moment Americans enthusiastically started drinking healthy imported waters at cocktail time instead of their usual gut-corroding liquors. Or take the case of wines. Famous old vineyards and ancient firms can go into decline and hitherto unknown ones unexpectedly flourish the moment drinkers in the United States shift their preferences en masse. Orvieto, long a favorite of Americans, had to uproot its vines and abandon the production of its century-old famous sweet abboccato to produce a much less distinguished dry wine. Champagne, too, turned from sweet to dry at the turn of the century, thus revolutionizing entire French provinces, where the old vines had also to be uprooted and new ones planted when the American taste, or as some labels said, the goût américain, turned to the very dry.

Let's imagine that enough Americans one day acquire a craving for zabaglione (a well known warm dessert of beaten eggs, sugar, and Marsala wine). This is not an absurd hypothesis, for the concoction is tasty and is believed to reinvigorate and multiply a man's capacity and zest for love. As a result, miserable Sicily (where Marsala comes from) would once again become an opulent island; the local Mafia would turn from Italian politics and drugs to the international control of the wine; the Spanish, the Portuguese, and the Greeks would spend millions pushing their own substitutes; Japanese chemists would find a way to make better and cheaper synthetic Marsala from whale blubber; the

Soviet Union would surreptitiously surround the island with its fleet; the Arabs would make military preparations to conquer irredent Sicily, Sicilia *irredenta*, once again . . .

Another cause of profound anxiety is the oscillating value of the dollar. The dollar is now the main currency of the world marketplace. All attempts at finding substitutes have failed. But unlike wampum, glass beads, sesterces, the drachma, the doubloon, zecchino, thaler, the Louis, the Napoleon, the sovereign, and the eagle in their days, or the plastic multicolored rounds or squares at Las Vegas and Monte Carlo, its value may change unexpectedly within hours inside a man's pocket, in the underground vaults or the ledgers of a bank. What is frightening about this phenomenon is that the reasons for the fluctuations are often provincial American reasons, usually incomprehensible to foreigners: the state of the American balance of payments, a political maneuver dictated by domestic needs, the testing of a new-fangled economic theory, decisions or nondecisions by the monetary authorities in Washington. On none of these factors do Europeans (as well as all other non-Americans) have any influence, let alone control. The uncertainty is enough to give a constant feeling of trepidation and insecurity to bankers, individuals, families, communities, and whole nations all over the world.

What actually causes uneasiness and dismay (occasionally verging on panic) among Europeans is not only the obvious fact that the United States is big, rich, powerful, and incredibly productive, or that Americans occasionally tend to shift preferences, political opinions, tastes, and hopes en masse at the same time, often unexpectedly, so much as the fact I pointed out that they seem not always to be exactly aware of their country's actual size, of its strength, and its influence. They occasionally underestimate the effect of their actions or words or they overestimate it optimistically with disappointing results. They do not seem always to be able to control, harness, and direct their awesome power. The consequences of some of their moves are in fact sometimes as surprising and shocking to them as to the rest of the world. At times the United States (as seen by foreign observers, anyway) still behaves as the small, peace-loving, homespun, philosophic Republic it used to be, which could afford to propose or proclaim any desirable, noble, or crackpot idea—the Open Door policy or the Kellogg-Briand Pact outlawing war—because nobody would take it very seriously and nothing much happened. At other times, the United States, overconscious of its weight and responsibility, tries to impose a solution to some of the world's tangled problems, as it did many times in the Middle East. Often nothing much happens in these cases either, but sometimes the results may be deeply disappointing, the contrary of what was wanted.

This, of course, could also be said of other great nations in the past and present, that they miscalculated on occasion the effects of their actions, as for instance, did Imperial Russia, Imperial Germany, and Austria-Hungary in August 1914. But there is one important difference. Few other nations in history were ever as powerful and capable of influencing events in 1914 as the three mentioned above and as the United States is today. Minor countries (and the United States in decades past) could often afford to make mistakes. The United States cannot afford to make mistakes today.

Conclusion

W HAT, THEN, are the obscure forces preventing the coagulation of western Europe into a solid whole, as easily as liquid milk curdles into a block of fresh cheese as soon as the rennet is dropped into it?

One, of course, is most evident. It is the apparently ineradicable survival of sensitive national prides. Perhaps the everyday people, the young especially, are not as attached to their countries' faded glories as the politicians presume. Perhaps the politicians, who are coldly skeptical by profession, stand by the honor of their flags, like Cambronne and the Imperial Guard at Waterloo, merely hoping to please the middle-aged voters back home. Maybe all these antagonistic patriotisms are merely considered by some as useful to ennoble the shabby contrasts about minuscule import-and-export problems or the squabbles about the division of the Common Market budget.

However, it is a fact that the cold atmosphere created by the stubborn defense of each nation's dignity contributes to discouraging the spontaneous flowering of European patriotism and to preventing a rapid progress toward effective integration. As de Gaulle once bitterly complained, "Il y a autant d'égoismes sacrés que de membres inscrits." (There are as many sacred egoisms as there are registered members.) He knew, of course, what he was talking about. His own and France's *égoisme sacré* was and still is the principal stumbling block. He, like all politicians in power, feared to see his prerogatives eclipsed by a superior authority and his freedom of action hobbled in a crisis. He admitted this only in private, and preferred to speak in public of his fear of seeing his country's precious identity vanish in the common cauldron. Before the foundation of the Reich, all German princelings were similarly reluctant to see part of their sovereignties, their incomes from customs duties, their flags and uniforms vanish. It took Bismarck two or three bloody victorious wars, against Denmark, Austria, and France, to conquer their reluctance and persuade them that there was nothing they could do about it anyway.

To be sure, there are excellent reasons why each member nation should cling to the memory of its glorious past, and should mount guard, jealously and suspiciously, over its unique heritage. Each nation is persuaded it has contributed in a decisive manner to European (and the world's) civilization, which would not be what it is without it. They all are, of course, right. France certainly helped shape Europe in many ways at all times; Italy too, to be sure; Britain, without any doubt; and Germany, undisputably, for good and evil. But even the smaller member nations are rightly attached to the memory of their contributions: Denmark, where the Normans mostly came from, who invented parliaments, conquered and brought order to Britain, southern Italy, Sicily, and the northern part of France which bears their name; Benelux, heir to Burgundy's prodigious flowering, the dawn of the Renaissance, and which even taught music to the Italians; and Ireland, whose holy men built monasteries and spread Christianity all over continental Europe. And what about Greece, the early teacher of all of us?

All, or almost all, represent glorious vanished empires, some of them two empires, a few three or more. They are:

- the three French empires (Napoleon I, Napoleon III, and the colonial empire)
- the British Empire, which once colored most of the world's map pink
- the Dutch East Indian empire
- the Belgian Congo
- the three German Reichs
- the many Italian empires or quasi-empires (Ancient Rome, the

Venetian and Genoese overseas possessions, and more recently,
Libya and Ethiopia)
· the Byzantine Empire of the Greeks

When Spain and Portugal enter the club, as they eventually
will, they will bring with them the proud memories of one empire
on which the sun never set and of possessions that stretched from
Brazil to India to China. If Turkey one day succeeds in being
admitted, the legendary Ottoman Empire will join the ghosts of all
the others. To be sure, some of these nations are prouder and
more jealously attached to their past grandeur than others. The
Italians, for instance, had a surfeit of their remote glories, of
which the Fascist regime reminded them every day. In view of the
consequences, they now suspect Ancient Rome brings *jettatura*, or
ill luck.

There is no doubt that these memories help stiffen the spines of
ministers meeting at Brussels and make most agreements slow and
extremely difficult. Curiously enough, other memories that could
inspire the same ministers and the European Parliament, fan the
flame of European patriotism, and miraculously facilitate all
agreements are seldom evoked. One is the memory of Christendom, at one time another name for Europe, when all sovereigns,
great and small, were theoretically united under the earthly
tutelage of the Holy Roman Emperor and the spiritual tutelage of
the pope. Not even the Vatican likes to be reminded of Christendom. Only on rare ceremonial occasions is the name of Charlemagne, the founder of the Holy Roman Empire, mentioned. The
memory of Europe's glorious centuries, when it dominated the
whole world, culturally, economically, and politically, until the
First World War, is seldom recalled. To be sure, European armed
forces organized only one common expedition, together with the
Americans and the Japanese, in 1900, to free the legations in
Peking from the Boxers' siege; nevertheless, all wars of conquest
and all the peaceful penetrations in distant continents for centuries, not all of them deplorable and dishonorable enterprises,
could be considered pan-European exploits. The evocation of some

could still make Europeans proud. This obliviousness to common adventures and common merits is significant. Maybe Europeans do not want to be reminded today of the uncomfortable fact that they were in a way one people for centuries, could be one again, and even when divided and competing, managed collectively to open up the world to modern ideas, not all of them harmful.

More than by the *égoismes sacrés*, European unification has been really retarded and possibly prevented forever by the delusion that a customs union would one day spontaneously generate a political and defense union. Not all were deceived by this. Many merely wanted the former and devoted to the latter only oratorical homages. The economic integration was apparently decided at first as a *pis aller*, better than nothing, something that could be safely organized to while away the time. But a few hoped it was the ultimate goal. By now everybody realizes it has led to nothing, at best only to an even closer economic integration within the next decades. But even this is not quite certain. Many interests are still successfully defending local privileges and protected activities, in particular the bureaucracies that continue to invent ever-new ingenious ways to stop the importation of some goods from other member countries by means of rules and regulations that they justify with sanitary, safety, phytological, or vaguely technological motivations. Furthermore, there are clauses in the Treaty of Rome itself that allow all members to block, temporarily at least, the entry of a particular product to save the local producers from bankruptcy.

The reason why the economic union is a dead-end street is that it is based on a limited, oversimplified, and inadequate philosophy that became predominant in Europe after the Second World War. It was believed to be the final solution of all problems. It holds these truths to be self-evident: one, that the economy is the principal motor of history; two, that an increasingly bigger GNP was the only and sufficient condition for progress; three, that many costly activities essential to the health of a nation, such as defense expenditures, had to be sacrificed to the spread of affluence and an ever-higher standard of living; four, that a larger state revenue permitted the abundant distribution of unemployment subsidies, health and old-age pensions; five, that a well-paid, well-fed, and amusingly entertained population would not give governments any trouble. For these reasons, each minister meeting at Brussels looks after the petty economic interests of his country, or of particular sectors in his country, defends its prosperity in good years and even more tenaciously in bad years, and seldom thinks of Europe as a whole.

There would be nothing wrong in this philosophy if man (single or en masse) were always a rational human being who knew what was best for him and his progeny and was always moved by the right economic choices. He is not. Not even the Swiss, the Dutch, or the French peasants would lay down their lives merely for the price of gold or a rise in the interest rate. The motivations of sudden and violent tempests in public opinion, revolts, revolutions, and wars notoriously have been many and irrational, religious, ideological, social, dynastic, patriotic, psychological, the hatred of a tyrant or a neighbor, and the defense of national honor. To be sure, the economic factor is often mixed up with others but materialistic historians usually have a difficult time isolating it. (They belong to the same school of journalists who believed the Americans fought in Vietnam and the British in the Falklands to get hold of oil deposits.) One revolution at least was started by boredom, the boredom brought on by increasing uneventful, unbearable prosperity, the July 1830 revolution against Louis Philippe. Most colonial people who fight bloody wars of independence know they are leaving a moderately affluent and secure life for hunger, disorder, misery, and impecuniousness, in the near future anyway. Therefore it is impossible to foresee (and prevent) the future convulsions of history if one only considers the economic factor, if one believes with Khrushchev that "people with a full belly do not think of starting trouble."

The delusion is as ineradicable as it is innate among the middle-class politicians who hold power, under many names, of the Left, Center, or Right in almost all European nations. It is also a natural reassuring dogma to which all businessmen are tenaciously attached. A very worried Italian banker asked me, a few months before the last war ended, "What do you think will happen after the war?" I said we would have to face terrible times because we would be governed by the middle class, the bourgeoisie, which is not a political class at all, as it knows only one thing. "What thing?" he asked. I said, "Buy low and sell high." He meditated a while and then said, "Is there anything else?"

One thing might shake Europeans from their complacent belief that a lame Common Market is all they need for the time being because any further progress toward political integration might be fraught with dangers. It is the same thing that prodded them in the first place to search for instant union after the war: the fear of the Soviet menace. This fear has grown weaker and weaker as time has passed. At the present moment the Soviet Union worries them (who could be its first victims) far less than the Americans. There are several reasons for this. Europeans are evidently aware that the Soviets continue to concentrate armaments in megalomaniac and senseless abundance on their border, ever more deadly and sophisticated weapons each year, and hundreds of thousands of trained men in uniform. They also know that the Soviet leaders are depriving their own people of many absolutely necessary things in order to spend untold sums on war preparations. But they evidently do not want to conquer Europe. If they did, they could have done so in the past on many favorable occasions. They surely would do it tomorrow morning, before the more diabolically modern American weapons are deployed. Why then do the Soviet leaders risk provoking their people's malcontent and eventual revolts? Why do they theoretically endanger their own hold on power for the sake of building up an unnecessary war machine? One answer is that they literally cannot stop. The economy is directed by the bureaucracy. Bureaucrats do not willingly abdicate their responsibilities in any country. Te reduce Soviet armaments might entail the demobilization of entire Moscow ministries. All industrial plants in the USSR have not only to fulfill a predetermined yearly quota but also to increase production by five, ten percent, or more. The directors and managers of plants who do not succeed risk spending the rest of their lives in a humiliating obscurity and penury, if not worse. They must give up the dachas and the long black cars. Their wives must go back to the breadline and their sons leave their good schools. Armaments come under the heading of heavy industry, and heavy industry had the highest priority in the five-year plans since the early beginning, a priority defended tooth and nail by the military, who constitute the most powerful pressure group in the Soviet Union. Allied to the bureaucracy they are unbeatable. Consumer goods can wait. They have been waiting since 1917 anyway.

Then there are psychological reasons. The first is the necessity for all wobbly authoritarian regimes or tyrannies, which are unable to solve normal everyday problems and feed all their people adequately, to magnify the threat of a dangerous enemy on the border, ready to pounce, if it was not sufficiently terrifying, and to invent one, if it did not exist. This has long been known to experts as the "obsidional complex." When I was in Moscow years ago after the break with China, people, ordinary people, not officials who mechanically repeated the party line, were talking nervously about the "yellow peril," the threat of an invasion of millions of Chinese, which they believed to be imminent. They were as serious about it as Kaiser Wilhelm II had been at the turn of the century. Their fears, of course, were artfully fanned daily by the mass media and by agitprop.

The danger from the West is easier to demonstrate. There are, to begin with, the official ideological motivations. If the Soviet experiment is the open road to the *real* liberation of man, the abolition of his enslavement and exploitation by millionaire capitalists and American imperialists, it is only natural that the enemies at bay should do all they can to try to destroy the "real socialism" before it destroys them. The Soviets are not deceived by the fact that their enemies often seem confused, divided, perplexed, the Europeans sometimes at odds with the United States, and inadequately armed. These are interpreted as ruses. To be sure, the ideological justifications are no longer firmly believed by a larger percentage of the people, perhaps by a majority. Nevertheless, they have an official validity that nobody, except a minority of heroic cranks, dares to contradict.

Then there are deeper, non–Marxist-Leninist-Stalinist reasons. One is the ancient fear of the Germans. Under the czars, Germans (or German descendants) were often entrusted with precise, delicate, organizational, and scientific tasks, in preference to the bungling and lackadaisical Russians. Many of the Soviet generals in command today, as well as Leonid Ilyich Brezhnev, were born in the Ukraine, and were young officers during the last war. They saw how irresistible and deadly the German war machine could be, how astutely commanded, and how many corpses it took for the less skillful Russians to stop it. The Germans awake Ukrainian ancestral fears, as the Turks do in Syria or in the Balkans.

But do the Soviets really want to conquer Europe? It all depends on the definition of the word. If "to conquer" means to destroy the West with nuclear weapons and become the masters of radioactive rubble from the Elbe to the Atlantic, at the price of millions of casualties and ruined cities both in the United States and the Soviet Union, one can eliminate war as a possibility. Evidently what the Soviets have in mind is a slow, careful, and peaceful "conquest" or penetration of Europe as is, with its scientists, skillful politicians, universities, inventors, expert financiers, bureaucrats, net of communications, staff officers, mines, and industries. With it the Soviets would keep the United States at bay and dominate the rest of the world. In order, however, to keep Europe functioning to their advantage, they know they must keep it politically and socially intact. If they abolished liberty, private initiative, the market economy, and the free flow of international exchanges, they would paralyze Europe and reduce it to the same level as the Soviet Union, slow to invent new technologies and incapable of feeding itself. If this is true, one should consider the armaments amassed against the West more a political and psychological problem than a purely military one. They are a loaded pistol pointed to persuade and seduce the Europeans to be friends, to accept the Soviet hegemony in foreign and military affairs, in exchange for another Thousand Years Peace under police tutelage.

The grand Soviet design is impracticable and unrealizeable. It counts on the expanding power of the friendly Communist parties of the West, which are now slowly withering, their very existence made more and more difficult every year by the Soviet's aggressively clumsy conduct of foreign affairs. The design also counts on the Europeans' passivity and reluctance to fight a conventional war, in case neither superpower dares launch a first nuclear strike. And a purely conventional war is an improbable possibility. The design counts on the fear of the Europeans, and the Europeans are far from scared as things stand now.

But then the Soviets are themselves afraid of their own plan. They are afraid, first, of the contamination of Western ideas, way of life, abundance of consumer products, culture, and civilization, which notoriously corrupts all Soviet citizens or soldiers obliged to live in the free world for a while. When they come back, they always tell idealized tales of the Western paradise and spread dissatisfaction, creating at times serious political problems. They are afraid, above all, of the impossibility of governing by indirect or direct means sophisticated, democratic, modern countries. The Germans tried it without success during the last war. Could the Russians, generally less adroit, less civilized and learned than the Germans, educated from childhood to believe reality obeys Marxist laws, do any better? Would a Europe in endemic revolt be of any use to the USSR? Would it not also fan revolts in the satellite countries?

In conclusion, Europeans are not particularly afraid, because they believe a war to be improbable for the time being and see the insane accumulation of Soviet armaments primarily as a domestic affair, a ruse to keep the people docile and resigned to their fate and to the sacrifices demanded of them.

We must admit that in a modest way the dream of European unity has been a success. It was really conceived to prevent a recurrence of the wars of 1870, 1914, and 1939 between France and Germany. This it has done. It has also established a shop-keepers' ideal continental market of sorts, which has encouraged exchanges and production. It cannot go any further. There cannot be a really united Europe without a common currency and a common foreign policy, but above all, a common defense policy. This, in the twentieth century, means nuclear weapons and space defenses. It entails a tangle of insoluble political problems among the member nations and the superpowers. But the principal obstacle is the German problem.

Germans dream of national reunification, whether they admit it openly or not. No great nation can survive cut in half. It is vulnerable psychologically and, being the West's outpost, also militarily. Adenauer thought the United States had the power, the will, and the capacity to force the Soviets to free their East German hostages. This, of course, was impossible. The United States may have had the power for a few years but fortunately lacked the will to start the Third World War for the sake of the Germans. Willy Brandt then thought the only way to reunify his mutilated country was to establish intimate and friendly relations with the Soviets, reassure them, placate the atavistic fears of their neighbors, and, with their consent, make the ties between the two Germanies gradually more intimate, to the point of almost erasing the border between them. He also failed. The Soviets' fears apparently could be placated only if Germany abandoned the Western Alliance and the Common Market, if it limited its armaments to those of Luxembourg, adopted strict neutrality, and accepted Soviet dominance in foreign affairs. The unification of Europe without Germany would be impossible and pointless, but with Germany would entail the acceptance, for all members, of the German problem. Everybody knows it could be nullified tomorrow morning if the problem were solved the Soviet way, by the neutralization of all Europe. This of course would be suicidal. It could not be accepted by the Europeans themselves and would force the Americans to retreat behind the bastions of their country, the only nation left in the world to defend man's liberty and justice.

Neither Europeans nor Americans cherish the idea of becoming political zombies in exchange for a mediocre, predictable, and safe future life. It is against the nature of things. This is probably the principal reason why the unification of Europe must wait. One must be content with what there is, for the time being anyway. The future is in the laps of the gods. It will probably be decided, once again, by Germany's decisions. And Germany is, as it always was, a mutable, Proteuslike, unpredictable country, particularly dangerous when it is unhappy.

ABOUT THE AUTHOR

LUIGI BARZINI was born in Milan on December 21, 1908. He graduated from the Columbia University School of Journalism in 1930 and returned to Italy to work as a correspondent for *Corriere della Sera*, covering most of the international stories of the succeeding decade. In 1940, Barzini was arrested for activities considered hostile to the Fascist regime. Four years later, when the Allies entered Rome, he began working again and published and edited two dailies (*Il Globo* and *Libera Stampa*). Later he began to devote himself exclusively to writing, both for Italian and English publications in addition to books and plays. He was elected to Parliament as Deputato of the Italian Liberal Party for Milan in 1958 and re-elected in 1963 and 1969. His book *The Italians* became a classic and a best seller all over the world.

Mr. Barzini lives in Rome and contributes regularly to scores of magazines and journals in several countries.